Gay Ski

Gay Skins

Class, Masculinity and Queer Appropriation

Murray Healy

CASSELL

For a catalogue of related titles in our
Sexual Politics/Global issues list please
write to us at the address below.

Cassell
Wellington House
125 Strand
London WC2R 0BB

215 Park Avenue South
New York, NY 10003

First published 1996

British Library Cataloguing-in-Publication Data
A catalogue record for this book is available from the British Library.

ISBN 0 304 333239 (hardback)
      0 304 333247 (paperback)

Design and typesetting by Ben Cracknell Studios
Printed and bound in Great Britain by Biddles Ltd,
Guildford and King's Lynn.

Contents

Acknowledgements

This book started out as my MA dissertation at Sussex University in 1993, where the advice of Alan Sinfield, the archive of Bill Osgerby and the supervision of Andy Medhurst were invaluable. This couldn't have been written without the enthusiastic support of friends and the many gay skinheads who were keen to share their knowledge. Thanks are due in particular to Louise Boruta, Jamie Crofts and Michael Dover, who were vital in tracing some of the key figures of the gay skin scene of the 1960s; to David Scoular and Michael Dow for their energetic contributions; and to all the gay skins who were willing to talk about their experiences and memories.

My thanks also to the photographers Anthony Burls, John G. Byrne and Richard Maude, whose works are reprinted by their kind permission.

Introduction

'I hope you don't mind me asking, but just why are *you* interested in gay skinheads?' It's a fair question that a number of skinheads, who have found themselves looking down the wrong end of my microphone, have felt the need to ask me. They were understandably wary of this nosey stranger with a list of questions, a tape recorder and an appearance about as far removed from 'skinhead' as possible. I must have looked suspiciously like an outsider sniffing round their subculture in order to debunk it. Given the political storms that have raged over the presence of skinheads in gay subculture for at least the past fifteen years, it would not have been the first time.

Initially I wasn't interested in skinheads at all. This book was inspired by an academic's challenge to disprove the matter-of-fact assumption that 'gay' was a middle-class identity and that, until about 1970, most working-class men could not identify with it. It was 1992, and furtive searches through libraries revealed a conspicuous absence of material on gay working-class men. I was disappointed, but not surprised – the ruling classes write history, and that goes for the history of sexual dissidence too. With homosexual histories necessarily inconspicuous until fairly recently, unearthing personal histories was the only alternative. But as I didn't know any gay men older than their early twenties at the time, my only recourse was speculation. A novel published in 1961 about two gay members of a hard biker gang, *The Leather Boys*, led me to investigate the possibility that delinquent working-class youth cultures might have allowed space for queers not only to have sex but to form an identity around their queerness. Even given the straightness imposed on these histories, it was possible to do this with every youth culture – except with the skinhead, which, given the look's prevalence on the scene by the early 1990s, seemed significant. Hence my interest in gay skinheads.

I'm not interested in skinheads for the reasons you might think. You're not the only one: a lot of gay men suspect this explanation is disingenuous. They think they know the real motive. A common reaction to my work has been, 'So you're writing a book on gay skinheads? Bet you're enjoying the research, eh, the *research*, know what I mean?' The book, they assume, is a clever excuse to maximize my sexual potential. Nudge, nudge, wink, wink, say no more.

And that's the trouble: so much more needs to be said. But it never is, because within gay subculture, that gay men should find the image of a skinhead a turn-on is beyond question. The assumption is never questioned because, apparently, 'it's simply common sense that a gay man should fancy a real man' – and already, within that commonplace, throwaway refusal to explain masquerading as an explanation, there are all sorts of loaded, contentious terms that need unravelling. This is . . . interesting.

Because he is so sexy (or so I'm told), the skinhead has become without doubt a homosexual phenomenon. Skinhead identities have become increasingly popular among gay men since the mid-1980s. At the time of writing – summer 1995 – there are five venues in London alone that cater specifically for gay men who identify as skinheads: The Anvil, the London Apprentice, the Coleherne, the Block and the sole exclusively skinhead club, Silks '95. There are established gay skinhead networks in other cities too, most notably Birmingham and Manchester. But London boasts the oldest, most diverse gay skinhead scene – not surprising, considering that it also has the biggest gay scene anyway and is where the skinhead first emerged. In addition, there are national gay skinhead social organizations, Skin4Skin and the Gay Skinhead Group. The leading scene magazine *Boyz* has included a column in the pages of its personal ads specifically for skinheads, 'Boots and Braces', since its launch in 1991. Furthermore, skinhead imagery extends its influence well beyond the distinct minority of gay men who would describe themselves as skinheads: sexual fantasies about skins feature prominently in phone lines, porn mags and illegal videos.

In addition to those who proclaim themselves to be skins, there are many more wearing the same gear who don't. A major reason for this is that being a skin almost certainly guarantees you sex. I discovered this when a thirty-year-old white colleague of mine shaved off his peroxide crop and shed his favoured designer clubwear in favour of a Ben Sherman, braces, bleached jeans and ox-blood DM boots to guarantee him entry to a men-only club that was holding a skin night. An Essex boy, he hardened his accent and perfected the stance. When he recounted his night out to me the following day, he acknowledged this as drag; but he had looked the part. 'They were *queuing up* in that back room!' he exclaimed in disbelief; it wasn't as if he hadn't been notoriously popular in such environments beforehand. 'And the harder I acted, the stroppier I got, the more they loved it!' Such were the benefits of being a skin that, although he disliked the look at the level of style, he kept the shaved head so he could slip into his skin drag whenever he felt the need.

But it's more than a matter of personal desire and individual private fantasies; it's also a question of identification and collective representational strategies. About the same time my colleague was first discovering the joys of skin sex, I ran into an old friend I hadn't seen for nearly five years; he was now twenty-five and a social worker. Whereas he had once favoured the anti-style aesthetics of the student-activist, he now had a shaved head and was wearing a bottle-green Fred Perry, red braces, rolled Levis, black DM boots and a green MA–1 flying jacket. When I asked him whether I could interview him for this book as a skinhead, he protested, 'But I'm not a skinhead.' I reassured him that it wouldn't be a matter of defending his self-presentational strategy because he was black. 'No, you don't understand', he insisted. 'I really am *not* a skinhead. I dress like this because I'm a gay man. It's sexy and it turns queens on.'

But what is it about a cropped head, rolled-up jeans, a flying jacket, and Doc Marten boots (to take one incarnation of the uniform) that encompasses an unquestionably sexually desirable masculinity for so many men? And here again as an outsider, as one who has never felt this attraction, I am well placed to ask this question.

Why do so many gay men, consciously and unconsciously, look like skinheads? This particular youth subculture seems to have informed the development of gay male presentational codes more than any other. Just go into any gay bar and tick off the elements from a skin wardrobe; the common urban gay uniform has consisted of Doc Martens, Levis, T-shirt, bomber jacket and cropped hair since the mid-1980s. It's hardly a controversial suggestion that this uniform is derived from skinheads. So widespread are these elements in British urban gay networks that they have ceased to signify skinhead, sending out the message 'I am gay' instead. So it isn't always easy to maintain a distinction between gay skinhead and broader significations of gay at a purely semiotic level: many bearers of the elements themselves are unaware of this resemblance until it's pointed out.

Tracing the history of the circulation of skinhead codes on the gay scene is therefore particularly difficult, but presumably there was a time when the sight of skinheads on the scene was so uncommon as to be conspicuous. When did gay men start using elements of a teen subculture of the late 1960s? Did they hijack a look after it went out of fashion? Or, given that the first wave of skinheads comprised a walking assemblage of macho signifiers that gay men had already come to fetishize, were gay men partly responsible for the creation of the look in the first place? In fact, were there gay skinheads right from the start?

Straight expectations

At the start of this project, my familiarity with gay subculture meant that the ubiquity of skinhead codes rendered them virtually invisible to me too. But I can remember my shock the first time I happened across a gay skinhead: it was in my early teens, on Channel 4 where I discovered the 'unashamedly homosexual' dancer Michael Clark. He had a poofy job, a bit of a poofy voice, but he could behave like a bit of a lad and dressed, at various times, like a punk and a skinhead. I was amazed. Straights might actually be scared of him!

Of course, it was a naïve reaction, but no more naïve than the assumption that, by 1992, everyone had become familiar with the existence of gay skins. In stark contrast to those familiar with gay male subculture, uninitiated heterosexuals have been puzzled by my project: 'Gay skinheads? Gay? Skinheads? Are there such things?' They assume that the skinhead and the gay man are unrelated species. If the existence of gay skinheads is beyond question for gay men, it's out of the question for the subculturally uninitiated.

Consider Peter Tory's review of *Skin Complex*, a documentary about gay skinheads shown on Channel 4's lesbian and gay series *Out* in July 1992:

JUST OUT TO SHOCK
Channel 4's programme, *Out*, the series for and about homosexuals, cannot often be recommended viewing for those of a nervous disposition. This week's offering would certainly have frightened old ladies. And pretty boys too, no doubt.

The question was asked: have gay men gone too far in their quest for the ultimate macho sex image? The answer from those who are not of the inclination must be yes.

Gay men, according to *Out*, now favour the skinhead look. They parade about, virtually cropped and with rings in their lobes, looking as though they would like to tear the noses and ears off old-age pensioners.

The majority, surely, find aggressively overt gay men offensive. And the majority, of course, find skinheads equally so. *Put the two together and you have a real fright.*

We can only hope that gay men one day revert to wearing suits and ordinary hair-cuts like the rest of us. Then Channel 4 can follow its programme, *Out*, with another one – perhaps – called In Again.[1]

The poor man has had a shock. Gay skinheads shouldn't exist, *but they do*. They shouldn't exist because the common understanding of masculinity to which he subscribes posits 'the skinhead' as the very opposite of 'the gay man'. Press coverage of what started out as just another teen subculture in the late 1960s has created a social mythology around skinheads to which the attributes of real man – working class, socially fixed, violent, with extreme right politics – have become attached. In contrast, 'gay man' is viewed as unnatural/effeminate, middle class, socially mobile, weak, with left politics. Restricted by such reductive definitions, the categories 'gay man' and 'skinhead' define each other in tautologous contradiction. Gay and skinhead operate as polar opposites – as reminders of what men shouldn't be. They demarcate the unacceptable opposite extremes of masculinity (for this reviewer, both are 'equally offensive') and thus stabilize the area of accepted masculinity in the space between them. Undermining this opposition exposes all sorts of inconsistencies and contradictions. That the two poles might actually converge in a single identity disrupts the dominant expectations of male behaviour. So 'put the two together and you have a real fright': the knowledge that gay skinheads not only might exist but are in fact common short-circuits accepted beliefs about real masculinity.

Of course, Tory doesn't want to have to think about skins, queens or the idea that masculinity might not be in any sense real anyway, so the assumptions mapped out in the accepted territory between 'gay' and 'skinhead' are never explicitly stated. *It goes without saying*, and these assumptions need to be left unsaid. To reiterate the 'common sense' assumptions about masculinity would be dangerous, because the fact that the gay skin *does* exist despite them risks exposing their inadequacy.

So instead the reviewer redeploys old, familiar stereotypes: skinheads are scary creatures that tear the noses and ears off old-age pensioners, and gay men are effeminate 'pretty boys'. But even these are undermined: where once he could assume that there could be only one kind of poof, one kind of skin, he has to acknowledge that there are poofy skins and hard queers. The homosexuality radically concealed in gay skins, but which is paradoxically 'aggressively overt', leads to the panicked generation of a counter-model: homosexuality safely contained in the bourgeois politeness of the suit.

The gay skinhead embodies a contradiction that endangers masculinity. This is because masculinity exists within the fragile interplay between the homosexual and what Eve Sedgwick has termed the homosocial: the consolidation of masculinity through the grouping of men together, the unity of gender sameness in opposition to the absent, abject other of woman. Male homosociality is expected in certain environments (the football terrace, the snooker hall) and rituals (stag nights) and enforced in institutions (the military forces, sport). Many gay men's unhappy experience of games at school, which in many educational establishments is now the only occasion in which the sexes are separated, may lead them to suspect that their purpose has nothing to do with physical fitness or teamwork, and everything to do with reminding you that you are a man, teaching you what is expected of you as a man, and testing how you meet those requirements by placing you in competition with other men. It is instruction in homosociality and it is a Good Thing, unlike homosexuality, against which it has to maintain its difference. Much cultural effort is devoted to concretizing the distinction between the two, which is why so much anger and embarrassment accompany debates about gays in the military, rumours about gay football players, and so on. The discovery of the homosexual within homosocial institutions threatens to sexualize the whole environment as individuals are eyed with mistrust – everyone is potentially queered, and being a man's man might arouse more than mere suspicion. Hence the masculine rituals of urinal etiquette: always look straight ahead, keep words to a minimum, don't talk to strangers, and keep your movements as macho as possible. Knowledge (and indeed experience) of cottaging is common enough for men's toilets to be queered, and the potential for homosexuality to rear its ugly head in this homosocial environment is disavowed by shows of manly hostility.

As if femininity were a symptom of homosexuality; and this is precisely the problem. Ostensibly homosexuality functions as the inverse of homosociality, so the two can never be present at the same time. This is predicated on the invert model of male homosexuality – female souls in male bodies manifest in feminine behaviour – so when gay men appear within the hypermasculine environment of the homosocial, gender expectations are troubled. When a safely homosocial icon such as the skinhead – masculine, gang-based, all lads together – is revealed as a gay subcultural identity, homosexuality and homosociality become dangerously confused, as indeed they always were. This is hardly a surprise for those gay men who for decades have moved in cultural environments where homosociality is strictly enforced in order to articulate their homosexual identity – in other words, queens cruising in men-only clubs. For some straight men – such as the *Daily Express*' TV reviewer, the realization that homosociality might be a requirement of homosexuals is a 'real fright'. The proximity and congruency of homosexuality and homosociality becomes horrifically apparent: queers want to be with real men, so being a real man might make you . . .

The confusions in Tory's review reveal the knock-on effect that the dissolution of homosocial/homosexual has on private/public. Sexuality is supposed to be a private matter, society obviously a public one. Tory claims he wants homosexuals to go 'in again' – to confine them to the closet, because what two men (and his concern is with men) do *in private* is not his concern; privacy affords this privilege. He proposes that individuals in the public space wearing a uniform, a suit. This would deny homosexuals a social identity by erasing markers of homosexuality in public, and deny the difference of their private lives, so he never has to think about it; they will all look like heterosexuals. But he has identified skinheads as straight, so gay skins can hardly be accused of publicly marking their difference: by his logic, gay men should have gone 'in again' in becoming skinheads. And yet he damns them for being 'aggressively overt gay men'. In fact, despite what he says, Tory wants gay men to be confined to the closet of the less troubling effeminate model – 'pretty boys'. Closets don't so much hide the homosexual as pronounce the homosexual's confinement. It's the unexpected ease with which homosexuals slip from the private and colonize the public space (the skinhead is a street identity) that alarms him. The gay skinhead has made nonsense of 'common sense' (i.e. straight) understandings of masculinity.

Unidentifiable bodies

The confusions at work in the review of *Skin Complex* were also evident in a news item in the *Sun* nineteen years earlier. On 12 May 1973, under the headline 'THE MYSTERY MAN IN LEATHER', the tabloid reported a suspected gangland murder after a body was washed ashore in Rotherhithe:

> The strange life of Wolfgang von Jurgen was as full of mystery as his death.
> Police had him on their files as Michael St John, small-time London crook. And when his hand-cuffed body was washed up on the Thames shore they treated the case as gang-land murder.
> But his death came as a shock to neighbours in Stratford, East London, who knew him as a young TV actor and drag artist.
> . . . Von Jurgen was the name he used on stage – and he told his landlady, in his 'posh, educated voice', that he was German.
> But he was really born in Stoke Newington, North London.
> And in his secret life of petty crime he used at least two further aliases: Bernard Cogan and Anthony Cohen.

The alleged murder victim, who had a criminal record and who worked under several aliases, is described as an 'actor' and 'drag artist'; he lead a 'bedsitter life'; his landlord declared, 'He lived on his own and we did not see many of his friends. We never saw him with any girlfriends', his wife added, 'His two close friends were Terry and Mark, who took part in the drag act with him.' Are these pieces of 'evidence' provided to suggest that he is a homosexual?

The deciding paragraph would seem to be, 'Recently, Wolfgang started wearing expensive leather clothes. The red-painted walls of his flat were covered in pictures of film stars, including Steve McQueen in motorcycle gear.' But although by this date leather had acquired kinky connotations in the mainstream, were these details intended, and could they be guaranteed, to signify queerness to the straight *Sun* readership? The photo accompanying the piece showed the man baring his muscly torso, sporting cropped hair with long sideburns, and braces on his jeans. In fact, the machismo signalled by his skinhead appearance, a wardrobe of leather, gangland connections and a bachelor lifestyle would seem to have *contradicted* the previous homosexual hints: otherwise, why would a neighbour feel inclined to insist, 'He was a cheeky, jovial character – *certainly not a Hell's Angel*.'?

With his decadently decorated home a shrine for macho iconography, we can identify the 'mystery man' as a conspicuously obvious gay skin. In fact Wolf, as he was known to other gay skinheads, was a famous face on the emerging macho scene of the late 1960s and early 1970s. But such knowledge was not available to straight (and indeed many gay) readers at the time. So while these details add up to a familiar identity for some of us in the 1990s, they remained conflicting and contradictory for the *Sun* reporter. Unable to be reconciled within one being, they constitute a schizophrenic nonsense: just as he has an excess of names, so he has an excess of contradictory character attributes. If he's jovial then he can't be a Hell's Angel; if he's a drag queen, he can't be straight; if he's a hardened criminal, he can't be gay; and if he's any of these things, he cannot be – and, conspicuously, is not – described as a skinhead, even though that's exactly what his picture announces him to be.

The essentialist discourse of the centred individual still dominates common understandings of identity: individuals are required to be comprehensible as consistent personalities, their biographies neat, linear narratives. Wolf's frustration of this requirement as a gay skinhead meant that he could not be conceived as a 'real' person. Hence the report's curiosity and confusion: the mystery was not so much who as *what* he was. So even when the unidentified body washed ashore on the south bank of the Thames was positively identified as Wolf's, as a gay skinhead he continued to remain an unidentifiable body. Under the excess of names and identities, irreconcilable within the given parameters of cultural organization, the 'Man in Leather' remained a 'mystery': 'So just who WAS the man whose body, after at least a week in the water, was pulled ashore at Rotherhithe?'

In *Bodies that Matter*, Judith Butler analyses the way in which bodies become real, achieve materiality, through their sexing: 'Sex is one of the norms . . . that qualifies the body for life within cultural intelligibility.'[2] Through this she exposes the false dichotomy of nature/nurture which has dominated debates on gender and identity for the past four decades – 'Are men born or made?', 'Is femininity innate or learned?', 'Is there a gay gene?' Gender is neither an essence expressed through the body, nor a cultural construct written upon the ungendered site of the body – the body seems to be always/already gendered because it is only intelligible, it comes to be a body, *through* its gendering: 'The body signified as prior to signification is an effect of signification' (p. 30).

For most of the twentieth century, homosexuality has been understood according to the invert model, which feminizes male homosexuals. Men cannot be sexually attracted to men, so homosexual men must really be women. Confined to the open closet of the effeminate type, the homosexual is conspicuous; any movement beyond this therefore renders the homosexual invisible, as his homosexuality is culturally unintelligible. The masculinizing discourse of the gay skinhead is not one of the norms by which homosexuality can be understood.

Butler describes how the exclusionary matrix of heterosexual imperative creates 'unlivable' and 'uninhabitable' zones of social life against which the subject constitutes itself, and she concludes that it may be precisely through practices which underscore disidentification with those regulatory norms by which sexual difference is materialised that both feminist and queer politics are mobilised. Such collective disidentifications can facilitate a reconceptualisation of which bodies matter and which bodies are yet to emerge as critical matters of concern.

This is precisely the kind of collective disidentification that I believe the gay skinhead represents. The heterosexual imperative preserves the cross-gendered nature of sexual desire: gay men love men because internally they are really feminine. Skinheads emerged in the East End of London at the very time when gay politics on both sides of the Atlantic was mobilizing various disidentifications with the invert model. For gay men in England, the skinhead represented the most potent representation of real masculinity available. What the gay skinhead is then is a mystery man: an unidentifiable, culturally unintelligible body identity precisely because masculinity as it was understood should have ruled out its emergence. So 'gay skinhead' must be left unarticulated (and Wolf is termed neither gay nor skinhead even though both facts are equally obvious) or willed away (as Tory does: 'pretty boys' are derided but at least they preserve the heterosexual matrix) because the very term demands a reconceptualization of bodies that matter.

The reviewer's anger then is due to the fact that his (common) understanding of homosexuality should preclude the existence of gay skins. Not only do they exist, but they have alerted him to their existence; they have become intelligible – they matter. Nineteen years divide the two newspaper reports. What is amazing is that it took so long for the gay skin to materialize in the straight press.

Mapping epistemology. who knows?

In the early 1980s, the broad-left daily the *Guardian* ran a TV advertising campaign in which, identifying itself in opposition to the strong right-wing agenda informing the rest of British newspaper editorial policy, it sold itself on the grounds of its objectivity in refusing to tow the line. The breadth of its perspective was illustrated in one ad that, filmed in black and white, showed a skinhead running towards an businessman in the street. The expectation that the man in the suit will be assaulted is reinforced by his raising of his briefcase as a protection against the oncoming skinhead. A final sequence, filmed from a different angle sees the skinhead pulling the businessman out of the way of falling debris, with a voice-over assuring the viewer that it is only the objectivity of a broader perspective that can take in the facts. Aha, suggest those liberal *Guardian* people, appearances aren't always what they seem; you thought he was a villain and he's saving someone's life.

They are exploiting the skinhead's unambiguous significance: the monolithic status of the skinhead is such that they can assume that he will only be read in one way, allowing them to counter this shockingly with an unexpected reading. The plausibility of this counter-revelation depends on the subject position of those watching the ad, of course. But even they are unaware of the extent of the skinhead's polyvalency; while a *Telegraph* reader snorts indignantly at the implausibility of it all, and a *Guardian* reader feels a warm glow of democratic fairness, some old queen, who may read the *Sun*, absentmindedly catches the ad and thinks he's just spotted his boyfriend on the telly. What the *Guardian* hadn't counted on was that the skinhead was already polyvalent.

By the mid-1980s the elements of skinhead dress were so ubiquitous on the gay scene that they were ceasing to signify 'skinhead' and starting to signify 'gay' instead. But such knowledge is restricted. One's social position dictates the breadth of the ways of reading 'skinhead'. Gay skinheads are still invisible as gay men to many straight people.

'I don't think the general public know about it at all at the moment,' says one gay skin in 1995. 'I think they're quite shocked to discover gay skinheads. My boyfriend's very very out, very bold, and if he feels affectionate, he'll show it wherever we are. We were holding hands in Oxford Street today, in our usual skinhead gear, looking straight I suppose, and we got a few strange looks. We'll actually sit on the bus holding hands and people are shocked. I still feel slightly conscious of it, but he doesn't at all, he's totally relaxed. Once and these straight lads got up to get off, and the last one noticed, and he said to his mate, "You see them geezers on the back seat? They're holding hands!" And they were quite shocked. We found that funny.'

The invisibility that skinhead clothes still seems to provide in the mainstream may be one of the factors that renders it attractive to gay men. Two gay skins interviewed on *Skin Complex* spoke of the protective cover their clothes provided. 'The fashion skin is replacing the classic clone look and maybe the leather look as well', claimed one; for reasons of 'security . . . if you walk out of a club looking like a skinhead, you're not going to get anyone coming up to you and calling you a poof and a queer . . . the last thing in their thoughts is a gay, a poof.' Another agreed: 'A lot of it's self-defence.'

This is controversial. Passing as straight frustrates the requirements of gay liberation that homosexuals be visibly identifiable. Anything which refuses to be so is symptomatic of desire not to be gay: it is self-oppressive. But even gay skins aren't sure how (in)visible they are as gay men. Chris Clive, who ran the Gay Skinhead Group until his sudden death in a car accident in 1995, agreed that the image provided protection from queerbashing, although this was a by-product, a secondary benefit, and not a primary motivation. 'You walk down Old Street from the London

Apprentice – maybe not late at night, because then people might know where you've been . . . well, certainly any other town, and people won't try and attack you.' His hesitation was significant. One question central to this entire project is how do different people read 'skinhead', and in how many ways? This is still debatable among gay skinheads themselves. These communities of knowledge don't map neatly on to 'gay ghetto' and 'straight mainstream'. Age, geography, time, and wilful ignorance all play a part in determining who can read.

Chris went on to say,

If I saw a cropped-haired guy, a skinhead, in Guildford, for instance, I'd assume he was straight and a proper skin. If I saw him on the tube or on the escalator and he kept looking round at me, I'd know he was gay. London's a *bit* different because there's more around. Straight people, a lot of them wouldn't really know a gay person unless he started waving his arms about, so I think most straight people if they saw even a gay person with cropped hair and boots and things on, they'd probably assume he was an out and out violent skinhead. And the further north you go, the more people assume that you are a typical, violent skinhead, I suppose, a bovver boy.

He felt that in London, being recognized as gay through skinhead codes was a signal to other gay men, and straight passers-by too; but the generally liberal, cosmopolitan tone of central London meant that this did not make him a target of homophobic abuse.

The extent to which geography dictates people's ability to decode 'skinhead' as 'gay' is illustrated by the experience of one Brighton skin.

It seems the hassle you get is sometimes anti-gay in nature. Obviously they are thinking that, so you win from both directions or lose from both directions, depending on which way you look at it. It's not like London. This is a small provincial town. It has a mixture of London indifference, laissez-faire attitude, and small town mindless stupidity. On Friday nights round the Steine, you get gangs of straight lads waiting for people to hassle.

Straights are more likely to be both aware and homophobic.

But the skinhead is not just any old straight signifier: it has a long history of association with extreme masculinity and violence which, in the late 1970s, was made official by its adoption into far-right movements. So there are further questions to ask about who can *afford* to read the skinhead as anything other than a threatening mode of hard masculinity that is significantly white. Given the skinhead's association with violence against communities on the grounds of their racial difference, who can afford to read the skinhead as anything other than a racist fascist? Given that there are still those who engage in homophobic violence who claim that identity, can white gay men be so ambivalent to the social meanings of skinhead? The gay skin presents a difficult problem in the politics of enunciation.

The variations in homosexual (in)visibility that gay skins today represent highlight the difficulties in recovering the histories of people who articulated some sense of same-sex attraction in the past. If a subculture as established as gay skinheads can still pass invisibly to most of the population today, how much more difficult it is to recover invisible histories. It is not just a matter of whether identities have been suppressed by a homophobic establishment. Given the violence with which homosexuality has been policed, it was in some people's interests to compose a self-presentational strategy that signalled to those with whom they shared an identity without alerting the attention of others. If they didn't want the attention of the contemporary press and police, how much harder for the historian thirty years later.

But recovering lost or invisible histories of homosexuality is even harder than playing 'Hunt the Homo (in Camo Gear)'. To further complicate this map is the fact that there have been many homosexualities. Official 'gay history' records but two: those such as Edward Carpenter who were materially privileged and well-connected enough to push for political reform in the name of sexual liberation, their class status ensuring that their efforts would be recorded; and those who had nothing to lose in advertising their sexual dissidence through conspicuous, gender-disruptive dress codes (most famously Quentin Crisp). There may have been many other homo-sexualities which we do not know about, that will remain hidden, either because they were disguised, or because they were not culturally organized in a recognizable way.

Dangerous knowledge

The communities of knowledge demarcated by those who read skinheads as gay are tellingly self-contained. This may be because the challenge that the gay skinhead represents to traditions in masculinity is too difficult to accept. There may be another, related reason. Philosopher Jean Baudrillard has identified the transmission of information as viral; homosexual knowledge is perhaps contaminatory. It implicates the bearer: 'It takes one to know one'. Much of the history of homosexuality has been written in double entendre, as much to protect the writer from accusations as to protect the reader from dangerous knowledge. This can be seen in objections to the broadcasting of safer sex information. 'It teaches people to be perverts; you catch AIDS from being queer.'

The sharp delineation of homosexual knowledge has been conspicuous since the birth of homosexuality (the term was coined in the mid-nineteenth century), and this may be for similar reasons of wilful disavowal. Double entendre has proved a vital means of communication for gay men, but it also provides straight commentators a latex glove with which they can handle hazardous knowledge. In his consideration of the life of Oscar Wilde, Neil Bartlett refers to Charles Whibley's review of *The Picture of Dorian Gray* for the *Scots Observer* in 1890, which claimed the play was intended to be read by 'outlawed noblemen and perverted telegraph boys'. That is, queers: the phrase referred to a newspaper scandal about a post office clerk who seduced young telegraph delivery boys and recommended them to a Soho brothel where the clients included titled gentry. 'This is hard to believe, because I thought that in 1890 we were invisible, that our invisibility was a fact,' says Bartlett.[3] But Whibley 'must have been sure that his readers remembered the headlines of four years earlier'. The title of Bartlett's book, *Who Was That Man?*, plays on the unintelligibility of the newly formed homosexual, which was yet to be successfully confined to the effeminate in the demonization of Wilde in the years that followed.

When the Marquess of Queensbury left his accusatory card for Oscar Wilde which precipitated the events that lead to the writer's imprisonment, he signed it, 'To Oscar Wilde, posing as a somdomite'. This misspelling is usually explained as a mistake provoked by Queensbury's anger. But did he in fact want to disavow his acquaintance with the word? The porter of the Albemarle club with whom the card was left 'looked at the card, but did not understand the meaning of the words'.[4] Indeed the phrase was recorded as 'Posing as a *****.'[5]

Perhaps, then, it is in some people's interests to ignore the homosexuality of the aggressively overt gay skinhead.

A shared mythology

Even within the fairly reductive definitions of 'gay man' and 'skinhead' in circulation in the mainstream, what both categories have in common is some interest and investment in the notion of an 'authentic' working-class masculinity. Given that society and gay subculture are white-dominated, and that the skinhead was asserting a whiteness against racial others, that needs one more specification: this is about a mythology of specifically *white*, working-class masculinity. Just as 'skinhead' usually means '(straight) skinhead', so 'gay man' usually means '(white) gay man': given the ideological centrality of some groups, certain categories are uninflected: it goes without saying. This is by no means to suggest that all gay skinheads are inherently, or subconsciously, racist: it does however highlight the extent to which the mythology of the skinhead has served the purposes of white men, gay and straight.

The existence of gay skins demands that we reconceptualize not only homosexuality but skinheads too – the way gay subculture has fetishized, utilized, rejected and appropriated the putative natural masculinity embodied in the skinhead. My suspicion is that skinheads hold an erotic fascination for gay male subculture precisely *because* they represent and preserve all these conservative notions of masculinity; this may of course lead to some troubling, unwelcome conclusions.

The circulation of conservative masculine signifiers within gay subculture may undermine the status of such a definition of masculinity, which relies on its unquestionable heterosexual authenticity to sustain its superiority. The image has powerful potential to refute straight expectations about gay men (which, even today, site them as the descendants of a line of queens from Oscar Wilde via Quentin Crisp), problematizing heterosexual masculinity's claim to authentic status in the process.

The contradefinitional function of 'gay man' and 'skinhead' preserves notions of masculinity in a tautology which places them beyond interrogation. What I hope the experiences of gay skinheads collected in this book reveal is the way that the supposedly bizarre juxtapositions of gender they embody shorts the closed circuit of masculinity.

Notes

1. 'Tory on TV', *Daily Express*, Saturday 1 August 1992 (my emphasis).
2. Judith Butler, *Bodies That Matter* (London: Routledge, 1993), p. 5.
3. Neil Bartlett, *Who Was that Man?: A Present for Mr Oscar Wilde* (London: Serpent's Tail, 1988), p. 94.
4. *Penguin Famous Trials 7: Oscar Wilde*, ed. H. Montgomery Hyde (Harmondsworth: Penguin, 1962), p. 76.

2

Kids, Cults and Common Queers

English may not have a grammatical gender, but the common usage of phrases such as 'male model', 'female doctor', 'male nurse' and 'lady driver' shows that many nouns are implicitly gendered. The fact that gendering extends beyond sex to sexuality, and that, even today, the phrase 'gay skinhead' exists is symptomatic of the assumption that skinheads by definition must be straight.

The official skinhead histories – sociological papers trying to understand the phenomenon, the cultural activity of those participating in it, and press reports condemning it – are not very useful if you're looking for gay skinheads. Not only was no one looking for them; by definition, such a thing could not exist. As for the gay skinheads who were enjoying themselves in the late 1960s despite their supposed non-existence, they weren't going to draw attention to themselves.

To understand how and why the categories 'gay man' and 'skinhead' define against each other, it is necessary to examine the other binaries of this opposition: working class/middle class, masculine/effeminate, natural/ unnatural, heterosexual/homosexual. These oppositions add up to the 'truth' that skinheads are working-class, violently aggressive, inarticulate, politically right-wing real men. Gay men, on the other hand, are middle-class, passive, creative, politically left-wing failed or false men. Yes, these are stereotypes; obviously there are articulate skinheads, gay Tories, anti-racist skinheads, macho queens, gay skinheads and so on. But these are the expected qualities used to define social groups, and conforming to those expectations can even be exploited by members for their own ends. It is through the creation and regulation of stereotypes that the dominant culture polices its subjects. I want to show how a certain notion of masculinity is made to seem natural, and how certain groups are excluded from this 'natural' masculinity, by highlighting the disruptive possibilities that these oppositions are supposed to exclude – the gay skinhead being a prime example.

Class divisions supposedly exclude gay men from skinhead subculture. The skinhead is a working-class youth cult from the late 1960s whereas gay or homosexual identities were supposedly available only to the middle classes until the late 1970s. Skinheads are expected to be rough and queens are expected to be a bit posh.

Common queers: who are you calling gay?

Axiomatic to lesbian and gay studies is the view that until the aftermath of the Gay Liberation Front, gay was a middle-class identity. 'It is impossible to come out as politically gay if there is not to begin with any culture in which we can identify ourselves.'[1] The argument runs that working-class men had no access to this culture. Working-class men had restricted social mobility, and this is particularly true when it came to access to homosexual subcultures. Bemoaning the sparsity of evidence with regard to working-class homosexuality, Jeffrey Weeks writes, 'We may hypothesise that the spread of a homosexual consciousness was much less strong among working-class men than middle-class – for obvious family and social factors.'[2]

The arguments that, until the 1970s, only middle-class men could identify as gay, can seem fairly convincing: the effete, posh Oscar Wilde, middle-class with aristocratic aspirations, has dominated homosexual identity in the twentieth century, making the homosexual identity which emerged in his wake particularly pertinent for other middle-class men; homosexual rights groups campaigning for political change and law reforms have been dominated by middle-class, university-educated homosexuals; professions which tolerated homosexuals – the theatre, the fine arts, fashion – were middle-class. Most of the inadequate existing material on homosexual identity in the first half of the twentieth century reveals that male homosexual identities only existed either as a part of the broader leisure industries for middle- and upper-class men by way of networks established through underground clubs in cities, or, to a lesser extent, as a political or intellectual identity within the cultural or academic élite. Both were extensions of upper-middle-class culture and carried its values, and both were inaccessible to most working-class men.

Also, the adoption of a homosexual identity for working-class men may have been precluded by material conditions. Changes in British society after the Second World War led to what has been referred to as a 'privatization' of sexuality. The Wolfenden Report, advising law reform in the area of sexual conduct, was published in 1957, declaring that the law should not 'intervene in the private lives of citizens'[3] but instead concentrate on 'the public realm'. It was radical in so far as it effected legal and political changes which put 'private' activity, including sex between men over the age of twenty-one, beyond the reach of the law. But this move privileged those who could afford private space – that is, the property-owning middle classes. As if to compensate, the law reasserted its moral function by redoubling its efforts within its newly restricted domain, and there was a sharp rise in cottaging offences in the years following the partial decriminalization of male homosexuality. As such, men who could not move within the limited areas of society that tolerated homosexuals found their efforts to find sex with other men more hazardous.

Cultural analysis informed by Marxist criticism has identified these moves as an attempt to create a 'privatized' sexuality in the post-war period which was inherently bourgeois, dependent on notions of private property and the individual: 'The structure of the middle-class environment . . . is based on the concept of *property* and private *ownership*, on individual differences of status, wealth and so on, whereas the structure of the working-class environment is based on the concept of community or collective identity, common lack of ownership, wealth, and so on.'[4] Illustrating how property ownership benefited middle-class homosexuals is the testament of Janine, a lesbian in 1960s' Brighton:

> If you were extremely middle-class and gay and you'd sorted yourself out and you had inherited money and you owned your own house, then you made a circle of friends and it was an extremely selfish life. You didn't think as much as I do now that you needed to support gay causes, I mean they were things, on the whole, that happened to other people.[5]

The 'privatization of sexuality' made the adoption of homosexual identity by working-class people, and the formation of a collective identity, more difficult.

So homosexual identities were not available to working-class men until fairly recently: they got married, had children and generally conformed to dominant notions of masculinity. If they did engage in same-sex activity, it was discreet and did not involve questions or problems of identity.

Or so the argument runs. But try putting it to working-class men who were gay in the 1950s and 1960s, as I have in the course of writing this book, and the response you are likely to get is concise, unambivalent and in the negative. Their own biographies renders the widely accepted generalization that 'gay' is a middle-class identity a nonsense. Even if one accepts that access to homosexual subcultures was restricted for working-class men, the adoption of an identity is not solely dependent on access to a subculture. Few children grow up with access to gay subculture or lesbians and gay men. Most people identify as gay, in their early teens, in isolation, before they have access to a scene or meet other homosexuals; it is this primary identification which motivates the formation of those links.

Knowledge of homosexual identity is what is required, and certainly post-war working-class epistemology did not fail to include deviants. Partly as a backlash against moves towards legislative change in favour of homosexuals, sensationalist stories about queers slowly started to appear in working-class newspapers at this time. In 1952, the *Sunday Pictorial* ran a series of articles called 'Evil Men'. It was about '"pansies" – mincing, effeminate young men who call themselves queers. But simple decent folk

GAY SKINS

regard them as freaks and rarities.'⁶ Censorship and taste meant that the issue could rarely be dealt with directly; disapproval had to be expressed, but in a way that did not educate those not already aware of it. However, according to the *Sunday Pictorial* feature, by 1952, 'Most people know there are such things', heralding a project of queer marginalization, allowing for a reverse discourse by many isolated gay men.

This series marked the end of what the paper's former editor, Hugh Cudlipp, tellingly referred to as a 'conspiracy of silence' about the 'spreading fungus' of homosexuality.⁷ Everyone knew about it, but *nobody dared write about it*. And a similar conspicuous silence characterizes our knowledge of homosexual identities of this period.

One problem is defining the parameters of 'gay'. The word was taken up by gay rights campaigners in the late 1960s to counteract the pejorative connotations of the alternative labels, and therefore its use formed part of a political project to build a positive sense of collective identity. These movements were dominated by middle-class tertiary-level educated men; if 'gay' refers to such politicized subjects, then it does exclude the likelihood of working-class involvement. However, in actual practice the word 'gay' is used to refer to sexual (self-)identifications well beyond these narrow limits. The word's homosexual appropriation derived from the nineteenth-century use of the word as a slang reference to prostitution. And although its revival by rights movements to some extent divided those people identifying as homosexual along generational grounds (there were objections from older homosexuals to the 'tainting' of an 'innocent' word), it was taken up, even at the time, by people who had no direct involvement with those movements. In the late 1980s, the postmodern critique of lesbian and gay identity politics, which later became known as 'Queer', alerted some lesbian and gay academics and activists to the historicist specificity of the word 'gay' and the folly of applying contemporary understandings to other periods of history. This too would seem to limit the definition. But I would question the motivation in such exercises of delimitation: even in the wake of Queer, labelling is perceived to be a matter of aesthetics rather than historicist semantics for most lesbians and gay men. A *Boyz* feature asking gay men at the Men's Ponds on Hampstead Heath how they liked to be termed evinced responses such as, 'I hate the words nancy and pansy – they sound so waspish and antiquated', 'I do like the sound of the word wussie', 'I don't like the word fag, it sounds American', 'I went off nancy because of Nancy Reagan', 'I hate the word homosexual, it sounds so medical'.⁸ Given that Queer set out to shake up the liberal lexicon of polite, acceptable, 'politically correct', terms, it is interesting that for one respondent the Q-word was a neologism he felt obliged to adopt: 'I suppose if I'm being really PC I should say I don't mind being called queer, though I'm still not used to that yet.' The most popular word by far was 'gay'.

But when considering and constructing 'gay history', the constituency denoted by 'gay' reverts to the very narrow definition of this single, politically informed, middle-class homosexual type. Much sociological work on post-war homosexual identity has taken this narrow definition of 'gay' and those who do not conspicuously conform to it are simply not going to register. And true, it was unlikely that you would come across many kids wearing GLF badges on council estates in the early 1970s. So working-class involvement is precluded literally *by definition*. Consider the tautology here: Working-class men had no access to gay identity. Why? Because 'gay' is a middle-class identity. Why? Because working-class men had no access to gay identity . . . . Whose interests does this exclusion serve?

Perhaps we should not be too surprised. The fact is that until fairly recently, most of the work being carried out on homosexual identity was within academia, itself a middle-class environment populated by a majority of people from middle-class backgrounds perhaps not best suited to understanding working-class cultures.

But it may be more than misunderstanding; it may be a motivated by a drive for fantasy-preservation. There is much effort in sociological analyses to preserve the working-classes as homo-free. For example, the rent boy, modern history's conspicuously visible working-class homo, is usually explained as a solution to a problem of economics, not sexuality: 'There is a subculture involving young boys in the gay world, known as "chickens". They can be heterosexual boys, using a market-place for prostitution.'[9] In *The Naked Civil Servant*, however, Quentin Crisp describes his involvement in a street culture of the 1950s, where working-class youths take to prostitution not so much for the money as for the access it provides to a homosexual identity and sex. We need to ask ourselves why the belief that rent boys are really straight is so persistent, even today. Could it be that working-class men embody a more authentic masculinity for many middle-class men, and the need to preserve that authentic masculinity as unqueerably straight has predisposed the analyses to the exclusion of working-class men? Middle-class gay men who have invested in fantasies about sex with 'real' men (as the posh queens themselves phrased it, 'rough trade') would have all the greater investment in this. Working-class lads have to be kept straight.

Or there may be a political explanation; one could go so far as to speculate that those gay academics themselves researching in this field may have had some investment in restricting and preserving gay for a political identity, leaving them little incentive to research into homosexual identities which did not contribute to radical politics.

Queer, in debt to Foucault, popularized the fact that there are many '(homo)sexualities', that the territory of sexual dissidence is ever-changing, and that we need to look beyond 'homosexuality' as it is positioned within today's cultural organization of sexuality, the very notion of sexuality itself being a recent phenomenon. Certainly Queer is a very useful tool with which to organize discoveries of sexual identities which do not fit the categories of hetero/homosexual. But my suspicion is that there were many working-class men articulating an identity recognizable as being somewhere in the orbit of 'gay' (by today's understandings of the word) in the post-war period.

I am not suggesting a conspiracy theory here – I am questioning motivation rather than making accusations of conscious exclusion. Given that categories create constituencies, I am not unsympathetic to the theory that 'gay' was a product of, and therefore made more sense to, liberal bourgeois discourses of the individual, identity, family and society. But although their *material* conditions differed from those of the middle classes, working-class people may have shared with them an *imaginary* relation to society; indeed, consensus politics would require any material differences to be negated by a shared imaginary relation, lest the perception of those differences provoke social unrest. *Whose* imaginary relation this was is hard to say, although obviously bourgeois ideology could assert itself all the more successfully in the changing lives of working-class people through various cultural sites (new housing, consumerism, TV scheduling). So even if 'gay' was a middle-class identity, to assume its class restriction is naïve. And to take this as read in the absence of any material to the contrary, and then to cite that absence as a reason not to bother discovering it, is suspect to say the least. That we know so little of pre-'Liberation' working-class homosexual identities is perhaps due not so much to an absence of such participants as the class identity of the analysts.

Working-class homosexuals

In fact, what recent, more grass-roots-orientated work in recovering gay history shows is that, despite the very real obstructions identified as limiting homosexual subjectivity to the middle classes, working-class men and women both felt the need to, and in many cases could, articulate a homosexual identity. For example, the Ourstory Project's book *Daring Hearts* and the documentary *Storm in a Teacup* (commissioned for Channel 4's 1992 series of *Out*) both show that in Brighton and the East End of London in the 1950s, pubs existed which catered for a more or less exclusively working-class clientele. *Daring Hearts* records the memories of lesbians and gay men in the Brighton of the 1950s and 1960s, where the scene was strictly structured on class lines because, as one participant recalls, 'there were queers among the upper, the middle and the lower classes, but in those days a lot of queers were inclined to be a bit snobbish, they mixed with their own set'.[10] So the scene was complex enough to accommodate gay men of various social backgrounds; the Regency Club 'was very much a working-class club' defining itself in opposition to other more 'gentlemanly' venues. These men then identified themselves as gay *within* a working-class culture. The East End homosexual community remembered in *Storm in a Teacup* was based around the dock pubs. Here the subculture was well-established enough to have its own language, *polari*, a mutation of nineteenth-century East End traders' slang influenced by the language of local immigrant communities.

As Daffyd Jenkins, the manager of a gay club in a working-class area of south-east London points out, the very history of the gay scene tends to contest the assumption that 'gay' is a middle-class identity:

> Most of the established gay pubs have grown up in rough working-class areas. The East End, for all its macho-ness, the people there are far more accepting of everything. The London Apprentice is in the middle of an extremely rough area, but they don't have bother. The Union Tavern was in a very rough area. The White Swan, too. Wherever you go – Swansea, Cardiff, Birmingham, Manchester – OK, the places nowadays tend to be in the city centres. But most of the gay scenes in cities started in the working-class areas. Plus – a lot of the gangs that ruled, that even rule now, in the East End, have faggot connections. The Krays, the Richardsons – lots of them had gay connections. It's not a problem. The average working-class man or woman has far more to worry about than who's screwing who. They really don't care.

His own experience as the manager of the Anvil contradicts the notion that working-class men are more hostile to homosexuality:

> The police didn't want us to open here, because it's a very rough, gang-ruled area. They said we'd be inviting trouble, but we've had absolutely no trouble. In fact, when the people across the road started objecting to our licence, it was the local people from the council estates at the back who wanted to start a petition in our favour.

He claims there was no difficulty in him identifying as homosexual growing up as a working-class man in the 1960s: 'My father was a miner, my mum was a cleaner; just because I now own a business, I don't consider myself any less working-class, as the Gay Tory Group found when they came round for a subscription the other week.' As a gay working-class teenager, he had no access to a local gay scene – it was not until his twenty-first birthday that he visited his first gay venue, after finding a copy of *Gay News* on the train. But there was a social and sexual network where he lived which centred on public toilets:

> When I was about thirteen, the headmaster gave us a talk about this cottage, telling us about how it was disgusting, how there were evil

people there, how we mustn't go anywhere near there. So I thought, oh good, and I made a note of the address . . . I had a wild time. Out in Surrey, in Caterham, where I lived, cottaging wasn't a sexual thing. You used to go to the local cottage to meet your mates. It was the local nightlife.

Cottaging is not used as proof of pre-'Liberation' working-class gay identities because it does not necessarily require any recourse to a queer model for those involved. Dennis recalls in *Daring Hearts* that before the Pill, cottages were much more popular for men wanting non-procreative sex: 'They weren't gay, these people, they were just randy and wanted serving.'[11] Daffyd himself recalls one particular cottaging episode: 'I walked in there and there was this massive great skinhead. I had a wild time.' He concedes that 'He was straight; one fuck does not a faggot make.'

But his experience of cottaging was that it provided a focus for working-class men who did identify as gay. 'Where I used to live in the wilds of Surrey, if you were gay you had to be a screaming Mary, there was no two ways about it, you couldn't be gay and macho. If you weren't a screaming Mary, you weren't a proper queen. The few that were around that were not overtly faggot were oddities in a way.' We know that Wilde's legacy, the effeminate stereotype, became available as a model of homosexual identity to lower-class men by the 1950s. This model has not been forgotten by history, and cannot easily be silenced, precisely because it is so self-proclaiming and defiantly visible. Indeed, it readily leant itself to demonization by the normalizing processes of mainstream culture.

Many working-class kids who desired same-sex activity found that it did involve questions of identity, and damning press coverage, such as 'Evil Men' in the *Sunday Pictorial*, at least made it known that other such people existed. Access to a scene where they could meet others like themselves might have been restricted, but there was at least the potential for identifying with this model (it was real – it was in the newspaper), however difficult.

But for lower-class men to affect this effeminate model took much commitment and invited much hostility. For those men who did not accept that their homosexuality was at odds with their masculinity, this was not a satisfactory identity. One such gay man of the 1960s:

Looking back to the sixties, we're talking of a time in which, when I was 15 in 1961, homosexuality was illegal; there was the whole threat of being thrown into prison. So there was no thought of being upfront gay in the street – apart from the Quentin Crisps of the world. But I couldn't be like that. That sounds like a criticism, but it isn't, I just wouldn't dare do what he did – I don't like being called names like that, for a start.

His lack of access to the gay scene compounded his identity troubles:

> I lived in a small working-class town, I didn't know where gay men met, there were no gay publications, you had virtually no chance of finding a gay bar; the society was secret. So being young and gay was almost hopeless. No wonder people from that time became neurotic; you just felt helpless.

The alternative for those who had no access to the commercial scene, cottaging, proved equally fruitless:

> I knew people my age at that time were getting jerked off in men's toilets, but I hadn't been, and in fact every attempt I made to try to be where I thought gay people might be, they weren't. It was just appallingly difficult. So I ended up getting to 21 and I hadn't had sex, I didn't know what a gay bar was, not really accepting I was gay, not expressing anything, totally neurotic about sex. I didn't know anything.

And yet this young working-class man could still identify as gay. Where he found solace was in youth subculture: first as a mod, then as a skinhead.

The Leather Boys

In 1963 *The Leather Boys* was published.[12] It seemed to be a teen schlock novel about the aggressive, violent, destructive, demonized youth culture of the day – gangs of leather-clad bikers. John Gross in the *New Statesman* dismissed it as a 'potboiler about motor-bike gangs bashing one another to death'.[13] However, contemporary reviews (either deliberately or through carelessness) overlooked the fact that the two heroes are gay. This oversight was redressed twenty-four years later, when the book was reissued by Gay Men's Press in its Gay Modern Classics series, earning a review in the Leather section of *Gay Times*.[14] The book, by the journalist Gillian Freeman, is perhaps best considered a 'social problem' novel about working-class identity, and, in particular, the difficulties in identifying as gay for working-class boys. The fact that she should be able to site what amounts to a gay romance so easily within the most aggressively masculine environment of the day without it appearing nonsensically contradictory is significant. (Interestingly, she originally wrote the novel under the name of Eliot George, inverting gender and literature in one fell swoop; I'll leave you to dwell on the queer implications.) Given the supposed absence of working-class homosexual identities of this period, this seems conspicuous, and raises questions about the possibilities that teen culture allowed working-class men to articulate some sense, albeit confused, of homosexual identity.

Men having sex with men did not necessarily make them queer, and the existence of sexual activity which did not problematize sexual identity is acknowledged in *The Leather Boys*: some of Reggie's biker friends openly have sex with 'leather johnnies' to make money and Dick realizes that 'men did do things with other men when they felt randy, everyone knew that. It didn't mean they felt anything special, though.' Similarly, Reggie thinks how 'blokes often had sex together if there were no girls around, in the army and things'.

But their knowledge of this circumstantial model of casual sex only serves to illustrate how it does not apply to either of them: they experience homosexual desire specifically, emotionally and individually as part of their identity. Reggie considers sex with Dick as 'deliberate and what he wanted', and although he cannot identify as queer, he cannot dismiss the possibility either: 'he thought, why should I feel like this over Dick, I'm not queer. But perhaps he was, if he felt as he did' (p. 70).

The young bikers do find access to gay subculture but feel alienated by it. Straying into a gay pub, Dick is chatted up by a man 'in jeans and an open-necked shirt, his fingers covered with cheap rings . . . Dick could see powder on his face and a metal bracelet on his wrist. His open neck revealed a silver cross on a chain . . . nestled among the greying hairs on his chest. In contrast his hair was brilliantly blond' (p. 101). But Dick cannot identify with such a model:

> He had never seen homosexuals like them before. He had never thought of his relationship with Reggie as being homosexual, he hadn't labelled it or questioned it. It wasn't like this. They would never be like these men. (p. 162)

After declaring his love for Reg, Dick says, 'It's funny, isn't it. I mean, we don't want to put on lipstick or anything like that, do we?' (p. 71). He cannot identify with this camp homosexual identity (although 'He had never seen homosexuals like them before' does suggest other models were available: the leather johnnies?). He does, however, feel an urge towards what we might recognize as coming out: 'there had been times when he had wanted to blurt out, cry out, we loved each other. But he couldn't. There was no one, no one, no one he could tell' (p. 126). But to come out as what and into what?

To what extent, then, could Reggie and Dick identify as homosexual? Brigid Brophy's review of Gillian Freeman's next novel, *The Leader*, identifies the author's project of writing about the difficulties of expression for people with no appropriate language, identifying her characters as having 'submerged identities' and referring to the 'unrealised homosexuality of *The Leather Boys*' where 'the two youths . . . have no idea they are homosexual until they make love'.[15] Are we to read *The Leather Boys* as a gay novel, a queer novel, or a novel about the emergence of a specifically working-class homosexual identity, or a tragedy of its absence? There certainly seems to be no linguistic or symbolic language available to the characters with which to articulate homosexual desire: 'He wanted to analyse his feelings and Reggie's, to talk about themselves and their relationship. But he didn't know the word analyse and he couldn't explain his longing' (p. 71).

Such intellectual devices are not available to Dick and Reggie by virtue of their class positions: their education has not provided them with useful tools, so they have to create their own identity, or go searching for one. The novel also shows how material restrictions affected them. The financial situation of many working-class men may have improved in the 1950s, but this ran to an accumulation of household consumables rather than the purchase of property. Dick and Reg significantly have sex in Dick's gran's house. Gran thinks nothing of Reggie and Dick sharing a bed in her house; their foregrounded masculinity as bikers renders them unlikely suspects of queer. Assuming effeminacy as a symptom of homosexuality rendered same-sex practices invisible to contemporary working-class people: James in *Daring Hearts* recalls that unwanted pregnancy was the most pressing sexual issue, so 'a lot of working class people, providing they didn't know what was going on, they didn't mind if you put two boys in a bed together . . . then no-one could get pregnant' (p. 16). Gran's house is a vital space available to them due to their position within an extended family network, a community which the imposition of the nuclear family model sought to destroy. The very architecture of post-war new housing projects, influenced by the need for quick-build programmes and the efficiency of modernist design, led to working-class terraces being cleared in favour of tower blocks. The middle-class town planners reshaped the family as a nuclear unit, culturally alien to the extended family networks that working-class communities had been used to. Sexuality was restricted to a reproductive function and physically confined to the private space of the home. When Gran falls ill and the house is threatened, so too is the relationship.

No satisfactory identity exists within their culture, hence Reggie and Dick's desire to escape to sea, and Dick's riding away at the close of the book: 'the engine beating beneath him promised a liberation'. This has been the (unsatisfactory) answer for many gay men from lower-class environments throughout the century: *Between the Acts* gives the accounts of Bernard, who ran away from his working-class home in Aberdeen, and John, who fled from Tyneside. Both had identified themselves as being homosexual before leaving home, and both made for London.[16] But even *The Leather Boys* mourns the tragedy of an absence of adequate working-class homosexual identities. It would seem that the disruption of masculinities inherent to working-class youth cultures provides the raw materials with which to build new formations.

Dangerous masculinities

The discovery of queers at the heart of a macho youth cult shouldn't be that surprising. After all, much cultural effort is spent upon valorizing all-male environments whilst denying their erotic potential; just consider the efforts made to exclude homosexuals from the British armed forces, to keep the homosocial separate from the homosexual. Indeed, the categories of homosocial and homosexual are kept not so much separate as mutually exclusive by definition – the opposition of gay man with skinhead is an example of this dynamic.

But most of the studies of youth subcultures that emerged in the post-war period assume that all participants were unproblematically, unquestionably heterosexual – after all, these lads were rough. This in itself shows the way working-class masculinity is made to conform to middle-class requirements: common lads mark the boundary of accepted modes of middle-class male behaviour. It is interesting that these accounts, so sensitive to the issue of class, cannot see the way in which class has constructed and fixed the discourses of masculinity.

Joseph Pleck has studied how the white middle-class male status of those conducting US universities' sociological research throughout the twentieth century has ensured that their methodologies and conclusions preserved certain notions about the authenticity and excessive masculinity in working-class men. 'One of the most consistent findings of m–f [comparative gender] research is that working class individuals are more sex-typed on average than those of the middle class.'[17] In other words, working-class men are masculine. He quotes several studies from the early 1960s claiming to prove this with the finding that working-class boys went on to find highly masculine jobs ('businessmen, farmers, athletes, engineers'), whereas the middle-class boys ended up in less masculine jobs ('teachers, psychiatrists'). Pleck point out that 'masculine' jobs generally have much lower social status. The studies failed to see this because 'White middle class behaviour is always the standard by which other groups are compared.'

It would be ungenerous to criticize early class-based subcultural analysis: most date from the early 1970s, long before the general availability of gender-deconstructive tools was made possible by developments in the field by Gender Studies. It needs to be stated that most of the people doing this work were middle-class men, but would the analysis of a working-class man make much difference? Working-class men buy into these myths too. I have known few men, of whatever class, who have been offended by the suggestion that they are extremely manly. Although it is poor compensation, excessive masculinity is one of the few privileges afforded to working-class men. (There are drawbacks too, of course, most notably in the way discourses about criminality naturalize links between gender and class.)

So queers could not be delinquents, queers could not be working-class, working-class boys were rough, queers were soft, working-class boys could not be queer, queers were always/already fully-grown men . . . . Each axiom defers to the next for proof, closing the categories of working-class rough lads and middle-class soft queens. This precludes any possibility of involvement of, or appropriation by, homosexual males.

In fact, there's something queer about all teen cults – just like dirty homosexuals, they're dangerous, delinquent and demonized by the press. Stanley Cohen's *Folk Devils and Moral Panics* identified the process by which youth cultures are demonized to redefine normality.[18] The paradigm fits gay men as snugly as, say, skinheads. Both act as conspicuous reminders of what men should not be. Both are transgressive in their style.

But gay subcultures were never subjected to this very analysis that places them with other demonized groups that resist through style and specific social rituals. Of course, there are specific problems in researching homosexuality in youth subcultures: male homosexual acts were illegal until 1967, thereafter restricted to certain conditions between men over the age of twenty-one; it wasn't until 1994 that this was reduced to eighteen. Fears of prosecution may have hampered attempts to collate information. But given the assumptions mentioned above there was no space for any overlap, as working-class youth culture was separated from gay subculture along the boundaries of both class and masculinity. Thus gay subcultures are seen to operate in isolation from other subcultures.

Michael Brake in his consideration of subcultural analysis was exceptional in at least noticing that 'Subcultural studies of youth never mention homosexuals, and this is hardly surprising given the masculinist emphasis of practically all youth subcultures. Young gay people are swamped by the heterosexist emphasis they find in peer groups and subcultures.'[19] Unfortunately he is restricted by the very masculinist assumption of the analysis he criticizes – he conflates masculinism with heterosexism, so 'gay people' are too soft to hang out with the lads. Such an assumption renders invisible queer goings on in youth cultures.

On the rare occasions when it is addressed, homosexual subculture is treated as a singular, distinct subculture which magically appears without any personal biography, as if its members were never young, never had to grow up within straight society, and were always already there.

Such an approach is inadequate. Even working within a straight mind-frame, the thinking in traditional sociological analysis is too rigid: the tribes are too distinct and results in terrible difficulty in explaining diachronic subcultural transformations (they distinguish between mods and skinheads when in fact for a while there was no distinction) let alone synchronic subcultural interaction. The phenomenon of teenage working-class youth culture has been assessed *only* in terms of class identity. This methodology cannot allow for the way some youth subcultures, in experimenting with identity, create a space where social and sexual deviancy can overlap which may allow for same-sex sexual activity. The formation of subcultural codes may be a viable and indeed urgent project for men articulating same-sex desire. In the post-war disruption of masculinities, there may have been space for a working-class homosexual identity to emerge within these stylishly dissident, 'delinquent' subcultures:

> Delinquency can be seen as a form of communication about a situation of contradiction in which the 'delinquent' is trapped but whose complexity is excommunicated from his perceptions by virtue of the *restricted linguistic code* which working class culture makes available to him . . . In the absence of a workingclass ideology which is both accessible and capable of providing a concrete interpretation of such contradictions, what can a poor boy do? Delinquency is one way he can communicate.[20]

In fact, working-class men who experienced homosexual desire, but did not want to identify with the nelly model, had as much investment in playing around with new ways of being a man as their straight mates. Both groups were interrogating or refusing unsatisfactory gender expectations. In the post-war period there were fears over how to make working-class masculinity useful. Lynne Segal's 'Look Back in Anger: Men in the Fifties' examines the confused map of sexual and gender definitions in the wake of the Second World War, that resulted in the disruption of familial and domestic arrangements until the establishment of a new liberal consensus under the new social order of welfare-capitalism. In an effort to reintegrate the sexes in marriage and mould men into responsible fathers, a new masculinity was promoted: 'The man's place was also in the home. Men too, in popular consciousness, were being domesticated . . . Both the popular and the academic writing of the 50s celebrates a new "together-ness", harmony and equality between women and men in the home.'[21] This new man was feminized in the sense that he was now expected to exist within the once female territory of the home. But of course with any move to engineer society, there are always sites of resistance.

Prosperity in the post-war economic boom saw an increase in leisure time and wages for many in the working class. With more money and more free time, working-class teenagers in the 1950s constituted a new leisure class which was worrying to the middle-class institutions which structured society: what do the working class do when they're not working? John Clarke and Chas Critcher have closely analysed these anxieties in their book, *The Devil Makes Work*: 'The dream of the leisure society is constantly undercut by the nightmare of "idleness" . . . This unstable mixture of "free time" and "anti-social" behaviour has been a persistent theme of nineteenth and twentieth century British capitalism.'[22] The nightmare is centred on youth subcultures in the blurb on the back of the 1963 edition of *The Leather Boys*, as it was in newspapers at the time: 'aimless, lawless, they spend a packet on their clothes and hairstyles. Working class boys with big wages and nothing much to do with their money.'

And indeed, this new leisure class could use its consumer power and free time to refute what was expected of them. In his consideration of the consensus politics of the period, Alan Sinfield identifies the new working-class dandies as political dissidents: 'Teds were the first significant dent in the post-war period, the first sign that not everyone was feeling consensual.'[23] This then is an era when constructs of masculinity, effeminacy and male homosexuality, and their relation to class, were all under interrogation.

Youth subcultures

The emerging subcultures of the 1950s exhibited a new form of dangerous masculinity, dangerous in the sense that it refused to be what was considered by the consensus to be useful or good: the grown-up responsible father and husband within the heterosocial environment of the home.

At this time the working class rarely had access to any form of self-representation; sociological studies of youth cultures more or less agree on the supposition that they were a confused but stylishly conspicuous attempt to articulate a sense of self against societal expectations within the realms of what was available to them – through their consumer power and by appropriating the products with their customizing skills. Capitalism managed successfully to channel these rebellious energies by catering for this new teen market; the Teds, and the subcultures that followed, were forms 'of protest within the accepted framework of materialism'.[24] Young working-class men with money to spend were happy to have signs through which to display their wealth: records, clothes and, later, bikes. The potential for leisure time was taken up with consumer-based activities; the conditions for the emergence of a new dandy were created, and the very signs of their resistance to usefulness were in fact useful to the economy.

Disruption of masculine identities and fears of leisured idleness had previously converged in the nineteenth century in the figure of the dandy, the decadent, overdressed, effeminate, aristocratic (or aspiring-to-be-so) male:

> In the face of middle-class validation of work and purity, there were two alternatives for the wealthy and those who sought to seem wealthy. One was to collaborate, appearing useful and good; the other was to repudiate manly, middle class authority by displaying conspicuous idleness, moral scepticism and effeminacy; in other words, to be a dandy.[25]

So, while their situations in terms of class and gender-relation differ, both the new dandy and the old are linked by the fears of non-productive idleness, class aspiration, shows of disposable income and disavowal of dominant modes of masculinity. Both the new dandies and the old were characterized by a similar investment in conspicuous shows of disposable income, non-productive idleness and class aspiration, all theatrically thumbing the nose at socially approved modes of masculinity. The Teds, like those *fin-de-siècle* dandies, were contesting middle-class expectations – in the 1950s, the social pressure to become a family man. The fears of feminization aroused by the cross-gendered environment of the post-war home was evident in the Teds' intensified recourse to homosocial gatherings: lads hung out with other lads. Both Teds and the dandies signalled a shift in the arena of male identities, the similarities due to economic changes effecting upheavals in Britain's class organization. But there were of course differences: the Teds were also contesting working-class expectations – a know-your-place puritanism – with their elaborate, socially aspirational styles. And the new dandy aggressively contested the alignment of such flamboyancy with homosexuality, which had been cemented in the wake of Wilde's trials.

Nevertheless, the new dandies were directly influenced by the inheritors of the older model: male homosexuals. Jon Savage traces the birth of the Ted look to 'an upper-class clothing style' from 1947 which was a reaction to modern American styles in that 'it harked back to the pre-First World War "Edwardian Era" . . . it was not a great success'. Savage says significantly that the look nevertheless 'was taken up by homosexuals'.[26] Dandyism was already doubly-queered, first though Wilde and then through the New Edwardians' popularity with homosexual men. This look was then appropriated in the early 1950s by young criminals in the London suburbs.

If, in this appropriation, 'the Teds' idea initially was to acquire status, it didn't last long, because the upper-class wearers quickly abandoned the style when it became associated with the Teds.[27] This left only working-class boys and male homosexuals dressing in the Edwardian style in the mid-1950s. Perhaps it was not for dissimilar reasons: Alan Sinfield has said that 'camp, as used in male homosexual subcultures, includes an allusion to leisure-class mannerisms, and may coincide, in effect or intent, with upward class mobility . . . the mode includes a recognition of its inappropriateness, of its impertinence.'[28] Homosexuals may have been constructing an identity on the foundations of the older model of the dandy, and the Teds dressing posh to display their wealth, but the effect is the same: the ironic use of an outdated upper-class image and the wish to display upward mobility linked the gay and working-class subcultures. The looks evolved separately, but there was potential for some (unacknowledged) crossover – indeed, Elvis sang of the fashionable cultural significance of 'Blue Suede Shoes' in a

decade when suede shoes also signified the wearer as *one of them*.
Jon Savage's assessment of the evolution of the Ted identifies the common
ground between homosexuals and the working class in this cultural shift.
This sartorial assertion was new, at least for working-class males.
Previously, 'dressiness was confined largely to homosexuals. Since they were
cut off from the mainstream anyway, both sexually and socially, they had
nothing to lose by outrageousness in their clothes . . . Both homosexuals and
Edwardians occupied a similar psychic space – "creatures of the moment,
living in an everlasting present" – and attracted similar hatred.'[29]
    The figure of the Edwardian represented a contradiction in gender. The
display of conspicuously expensive clothes could stand as evidence of his
status as a successful worker – a real man. The clothes also provided a sense
of a male group identity in the gang; the homosocial ethic of 'all lads
together' was stressed as a disavowal of the potential for feminization both
through consumerism and contact with women, as was male ritual violence:
because the Teds 'expressed a concern with dress which was unusually
extrovert and which challenged what was a traditional female expression
. . . any insult to it, real or imagined, had to be met with toughness or
violence. It had to deny any hint of effeminacy'. The Teds' 'butchness set off
their dandyism and protected their masculinity.'[30] But this disavowal of
effeminacy does not mean an exclusion of homosexuality.
    Men from a homosexual subculture may have been able to pass to some
extent invisibly at the edges of or even within Ted gangs, and working-class
men may have been able to dress in a style that was seen as signifying
perversion yet simultaneously confirming their masculinity and class.
    Teds may have made an impact on the public consciousness through
media coverage, but Ted subculture enjoyed minority participation:
according to Kevin Leech, even at their peak Teds 'represented only a fringe
group', whereas the subcultures that followed, mods and rockers, 'affected
large sections of young people'.[31] 'Rockers can be seen as two groups, firstly
the bikers . . . hanging around transport caffs, in black leather and studs,
performing ton-ups on the new motorways.' These are the Leather Boys; like
the Teds they are 'violent, loyal only to each other, anti-authority and anti-
domesticity, the male free wonderer dream, living only for the present'.[32]
    Rockers and greasers were the most aggressive in their assertion of
traditional masculinity until the emergence of the skinhead. If we keep
homosociality and homosexuality safely separate, then Reggie and Dick's
desire for all-male company simply makes them one of the lads. Reggie's
rejection of Dot is perfectly in keeping with masculine disavowal of
domesticated (castrated) masculinity as experienced in the roles of husband
and father. Neither would the fact that Dick had 'never had a girlfriend'
necessarily (as indeed it does not in the book) arouse suspicion about his
sexuality. Nor does his motivation for dressing up:

one didn't only dress up for girls. One didn't only have clean shoes and a brushed suit because one wanted girls to admire one. His appearance mattered to himself. The time he spent on it was entirely for his own satisfaction. Well, perhaps not entirely. Some was for the other boys, in peacock competition. They were the ones who judged and criticised and appraised. (*The Leather Boys*, p. 26)

Men dress up to impress the lads rather than the women – it is another form of masculine competition, inviting male approval. Again, there is nothing poofy about that. Interest in other men is acceptable and expected within the (assumedly heterosexual) convention of homosociality. At one point, Dick and Reggie literally flee from the women they pick up during a day at the beach, in keeping with the macho rejection of the feminine/domestic.

However, once homosexuality is revealed in the midst rather than at the margins or outside, the homosocial becomes sexualized; but Dick and Reg do not come out to anyone else in the book other than the reader, showing how easily and *invisibly* the homosocial can collapse into the homosexual. This is a virilizing model of homosexuality which comes about as an extension of homosocial relations: to Dick's question, 'when you kiss me and that . . . you don't pretend I'm a girl or anything?', Reg replies, 'Don't be daft . . . I don't want to pretend you're a girl neither' (p. 71). The male competitive ritual at the close of the novel, with Dick racing the unknown biker, becomes transformed into an erotic and even romantic scene of the two men riding off into an unknown future together.

The leather-clad biker was a refusal of the domesticated, emasculated, home-focused husband; as a hyper-masculine model, it provided a site of erotic interest for gay men. The gay poet Thom Gunn produced work in the 1950s which sexualizes the male biker culture; his poems 'On the Move' and 'Leather Jackets' are homoerotic in their treatment of biker culture (though this was significantly overlooked by contemporary straight critics). In hindsight it is easy to trace the leather queen image back to this time. The biker was a site of erotic interest and even identification for men looking for male sexual contact. But what space did the formation of this subculture open for queers? Did biker culture provide an opportunity for identification? Certainly there was a gay leather scene in Britain in the post-war years, which fetishized masculine performance, bikes and associated paraphernalia. The leather scene of the 1950s and 1960s was submerged within the already underground broader homosexual subculture: James recalls in *Daring Hearts*, 'There were other things we didn't know a lot about in those days. Even among the fraternity, variations of interest like S & M or leather were kept very, very hush-hush and nobody knew except those who were intimately involved.'[33] The late

1950s saw a gang of gay Leather Boys congregating regularly at Hyde Park in London, later making the Earls Court pub the Coleherne their regular (see chapter four). Joe Orton refers to the leather scene in his 1964 play *Entertaining Mr Sloane*, where the object of lust, Mr Sloane, is employed as a chauffeur by the vociferously manly Ed and given a uniform:

Boots, pants, a guaranteed 100 per cent no imitation jacket . . . and . . . er . . . a white brushed nylon T-shirt . . . with a little leather cap. *(Laughs)*.[34]

Orton would seem to be signalling the blatantly fetishistic function of the uniform in Ed's embarrassed hesitations and laughter. In the next act, we see Sloane remodelled as a gay icon, lying on the sofa in his uniform: 'boots, leather trousers and white T-shirt'. The uniform has an obvious signification for Orton, although we cannot know how many in his audience recognized the signs; Ed's clothes are a semiotic double entendre as they form, after all, a highly practical chauffeur's uniform.

It is precisely the invisibility of this gay uniform that provides the two subcultures with the potential to overlap, which they do in *The Leather Boys*. Some men were attracted to Reggie's gang who

came along dressed in the whole kit, yet Reggie knew they hadn't motor-cycles, but cars parked a mile down the road. The boys laughed at them. They called them 'kinky', and 'the leather johnnies', but some of them went off with them. They said it was good for an easy quid or two. (p. 13)

Leather boys and leather johnnies shared codes and indeed icons: Michael Brake identifies 'Brando, the menacing biker hipster' in *The Wild One* as an iconic representation of masculinity adopted by biker subculture.[35] But Marlon Brando had already confirmed his status as a sex symbol for homosexual men with his steamy portrayal of the scantily clad Mitch in *A Streetcar Named Desire* in 1956. So the subcultures shared fetishes and icons. If not completely compatible, the two were probably indistinguishable to outsiders.

Masculine rockers defined themselves in opposition to effeminate mods as bad boys against the mods' clean boy image. 'For them mods were contemptibly unmasculine.'[36] 'Rockers thought that Mods were weedy, dressed up, stuck up, cissified poncey and effeminate nancies. A bunch of prissy little jerks.'[37] As *The Leather Boys* was published in 1961 this latter subculture was only just emerging from Soho, although Dick does seem to be closer to a 'Mocker', which Richard Barnes defines as a deliberate confusion of mods and rocker styles:

He always took great care of his shoes, which he had hand-made and which cost him a lot of money. Tonight he was wearing a suit but sometimes he wore a narrow-shouldered jacket with plum-coloured stripes, and sometimes a leather jacket with saddle stitching. He tied his tie carefully in front of the little looking-glass, and then bent his knees so that he could see to do his hair. It was thick and dark and wavy and grew to the tops of his ears. (p. 11)

In mod subculture we see perhaps the most conspicuous signs of social aspiration, but here the effeminate overtones of dressing up and moving up-market are not so strenuously disavowed: mods wore 'traditionally feminine fashions, such as long hair, make up, hair lacquer, brightly coloured and flimsy clothes, and high heels'.[38] '"Mod" meant effeminate, stuck up, emulating the middle classes, aspiring to be competitive, snobbish, phony.'[39] Brake sees the mods' 'practice of cool' as 'the attempt to abstract oneself from one's ascribed class location by a sophisticated distance',[40] and Phil Cohen agrees:

The original mod life-style could be interpreted as an attempt to realise, but in an imaginary relation, the conditions of existence of the socially mobile white-collar worker. While the argot and ritual forms of mods stressed many of the traditional values of their parent culture, their dress and music reflected the hedonistic image of the affluent consumer.[41]

We see this class contradiction acknowledged in a divided reaction to Dick's smart clothes: '"Proper peacock," said Gran, half admiring, half jeering. "Proper toff"' (p. 11). This emphasis on clothes and consumerism was common to all teen cultures; it was simply more pronounced in the mod. Dressing up, even in 'traditionally feminine fashions', was no longer incompatible with the violence and aggression traditionally associated with masculinity, and mods were demonized in popular culture and feared as much as other teen cultures. The money Dick spends on clothes and his preening in front of the mirror confirm him as one of the lads.

As with the Teds, the roots of the look were derived from a recognized gay culture: in his definitive record of the cult, *Mods!*, Richard Barnes writes of the first mod clothes he bought:

I realised that homosexuals had been buying that stuff for years. They were the only people with the nerve to wear it, but in the early sixties the climate of opinion was changing, and the Mods were wearing the more effeminate and colourful clothes of Carnaby Street.[42]

Leech rightly states that 'the Mod image was in sharp conflict with the conventional picture of masculinity'. What this subcultural development signalled was a further common symbolic ground shared by male working-class and homosexual subcultural codes. But the assumption that effeminacy was a symptom of homosexuality was so strongly established that it created confusion and anxiety in the accounts of contemporary observers. Leech concluded from the relative androgyny of some areas of mod fashion that 'it was an implicitly homosexual, or, more accurately, bisexual phenomenon; girls were not popular in the Mod world, and it was in this period that homosexuality became more culturally acceptable to British youth'.[43] In fact, wearing a little make-up and the occasional brightly coloured item of clothing is not likely to predispose boys to sleeping with other boys.

Barnes anxiously concedes that 'Mods were more interested in themselves and each other than in girls' and that 'the boys *were* effeminate and used to fuss about and preen in front of the mirror . . . There was a time when Mod boys used eye make up and mascara.' He draws the opposite conclusion from Leech: 'they weren't homosexual. There might have been a homosexual element, though, but then there might also have been among rockers, and it wasn't particularly important.'[44] Barnes's attempt to disavow the accusations of homosexuality made about mod culture, his realization that this sweeping disavowal is unconvincing, and his subsequent attempt to downplay its importance, however, are suspect; anxiety over the mods' reputed lack of (heterosexual) sex drive leads Barnes to go so far as to suggest that this was due to their use of amphetamines. Leech was wrong to assume that feminine representational codes evidenced homosexuality; Barnes is wrong to contradict this. Mod potentially provided access to a homosexual identity. What is interesting is that no commentator was willing to discover how many participants realized this potential. Mod was neither essentially homosexual nor heterosexual; like all youth cultures, in sharing elements with established gay subcultures, it was potentially transgressive, delinquent, deviant and a little bit queer.

Perverted adolescents

Despite the occasional sensationalist newspaper headline or more prolonged spate of demonizations, teen subcultures rarely troubled the capitalist establishment because they provided a rich new market of consumers. What was worrying was if some fixation should halt the socialization in this brief period between work and school. 'The relation of subculture and age are important, because adolescence, and the period of transition between school and work, and work and marriage, is important in terms of secondary socialisation.'[45] Working-class rebellion was therefore allowed and even welcomed if it could be contained within existing capitalist structures and as long as the lads conformed eventually and grew up into responsible husbands and fathers; delinquency is forgivable as long as it's 'just a phase he's going through'.

However, there is a danger that '[f]or the kids who are caught up in the internal contradictions of a subculture, what begins as a break in the continuum of social control can easily become a permanent hiatus in their lives'.[46] This break – delinquency – must not be allowed to lead the subject off the path completely, to become a deviant. Cohen wishes to observe 'a distinction between delinquency and deviancy, and to reserve this last term for groups (for example, prostitutes, professional criminals, revolutionaries) which crystallize around a specific ideology, and even career structure, which cuts across age grades and often community and class boundaries'. Jonathan Dollimore most clearly expounds Freud's interpretation of perversion as a straying or delay on the 'natural' course of (sexual) development.[47]

The delinquent teenage boy should disappear with his reaching the end of his teens and his starting a family (a resumption of the true path); 'alternatively, subcultural affiliation can provide a way into membership of one of the deviant groups which exist in the margins of subculture and often adopt its protective colouration, but which nevertheless are not structurally dependent on it (such groups as pushers, petty criminals, junkies, even homosexuals)', delinquency 'often serving as a means of recruitment into deviant groups.'[48] Juvenile delinquency can therefore lead to deviancy.

This would support my thesis that gay men not only existed, visibly indistinguishable, at the margins of various working-class subcultures, and informed those subcultural codes; but that they may have provided access routes to emerging homosexual subcultures. Not only did distinct deviant homosexual environments exist at the margins of delinquent youth subcultures; this invisibility and cultural cross-fertilization might have provided a space for men to identify as homosexual within the boundaries of class and move at the centre of these cultures. Indeed, I might go further and state that to distinguish the queers from the other participants is a dangerous misrecognition: *teen cults are inherently queer*. As far as dress codes are concerned, there is very little difference between Leather Johnnies and Leather Boys.

Notes

1. Joseph Bristow, 'Being Gay – Politics, Identity, Pleasure', *New Formations* 9 (1989), p. 67.
2. Jeffrey Weeks, 'Discourse, Desire and Sexual Deviance', in Kenneth Plummer (ed.), *The Making of the Modern Homosexual* (London: Hutchinson, 1981), pp. 105–6.
3. (London: HMSO, 1957), pp. 9–10
4. Phil Cohen, 'Subcultural conflict and working class community' in Hall (ed.), *Culture, Media, Language* (London: Hutchinson, 1980), p. 81.
5. *Ibid.*, p. 93.
6. Quoted in Jeffrey Weeks, *Coming Out: Homosexual Politics in Britain, from the Nineteenth Century to the Present* (London: Quartet Books, 1977), p. 162.
7. *Ibid.*
8. 'Call Me . . .', *Boyz*, 12 August 1995, p. 18.
9. Michael Brake, *Comparative Youth Culture* (London: Routledge and Kegan Paul, 1985), p. 181.
10. Brighton Ourstory Project, *Daring*

Hearts: Lesbian and Gay Lives of 50s and 60s Brighton (Brighton: QueenSpark Books, 1992), p. 71.
11. *Ibid.*, p. 99.
12. Gillian Freeman, *The Leather Boys* (London: Four Square, 1963). All quotations from this text refer to this edition. (Originally published by Anthony Blond in 1961 under the name Eliot George.)
13. *New Statesman*, 24 November 1961.
14. Michael Griffiths, 'Leather Chaps', *Gay Times*, (January, 1986), p. 77.
15. *New Statesman*, 27 August 1965.
16. Kevin Porter and Jeffrey Weeks (eds), *Between the Acts: lives of homosexual men 1885–1967* (London: Routledge, 1991), chapters 12 and 14.
17. Joseph H. Pleck, *The Myth of Masculinity* (Cambridge, MA: MIT Press, 1981), p. 88.
18. Stanley Cohen, *Folk Devils and Moral Panics* (Oxford: Martin Roberston, 1980).
19. Michael Brake, *Comparative Youth Culture*, p. 11.
20. Phil Cohen, 'Subcultural conflict . . .', p. 86.
21. Lynne Segal, 'Look Back in Anger: Men in the Fifties', in Rowena Chapman and Jonathan Rutherford (eds), *Male Order: Unwrapping Masculinity* (London: Lawrence and Wishart, 1988), p. 70.
22. John Clarke and Chas Critcher, *The Devil Makes Work: Leisure in Capitalist Britain* (Basingstoke: Macmillan, 1985), pp. 4–5.
23. Alan Sinfield, *Literature, Politics and Culture in Postwar Britain* (Oxford: Blackwell, 1989), pp. 155–6.
24. Kevin Leech, *Youthquake* (London: Sheldon Press, 1973), p. 6.
25. Alan Sinfield, *The Wilde Century: Effeminacy, Oscar Wilde and the Queer Movement* (London: Cassell, 1994), p. 69.
26. Jon Savage, 'The Enemy Within: Sex, Rock and Identity', in Simon Frith (ed.), *Facing the Music: Essays on Pop, Rock and Culture* (London: Mandarin, 1988), p. 147.
27. Sinfield, *Literature, Politics and Culture*, p. 153.
28. Alan Sinfield, *Effeminacy: Some Parameters* (a preliminary paper presented at Queory seminar, Sussex University, Spring 1994).
29. Savage, 'The Enemy Within', p. 148, quoting Nik Cohn, *Today There Are No Gentlemen* (London: Weidenfeld and Nicholson, 1970).
30. Brake, *Comparative Youth Culture*, p. 73.
31. Leech, *Youthquake*, p. 5.
32. Brake, *Comparative Youth Culture*, p. 76.
33. Brighton Ourstory Project, *Daring Hearts*, p. 107.
34. *Orton: the Complete Plays* (London: Eyre Methuen, 1976), p. 88.
35. Brake, *Comparative Youth Culture*, p. 73
36. *Ibid.*, pp. 76–7.
37. Richard Barnes, *Mods!* (London: Eel Pie, 1979), p. 126.
38. Leech, *Youthquake*, p. 5.
39. Brake, *Comparative Youth Culture*, p. 75.
40. *Ibid.*, p. 74.
41. Phil Cohen, 'Subcultural conflict', p. 83.
42. Barnes, *Mods!*, p 15.
43. Leech, *Youthquake*, p. 3.
44. Barnes, *Mods!*, p. 15.
45. Brake, *Comparative Youth Culture*, p. 16.
46. Phil Cohen, 'Subcultural conflict', p. 85.
47. Jonathan Dollimore, *Sexual Dissidence: Augustine to Wilde, Freud to Foucault* (Oxford University Press, 1991), pp. 212–27.
48. Phil Cohen, 'Subcultural conflict', pp. 85–6.

3

Getting Harder:
Skinheads and Homosexuals

A new cult for working-class kids in the East End of London was identified as the skinhead in 1969; homosexuality was partially decriminalized in 1967, making it legal for a man to have sex with one other man in a private place if both were over the age of twenty-one; the Gay Liberation Front was formed in London in 1970. All these events signalled changes in the way people thought about masculinity, and, as the heterosexual(izing) accounts of working-class youth cultures had nevertheless allowed space for queer involvement, there should have been some evidence in the straight accounts of the emergence of the skinheads.

But no. Such evidence seemed conspicuous by its absence, given the historical and geographic proximity of the events surrounding the formation of the skinhead and the modern political 'gay community', never mind the fact that this look has more readily leant itself to appropriation by gay subculture than all the others.

Contemporary journalistic accounts of the rise (and the later return) of the skinheads are by and large discredited as simplistic sensationalism by the various 'official' histories that followed. First of all, in the wealth of analyses that appeared from the early 1970s from various forward-looking University and Polytechnic Sociology departments (most notably the Centre for Contemporary Cultural Studies at the University of Birmingham) which were making breakthroughs in communicating the significance of working-class lives which had hitherto been largely ignored or dismissed as culturally irrelevant. Secondly, in the glossy photographic works, which came later in the wake of the post-punk revival, concentrating on the skinhead as a style, the brevity of the accompanying text is perhaps due to the skinhead being, as one commentator put it, 'the cult of inarticularity' and as such defying analysis. However, Nick Knight's seminal *Skinhead* did include a detailed, historically sensitive and style-oriented account by the photographer, who, as a skinhead himself, knew what he was talking about. And then, the final word, the skinheads' own folk history as documented in George Marshall's *Spirit of '69* (fittingly subtitled *A Skinhead Bible*), which came along to set the record straight in the wake of these trendy academics and style gurus who had got it all wrong.

As if the record needed to be any straighter. The trouble is that, unlike the Ted, the rocker and the mod, which had all to some extent contested the requirements of masculinity, existing accounts read the skinhead as a nostalgic evocation of a particularly conservative notion of working-class manliness.

Instead of questioning the nature of that mode of being a man, these accounts not only assume the reader's understanding of and complicit agreement with old-fashioned, authentic masculinity, but share the same uncritical belief in the skinhead's status as such. Joseph Pleck's consideration of the way in which class constructs masculinity so implicitly as to be invisible to class-based sociological analysis is particularly relevant here. The masculine codes in operation within skinhead culture were (and often still are) seen as natural to the extent that the nature of that masculinity is never interrogated. Marshall in *The Skinhead Bible* claims that the 'Skinhead values' were 'masculinity, male dominance and male solidarity'[1] but he does not explain what those concepts mean. He doesn't need to – we already know. Skinheads (white, male, heterosexual, naturally) are so hard that their masculinity *goes without saying*. Working-class men are authentically masculine, real men; skinheads simply more assertively so. Analysis of previous youth cults required some account of what they were doing with masculinity. Skinheads were merely reasserting it, and, as we all know what *it* is, we can leave *it* alone.

Dick Hebdidge was exceptional in his consideration of skinheads in *New Socialist* in 1981, where he identified the mythological nature of the authenticity of working-class masculinity. He warned that 'a myth of authenticity informs much of the writing produced by the left on working class culture' so that 'skinheads have been celebrated . . . for symbolically recovering the cohesiveness of the pre-war working class community'. But, again, this analysis privileged class over gender, rather than seeing how each term constructed the other. His mythology simply invited the reader to interrogate 'a conception of "working-classness" which informed the common notion of the "working man"'.[2]

Nevertheless, these flawed accounts – flawed in so far as their lack of gender critique precludes any overlap between skinhead and gay sub-cultures, let alone the actual convergence of the two – are worth reconsidering. In his 1980 introduction to the second edition of *Folk Devil and Moral Panics*, Stanley Cohen writes:

I do not believe that anything which has actually happened or has been discovered (about youth, popular culture, delinquency, mass media reporting) in the decade since the research was completed . . . there are no new archives to be opened, no secret documents to be discovered, no pacts of silence to be broken. There are just the same (rather poor) sources of information from the same (often inarticulate) informants.[3]

The data is already collected; the Birth of the Skinhead is a closed chapter. But Cohen called for this chapter to be reread, to see 'what new sense can be made of this "same" data' given 'the quite phenomenal growth in the relevant "making sense" fields'. His invitation to reassess was not motivated by the growth in critical approaches alone: there was a need to redress the tendency among contemporary sociologists to turn juvenile delinquents into working-class heroes.

But this invitation assumes that the data is complete. It fails to address the fact that the social status of the analysts, which predisposed their reading of the data, actually impacted on their collection, and subsequent reliability. There were certain questions those researchers could have asked, there were certain avenues they could have explored, but their understanding and assumptions about their subject prevented them. The fact that these studies render the emergence of gay skinheads, or the possibility that skinheads might be queer, structurally unviable reveals the way in which researchers' assumptions about class, masculinity and sexuality characterized their material, precluding certain formations and thus rendering them resistant to certain rereadings.

By these accounts gay skinheads should not exist; and yet, we know very well that they do. To understand how and why they do, it's important to examine how and why they shouldn't. Although we can't play Hunt the Homo (or even the Homo-shaped Space) with these accounts, the figure of the gay skinhead allows us to interrogate the implicit and important assumptions about masculinity which limit use of the material.

Class acts

Skinhead subculture was read, like its predecessors, as a symbolic attempt to rediscover or replace the social cohesion destroyed in the parent culture: Phil Cohen's famous thesis is that the 'latent function of subculture is to express and resolve, albeit "magically", the contradictions hidden, or unresolved, in the parent culture'.[4] Most of the sociological theorizing about all working-class youth cultures centres on their attempts to re-create a mythical working-class identity in the face of the bourgeoisification of the parent culture – the imposition of middle-class values which passed itself as consensus. Clarke and Jefferson describe how 'by mitigating the most visible forms of class inequality and conflict, at least at a symbolic level, the ground was laid for the consensual politics of a supposedly affluent and classless society'.[5]

Working-class youths who were aware of their class identity were not sold on the idea of a new meritocracy; they had little faith in the belief that anyone could aspire to any area of society. *The Painthouse* is an invaluable study of a skinhead gang on the Collingwood estate. The kids there identify 'traitors' among their community who adopt middle-class attitudes 'in direct conflict with their working class values' as a result of 'building flats instead of little houses', and 'the sort of wage increases there 'as been'.[6] This ideology of classlessness, and resistance to it, was manifest in three cultural and material sites:

In housing: the community – terraces and extended families – was divided into redevelopments and tower blocks built around the bourgeois ideal of the self-contained nuclear family.

In the mainstream youth culture: products marketed with a mass appeal tried to elide class differences for reasons of profit, so that a potential market could expand across class boundaries. 'The sense of classlessness conveyed by much contemporary pop music and youth cultural style is merely a reflection of the creation in a consumer capitalist society of a one-dimensional economic product for universal consumption'[7] – i.e. capitalism's attempt to involve youth 'as passive teenage consumers in the purchase of leisure prior to the assumption of "adulthood", rather than being a youth culture of persons who question . . . the value and meaning of adolescence.'[8]

And in existing working-class subcultures: in contrast with the skinheads, the mods were 'living out the lifestyle of the upwardly mobile affluent worker'[9] and the new ideology of spectacular consumption and affluence (neat hair, clothes and bike, make-up): they were bourgeois-aspirational in their espousal of consumerism.

Existing accounts see skinheads as articulating a heroic, if doomed, resistance to dominant forces: the reassertion of a homogeneous identity and geographical boundaries in terms of class created a sense of community lost as a result of geographic upheaval, slum clearance and town planning. This is described in great detail in the first chapter of *The Painthouse*, 'The Community'. 'It is also very important from what the members of the Collingwood gang said that they belong to a one-class community. "You don't get no fuckin' toffs 'roun 'ere, middle class people."'[10] The integration of various classes within a geographical location is identified by the authors as a specifically middle-class ideal. 'The suggestion of middle-class people moving into the East End itself is seen as an infringement on the "working class territory" by members of the Collingwood, as a threat to their identity.'[11] Identity is materially aligned with territory.

But Teds, mods and rockers were symbolically articulating similar problems of class identity. Many of these analyses fail to explain why youth subcultures emerge as they do in their specific historical contexts. The skinhead is not the first to realize that being white, male and heterosexual is not enough; class is what separates him from the dominant culture, hence the class basis of these analyses. But examining skinhead identity through vectors of power other than class may explain why it emerged as and when it did.

41

Policing the borders

The late 1960s saw a political contesting of the universalized concept of 'Man' inherent in the liberal consensus, as people congregated under banners which alienated them from such a normalizing concept: women, people of colour, gay men and lesbians. After decades of struggle, these groups began to effect recognition and change in the order that oppressed them with unprecedented vociferousness, attention and political organization. Working-class male youths found themselves just another group competing with these other disenfranchised voices. Skinheads, however, differed from their ideological rivals in their sense of centrality, which they now considered to be under attack from these other groups. 'Ethnicity – the identification with real or imagined racial or national traditions – is usually associated with oppressed minorities', writes Dick Hebdidge. 'But ethnicity is also an option for whites who feel neglected or excluded.'[12]

Whereas it was once assumed that heterosexual, male and white were the unmarked terms dominating homosexual, female, and black respectively, now straight slipped perilously towards becoming just another sexuality, white another ethnicity, male not necessarily the more powerful gender. What dominant British culture had once presented as a natural power balance in these binaries started to shake. The other groups, alienated by consensus and informed by socialist thinking, used their exclusion to identify themselves in radical opposition to a dominant culture where they had never been welcome: they were making claims. The skinheads on the other hand were reclaiming, hence the conservative discourses of nostalgia and authenticity. They did not believe these other groups should have the rights they once enjoyed and felt were under attack. In *The Painthouse*, 'The mob used the four groups described as "being on our backs" ("Jews", "blacks", "Pakistanis" and "hippies") as "scapegoats" for their lack of access to the opportunities supposedly offered by the dominant.'[13] Not all, however, were unaware that in fact skinheads, as white working-class men, were one group equal to these others: 'There tends to be a begrudging recognition of scapegoat groups very often having an equal status to themselves, at least the coloured immigrant groups. "White working class attitudes the same as black power? Against society? Well, I suppose I am a bit," admits one skinhead.'[14]

'Skinhead enemies', according to the *Skinhead Bible*, were 'Asians . . . hippies, gays, perverts, grease and anyone else who looked at you the wrong way'.[15] Because of its historical context, skinhead identity was articulated not only in terms of class but consciously in relation to race, gender and sexuality as well.

Skinheads and racism

Instances of skinhead racism from this era are well documented. It was an urgent contemporary issue, even for the popular press. A special report titled '"Paki-bashing": Police plan to fight the gangs' appeared in the *Sunday Mirror* on 12 April 1970, claiming that 'Britain first became aware of the term "Paki-bashing" last Wednesday' when 'a group of skinheads boasted on television that they beat up coloured immigrants in East London "for the fun of it". Special police squads are being set up to combat gangs of youths who beat up Pakistanis . . . their aim: to stamp out the first signs of violence by gangs of trouble-bent "skinheads" roaming dimly-lit streets.' The piece interviewed victims of the new wave of racist aggression in London's East End, and looked at the first police operation to combat it in Bethnal Green.

The report on skinheads which had featured in Thames TV's *Today* programme, broadcast on Wednesday 8 April, had at least prompted a reassuring attack from some areas of the popular press: a leader comment in the *Daily Mirror*, headlined 'Ugly, Vicious, Cowardly', called for changes in the law to 'stem racial violence . . . All races should walk free from fear.' But articles such as the *Sun*'s 'Picture Special Inquiry' titled 'Down Among the Bovver Boys'[16] reveal the way the coverage of skinhead racist attacks, even while purporting to condemn racism, allowed the press to reiterate racist beliefs – in this case, with the stamp of academic authority. Professor John Cohen, head of the Psychology Department at Manchester University, is quoted as saying that the skinhead is merely the latest manifestation of harmless teenage rebelliousness, 'although the skinheads are creating a potentially explosive situation now that they have moved into the racial field. If Paki-bashing was happening in the States, it would be a turbulent situation. Fortunately the Pakistanis, unlike the Negroes, like a quiet life.'

It would seem that the press and some areas of academia shared with skinheads certain ideas about the centrality of whiteness; this unfortunately has changed little in the following decades. Recent lucrative developments in the field of genetics have allowed psychology departments to validate research which sets out to reconstruct the 'natural' link between race and behaviour. The Queer film-maker Richard Fung underlines the way research reaffirms and naturalizes the ideological centrality of whiteness in his analysis of J. Philippe Rushton's research in this area at the University of Western Ontario in 1988.[17] His thesis posits that

> degree of 'sexuality' correlates positively with criminality and sociopathic behaviour and inversely with intelligence, health and longevity. Rushton sees race as the determining factor and places East Asians on one end of the spectrum and blacks on the other. Since whites fall squarely in the

middle, the position of perfect balance, there is no need for analysis, and they remain free of scrutiny . . . The contemporary construction of race and sex as exemplified by Rushton has endowed black people . . . with a threatening hypersexuality. Asians, on the other hand, are collectively seen as undersexed.[18]

Understanding how this white-centralizing paradigm, which Rushton summarizes as 'Orientals>whites>blacks', is gendered may explain how white working-class males' perceptions of racial difference converges with anxieties about their own masculinity.

A study of attitudes to race among young people carried out by Les Black on a racially mixed working-class estate in the early 1990s charts a similar white construction of 'whiteness' between poles of racial difference.

The articulation between gender and racism is clear. Black and 'Oriental' youth are characterised by white working class youth in terms of a set of gendered positions . . . An image of blackness [is] associated with the hardness and assertiveness which is valorised among white working class males results in the definition of black young men and young women as contingent insiders. By contrast, the young Vietnamese men are feminised and excluded.[19]

Black's conclusion is nevertheless cautiously optimistic. He sees some racial interaction among the youths, certainly between black and white, articulated in terms of respect and emulation in the way white working-class boys appropriate signs of 'blackness'.

Twenty years earlier white youths' relation to racial otherness was being articulated in terms of violence. Academic analysis of this first wave of skinheads distinguished a hostile attitude to members of local Asian communities from an uneasy and questionable tolerance for African and Caribbean communities, which was explained (as always) in terms of class:

'paki-bashing', unlike the dominant public expression which had found little to distinguish between different cultural groups of immigrants, was overlaid with a significant cultural dimension, which distinguished between Asians and West Indians. The latter were perhaps less of a threat to the cultural homogeneity of an area because many of their cultural patterns were much closer to those of working class youth than were those of the Asians whose introspective, family-centred and achievement-oriented way of life were closer to a middle class outlook. In addition, West Indian youths were more likely to gain respect by being willing to defend themselves physically.[20]

If we take the middle class to be the feminized Other to white working-class youths, then this analysis constructs the category 'West Indian' with working-class masculine (evidenced in this analysis by physical assertiveness), and 'Asian' with middle-class feminine. The way working-class whiteness here defines itself against poles of racial otherness is not dissimilar to the white-centralizing racial paradigm identified by Fung. But skinheads wanted their white working-classness to occupy that hypermasculine site in which white ideology constructed 'blackness'. This may explain why early skinhead styles and musical tastes were dominated by the masculine mythology of 'the notorious and much-feared streetcorner ruffians of Kingston',[21] the Rude Boys. This subcultural style became visible in British West Indian communities in the 1960s. 'The effect upon British streetstyle was both profound and continuous', writes Ted Polhemus in *Streetstyle*. 'It was the skinheads who . . . were most explicitly inspired by the Rude Boys' image and music'[22] because it provided an image of tough masculinity when youth culture seemed to be going soft and posh: 'the Rudies' style was hard at a time when everything from frilly Carnaby Street shirts to Hippy embroidered kaftans was soft in a deliberately feminine way . . . Hard Mods discovered that they had more in common with the Rude Boys than with the so-called Mods.'[23]

But skinheads provide Black's optimistic study of white appropriation of black signifiers with a paradox: 'Skinhead style incorporates Jamaican music, yet proclaims white power and white pride. In this case, black culture was an emblem of white chauvinism.'[24] In the late 1960s, although many skinheads were articulating a white ethnicity through racial violence, the less ambivalent association with white supremacist politics that Black writes about was more than a decade away. The skinheads' questionable respect for black Rude Boy culture in this early phase (questionable because it isn't necessary to respect a culture to steal from it) was motivated by a competitive jealousy, a wish to be seen to be as hard and unacceptably masculine as white people saw young black men. This theory is borne out by one skinhead's retrospective consideration of the subculture's attitudes to race: 'The racism of skins is based on envy and self-hatred . . . Above all they envy the Blacks, for . . . the way they are always more alien to suburban England than skins can ever hope to be.'[25]

However, skinheads themselves from this period don't seem to be aware of the sensitivity of their racial discrimination: many accounts reveal equal hatred of and violence towards *any* culture they considered to be not British. Alongside the *Sunday Mirror*'s report on racist attacks quoted above was an article titled 'My Son the Skinhead' profiling Chris Harward and his gang. The Blue Diamond Boys, named after their local funfair, 'go hunting Frenchies (French students)' because 'We ain't got no Pakis here, and the blacks . . . are all down Brixton way.' The journalist Bruce Maxwell met him in a south London bowling alley coffee bar where he 'made this comment with chilling thoughtlessness'. (Two days later, however, at home with his parents and 'without the gang, all the bravado had left him. I began to wonder if it was the same boy'. His father commented, 'I wouldn't stand for Chris going out and bashing up Pakistanis or anyone else. We are strict.' The piece then perhaps served to question the skinheads' reputation for violence.)

Racism and homophobia therefore, like class-consciousness, are aspects of the skinheads' concern with *territory*, most clearly shown by their loyalty to local football teams. When George Marshall unconvincingly argues that 'Paki-bashing' is not a racist activity on the grounds that it is about 'territory rather than colour',[26] he fails to recognize that racism itself is a matter of territory.

The new conservatives

In terrorizing those groups who were marginalized from 'Man', the skinheads were policing the deviants, and preserving the given definitions, for the dominant. Skinheads were thus a conservative hegemonic force in their nostalgia and reassertion of the natural, fixing things the way they (seem always to) have been. Stanley Cohen critiques the tendency of Marxist cultural analysis to create class heroes out of working-class kids and criticizes the 1970s accounts' 'constant impulse to decode the style [of youth cultures] in terms *only* of opposition and resistance. This means that instances are sometimes missed when the style is conservative or supportive'.[27] Much of the analysis of skinheads is guilty of this.

Aside from occasional sensationalist indulgence in the tabloids, contemporary journalistic consideration of the subculture seemed more sensitive to its conservatism. A report in *New Society* from 1969 did not fall foul of the class romanticism of much of the academic consideration that was to follow: 'The conventionality of the skinheads, in urban working class society, is paramount. They endorse accepted values. Ask skinheads whether they want to change the political system and most will say no – they just want a better deal out of it.' Skinhead goals are: 'Marry. Settle down. Have kids.' They have 'a great puritanism about them', endorsing 'the virtues of hard work and cleanliness, of stick to the lathe and don't ponce off the state . . . All the Palace group I talked to had an obsession about work, and its opposite, scrounging' which is used as an excuse for their attacks on immigrants, hippies and unions. They give the same reactionary answers as their parents on 'liberal issues – say hanging and homosexual reform. The principal thing is the skinheads do it more defiantly.'[28]

The focus of that conservatism – how things were better for the working man in the good old days – was historically distant and highly mythologized. Nick Knight believes that skinheads were trying to recover 'a way of life, a set of values which, according to some social historians didn't emerge until the late 1800s when the British empire was at its most powerful, when imperialism, nationalism and Toryism were beginning to figure prominently in the language of pubs and the music halls'.[29] In fact, conservative projects don't try to preserve the status quo so much as invest a cultural programme with authority by siting its goal in a mythic past; the golden days of white working-class wonder that the skinheads were reclaiming never actually existed. Nostalgia simply reinforces the fact that fings ain't wot they used to be.

Many academic and journalistic accounts claim that the elements of the skinhead wardrobe were assembled in direct contrast to the androgyny of hippies, articulating a traditional masculinity, read as traditional and working class, in reaction to the feminization of middle-class youth culture.

Whereas the Mod had seen his 'enemy' as the Rocker, and had rationalised his style accordingly (Cleanliness vs. Grease; Scooter vs. Motor Bike; Pills vs. Booze), the new skinheads reacted against the hippies. Their hair was short to the point of absurdity, they were tough and they went round in 'bovver boots' for the express purpose of beating hell out of deviants.[30]

However, this is disputed by those from within the subculture:

The word skinhead didn't come into general circulation until 1969, but kids wearing boots and sporting crops were seen in Mod circles as early as 1964. They were the forerunners of the skinhead cult, which was slowly to develop from the ranks of the mod from that year onwards. All the love and peace bollocks didn't come along until three years later so to argue that skinheads were somehow a reaction against hippydom is to firmly put the cart before the horse. Rejection, maybe, but a reaction never.[31]

Whether the skinhead first emerged in reaction to the working-class mod or the bourgeois counter-culture is less important than the fact that he was articulating a masculinity against the feminine appearance of *both* groups. Male hippies had long hair, wore dress-like kaftans and robes, were students rather than workers, wasted their seemingly endless leisure time with women, were believed to grow soft through their enjoyment of cannabis. The puritan skinheads, driven by the working-class work ethic, were as contemptuous of this decadent, effeminate superior class as the late nineteenth-century meritocratic middle classes had been of the decadent, effeminate aristocracy. 'I hate hairies . . . it's all that talk about love and peace and all those clothes. I mean, I work for my pay so I pay them on the dole. Most of them have posh accents and they all went to public school anyway', says 'Jimmy, 17 year old skinhead from Bethnal Green, East London'.[32] The Collingwood gang's objections to hippies centre round the points 'They are only middle class' and 'they want to be different'.[33] 'We was the 'ardest of our time, people with long 'air was cowards', says one of the gang-members.[34] In the face of the womanliness of the male hippy, skinheads were predominantly homosocial, had very short hair and wore tight clothes derived from male workwear.

The skinheads' evolution from the mod, in opposition to the subculture's commercial exploitation, also reveals gendered anxieties about class. If hippies were the middle-class Other, mods were the enemy within. Both mods and skinheads were working-class subcultures, but Clarke and Jefferson cite the socially mobile mods as an example of cultural embourgeoisement and position them against the 'lumpen' ghettoized, culturally fixed skinheads.[35] Mods sold out to middle-class aspiration, to the values of the enemy. As it is told in the *Skinhead Bible*, the skinhead developed from fractures in the mod movement along class lines, between the 'cool, stylish kids who were one step ahead of the pack', newcomers who were wearing a High Street (and therefore approved and defused) version of the image, mods who made it to college and became hippy-tinged, and 'rough Mods'.[36] So the subculture does have its roots in contradictions of class identity, and if violence against 'hairies' came later, it only served to strengthen the basis of that gendered class anxiety.

Skinheads were safeguarding conservative definitions of 'Man' by reasserting an 'authentic' working-class masculinity in the face of challenges to male identity from middle-class counter-culture and working-class aspiration. The assembly of the look, as described in *The Painthouse* by early skinheads themselves, is seen as an expression of innate hardness:

> as soon as Bob came round he wanted to make 'imself look 'ard or something and when 'e 'eard about all them 'ard lots like, all them older kids and Farris, they all used to 'ave their 'eads shaved, didn't they? . . . Bob wanted to make 'imself look 'arder like them so he 'ad 'is 'air cut short like them.[37]

Such hardness is the property of the male: 'The role of a man is to be domineering and violent' says a young skin. 'It is the male instinct to be dominant over the bird.'[38]

Central to Nick Knight's consideration of skinhead culture is his thesis that 'Two obsessions dominate the style: being authentic and being British.'[39] Working-class masculinity is authenticated by a putative genetic predisposition to physical activity. The physical requirements of manual work mean that *it goes without saying* that the (romanticized) working man is naturally physical; his authenticity is vindicated by the natural body, appealing to the authority of biological, empirical realness: Nature. John Clarke's work on skinheads has at least noticed this, even if he has not attempted to denaturalize it:

Working-class life placed a high value on physical prowess, partly because the work experience centred round largely physical tasks . . . and partly because of the strong cultural emphasis on toughness, masculinity, virility and connected values. There was no place either in the factory or on the football field for the 'pansy'.[40]

These qualities as foregrounded and epitomized in the skinhead place him in direct opposition to the soft queer. As this also *goes without saying*, queerbashing is given only the occasional mention in the accounts, simultaneously assuming and reinforcing the 'naturalness' and the breadth of the divide between the two identities. Queerbashing safeguards the territory of masculinity by policing the boundaries of acceptable (i.e. 'natural') behaviour at a time when masculinity was being interrogated, politically by feminism and, at the level of appearance, by mod and hippy fashions. Androgynous styles were becoming acceptable across class. A fashion spread in the *Sunday Mirror* (15 March 1970) showed Pierre Cardin's latest collection for men to be so effeminate that it was modelled by women at its unveiling in Paris. Under the headline 'All Boys Together' was a write-up astonishingly devoid of any ridicule: 'Girls want a boy who looks like a girl and makes love like a man.'

You don't have to be queer to get queerbashed, just not hard enough to look like a real man, not faithful enough to the 'naturalness' of the gender. 'Queers and anyone else who looked remotely like one were usually easy and regular targets', declares Marshall.[41] 'The skinhead definition of "queer" extended to all those males who looked "odd", that is, to all those who were not overtly masculine-looking' wrote sociologists Clarke and Jefferson,[42] and they support this by quoting a skinhead:

> Usually it'd be just a bunch of us who'd find someone they thought looked odd – like this one night we were up by Warley Woods and we saw this bloke who looked odd – he'd got long hair and frills on his trousers.

Sexuality converges with class: the man was just as likely a hippy as a homosexual. With the skinhead image being the ultimate sign of hard, white, working-class masculinity, anyone who wasn't a skinhead wasn't hard enough, so potentially the category 'queer' encompassed *all* non-skins. 'Other kids who weren't skinheads, we just used to punch the fuck out of them, didn't we? . . . we used to say "fairy", didn't we, 'member?' recalls one of the Collingwood gang.[43]

'I like violence, violence and, er, violence.'

'Anyone who didn't belong on your patch was pencilled in as a legitimate target for skinhead aggro.'[44] The borders of acceptable identities were policed with violence. 'Because of the valuation placed on "hardness" . . . violence was an accepted part of life for most working men . . . It was not seen as problematic, or in need of an explanation.'[45]

Violence was seen both by outsiders and skinheads themselves as an unquestionable and unproblematic expression of authentic working-class masculinity: 'The necessity for violence is more understandable when seen in the context of the male role as being dominant and aggressive, and anything less as being effeminate and "spineless".'[46] But it is also the particular characteristic of the skinhead, thus rendering him more working class and more masculine than any other youth culture. One of the Collingwood skinheads summarizes: 'Fighting's the main thing . . . when it was Mods, it was all clothes and fashion, when it was rockers, it was all motorbikes, and skinheads it is fighting',[47] and a teacher at the Collingwood gang's local secondary modern school described the skinhead cult as 'a new craze to be violent'.[48] In *The Skinhead Bible*, George Marshall celebrates the cult's association with aggro, quoting from a 1969 TV interview with a skinhead: 'I like violence, violence and, er, violence.'[49]

Academics consider physical aggression as an ambivalent expression of the working class's distance from intellectualism. Richard North calls it 'the skinhead cult of inarticularity'.[50] Clarke and Jefferson rightly align violence with anxieties over class and gender: 'For working-class youth, masculinity is a problem. It is the mark of one's independence, especially in a context such as school, where the dominant mode is rational discussion. If one can handle oneself then this means that all discussion can be settled as a direct challenge.'[51] Educational institutions are rightly identified as middle class, so intellectualism is feminine, fake; in contrast, violence is working class, masculine and real. John Clarke, commenting on the moral panic over hooliganism, 'publicly defined as a serious problem from the middle of the 1960s', says 'The stereotype of the hooligan is that of the ignorant working-class "yob" . . . His violence . . . is perpetually described as "mindless, senseless, illogical and irrational".'[52]

'As the media caught on to this aspect of the cult,' writes Knight, 'it caused some skins to leave the movement and more violent people to join it. Eventually, this was one of the reasons which led to its decline by 1971. There was no point being a skin if you simply got nicked by the police wherever you went.'[53] Marshall blames one particular area of the media for the decline of the skinhead, whilst acknowledging that the sensationalism was not without foundation: 'The tabloid newspapers had successfully defined skinhead as little more than a brainless, vicious thug. A few were indeed just that and a lot more did their best to live up to the tag . . . Being picked up by the police before you even get to the football ground isn't quite as funny the third time round.'[54] Thus the skinhead is subject to deviancy amplification: the dominant media stereotype 'may attract new participants who feel that the behaviours and characters described fit their own experience . . . thus the phenomenon tends to become more like the public image of it, a self-fulfilling prophecy takes place through the forcefulness of that public definition.'[55] The skinhead image then unequivocally (and not unreasonably) comes to signify 'mindlessly violent thug'.

The resulting effects on skinhead subculture are best described by Marshall as an active participant. The association of skinheads with violence brought severe reaction from the police: 'Being a skinhead soon became bovver in itself and you couldn't drop a sweet wrapper without being nicked. Once a copper saw your crop that was it. You were assumed to be trouble'.[56] Curfews were placed on skins in some areas and bovver boots removed before matches as offensive weapons.

The tabloid press, who in the 1960s came to prepare the front pages following a Bank Holiday Monday for seaside violence, celebrated such moves as victories of common sense over the new demons. 'BRACES SWOOP FOILS THE SKINHEADS' declared the front page of the *Sun* on Tuesday 31 March 1970, while the *Daily Mirror* ran with 'NO BELTS SO NO BOVVER!' 'Hundreds of skinheads – the crop-haired "bovver boys" – were stripped of their braces, shoelaces, and belts by police yesterday' at the Easter Monday 'teenage invasion' of Southend on the Essex coast. A double-page photo-spread showed skinheads trying to reclaim their laces from a tangled web. The idea was credited to 'two lone policemen who had to face twenty skinheads' who reckoned that 'The teenage toughs would not be able to hit out at anyone if they had to hold up their trousers, or kick out if they had to try to keep on their laceless "bovver boots".' The idea was quickly taken up by other forces, but 'Easter Monday "bovver" still managed to break out at other seaside resorts: thirteen youths were arrested at Great Yarmouth, Norfolk' and 'more than 200 chanting skinheads kept police on the alert at Brighton' while another 200 cropped teenagers fought for two hours at Rhyl.

Skinhead violence interrupted Luton Town playing away to Rochdale and a televised Rugby League match in Leeds on 25 April 1970, which prompted what almost amounted to a sociological analysis of the youth cult the following Monday. 'DOWN AMONG THE BOVVER BOYS' was headlined on the front page of the *Sun* and the piece contained quotes from experts that skinheads were normal. A 'leading psychiatrist' said that 'he did not believe there was anything psychologically wrong with the boys who got kicks out of being destructive . . . "It is not abnormal to get fun out of breaking things and from a certain amount of mild destruction. They are not delinquent compared with most boys who commit crimes."' The Labour MP for an area of London that had become notorious for skinhead aggro, West Ham, said, 'I don't condemn them. The Bovver Boys of 30 years ago were the Battle of Britain pilots. The difference is that the pilots had something to fight against and these lads don't.' Professor John Cohen, quoted in his capacity as the head of Manchester University's psychology department, was equally magnanimous:

> Every generation has its named group of aggressive, revolutionary teenagers . . . They will fade away in time, just as the others did, only to be replaced by some other group . . . I wouldn't run down our young people at all. My only quarrel with them is that the majority aren't rebellious enough.

However, these seemingly generous attempts at understanding were framed within a typically emotive leading paragraph.

> The skinheads were at it again this weekend. Clashing with police and frightening fans at football grounds. Looking for bovver, as they like to put it . . . This cult of violence has been spreading for a year now, with skinheads hunting for trouble in packs, standing out with their cropped hair, their braces and their bovver boots.

The images accompanying this 'Sun Picture Special Inquiry' were a picture of police clashing with skins on the terraces of Rochdale FC, and a threatening line-up of skinheads' rolled jeans and DM boots.

It has to be said, however, that as time went on, coverage of skinhead activity became less condemnatory. The *Sun* on 22 May 1970 carried a good-humoured report on a meeting held by the new Mayor of Reading with 'two skinheads in bovver boots and two Hell's Angels' about the lack of local facilities for young people: 'They told him straight there was nothing to do in the town.' There was a similar attempt to redeem skinheads by giving them the approval of authority in the *Daily Mirror* on 17 November 1970: Sam Shepherd, a nineteen-year-old East End apprentice who starred in the first skinhead film *Bronco Bullfrog*, protested with two hundred teenagers at the Cameo Poly in London's Regent Street as Princess Anne arrived to see Laurence Olivier's *Three Sisters* because his film had been dropped from the programme. 'ANNE HAS DATE WITH BRONCO BULLFROG' ran the headline, as she promised to attend the première at the ABC Cinema in Mile End Road the following Monday.

'By the end of 1970, a lot of the older skinheads were beginning to move on anyway,' writes Marshall. 'The cult was becoming associated with just violence and younger kids thought that's all skinhead was about.'[57] He describes how deviancy amplification leads to deterrence: 'Large numbers of skinheads began to grow their hair just that little bit longer so they weren't instantly recognised as a member of the bovver brigade.' The skinhead evolved into the suedehead, growing their hair just long enough to run a comb through and adopting a sense of sharp, sartorial elegance that had characterized the mods. 'A few, in black "Crombie" overcoats, bowler hats and carrying black umbrellas, almost resembled city gents.'[58] But soon even the suedeheads were letting their hair grow and, according to Marshall, by about the spring of 1971 large numbers were beginning to evolve into smoothies. 'To a lot of people, smoothies appeared very ordinary with no obvious uniform or identity.'[59] As skinheads were forced to adopt less masculine, uniform, militaristic styles, it appeared as if the skinheads had suddenly vanished.

This was how it seemed to the *Daily Mirror*, which was all too keen to dance on the grave of the seemingly extinct cult. 'WHERE HAVE ALL THE SKINHEADS GONE?' they asked on 8 March 1971. 'Two years ago you couldn't spend a quiet summer weekend anywhere on the Kent coast for the fear of "bovver" boys.' But now 'they can't be bothered with bovver'. The piece featured interviews with four ex-skinheads and the introduction suggests that 'their peaceful re-entry into normal life', signified by long hair and a greater interest in girls, is a transformation towards hippiedom. It's questionable just how much had changed apart from the fashion – one admitted that he still got into bother 'up football like with the other fans' and another said 'if the greasers get a bit lippy down the Starlight club then there's trouble'. But the censure invited by skinhead signifiers had lead to their rejection. 'If you had short hair it labelled you right away with the coppers and everyone.' Interestingly, they believed their feminine appearance won admiration from women; female association feminized them, so that 'Now if they see you with long hair they think you're queer, you just can't win.'

The borders erected along the lines of class and gender gave way to the androgyny and cross class appeal of Glamrock. The components of the skinhead uniform seemed to disappear to outsiders, and this may be why the skinhead has survived in popular memory as the ultimate terror of unsocialized masculinity. Marshall believes that 'Skinheads were being condemned to life's scrap heap of folk devils'.[60]

But the previous youth cultures had not been scrapped, they had been put on sale in high street shops. In order to keep attracting its market, mainstream commercial youth culture had to incorporate subcultural styles, assimilating them into the broader mainstream youth market. The centrality of the consumer commodity to mod culture, for example, and the mods' smartness, sanctioned by the mainstream, allowed the look to be easily sold back to a wider youth market. 'By the end of the '60s, Mod had become a highly organised commercial enterprise and had become institutionalised.'[61]

But whereas the aspirational mods had looked forward to the Golden Age of classless consumerism, the skinheads looked back to a Golden Age of working-class harmony, giving the look an always-already-thereness in the cultural mythology. Their concern with authenticity, as opposed to artifice, to style, may also have made them unsuitable for appropriation by consumer culture in the early 1970s. In many ways, the most prominent features of skinhead dress codes, derived from utilitarian worker and military uniforms, purport to be anti-style. So skinhead styles did not lend themselves to consumerist assimilation. And the fact that the skins' successors, smoothies, concentrated less on aggro and utilized more 'feminine' dress codes (longer hair, more flamboyant clothes) meant that, to those on the outside, skinheads seemed to disappear rather than evolve. Remembered as the most masculine and aggressive youth cult, skinheads were not destined for the recasting of earlier folk devils to 'relatively benign roles in the gallery of social types'.[62] Therefore the skinhead sticks as the ultimate thug in social consciousness.

Macho queens

It seems that, whereas masculinity in working-class youth cultures went without saying, masculinity in gay subculture needed to be accounted for. While the masculinity of hard youth subculture, invisible in the very ubiquity of its understanding, was rarely addressed, much academic work has been devoted to explaining the emergence of the macho queen in the late 1960s.

Although Jeffrey Weeks cautions those romantic about the political liberation movements of this time with the reminder that 'there was little in the original British or American counter-culture that indicated any rejection of stereotypes of women or gays',[63] the very attempt to question dominant ideology did at least open up a space for these other groups to get in, organize themselves and make themselves heard. Homosexuals were another of those disenfranchised groups claiming a voice through political action in the late 1960s. Skinheads had two reasons to target them: not only were they perverted, they were also part of this political (therefore intellectual, therefore middle-class) movement. The new homosexual identity emerging at this time – the gay – was bourgeois: 'Inevitably GLF in its early days drew from those who had been touched by the New Left or the counter-culture . . . most of the supporters were middle-class, though often marginally or first-generation middle-class; but there were few working-class gays.'[64]

This politicization, however, marked a transition in the identities available to men who identified themselves as homosexual. By the late 1970s Gregg Blachford can write of 'a new masculine style which has become the dominant mode of expression in the sub-culture' in Britain and America. This was a move 'away from the previous stereotype of "swish and sweaters"'[65] which had dominated so strongly that one elderly man talking of homosexual roles before the 1960s. 'There was certainly no appreciation of the fact that (to use a modern term) there could be "straight-looking gays".[66]

Soft and posh

According to most accepted sources, for most of the twentieth century homosexual identity has been closed to the effeminate model, both in dominant heterosexual culture, and in homosexual subculture. As I suggested in the previous chapter, there were probably other queer identities available to working-class men which we do not know about; the expectation of homosexuals to be conspicuously nelly has dominated studies of homosexuality to such an extent that anything other would have been invisible.

In the late nineteenth century, effeminacy was associated with the idle aristocracy, objectionable on the grounds that it was a symptom of excessive cross-gender attachment which resulted in the disorder of men's 'natural' mastery over women. According to Eve Sedgwick, the nineteenth-century aristocracy becomes seen as 'ethereal, decorative and otiose in relation to the vigorous and productive values of the middle class'.[67] This utilitarian gendering of class is still evident in the skinheads' puritan endorsement of the work ethic and repudiation of lazy middle-class hippies.

Alan Sinfield writes of Oscar Wilde, in whose image the homosexual was retrospectively cast, that 'Homosexuality was not manifest from [his] style. His effeminate, dandy manner did not signify queerness . . . Up until the time of Wilde, effeminacy and same-sex passion might be aligned, but not exclusively, or even particularly.'[68] Instead, it signified instead upper-class identity or aspiration. The effeminate model is also informed by the older molly tradition, where male prostitutes cross-dressed and adopted women's names without necessarily acting effeminately, and nineteenth-century sexologists' theories of inversion, where a person's psychic and physical gender do not concord, resulting in effeminate men and masculine women.

The beginnings of the modern gay subculture emerged in the late nineteenth century, where sexual perversions were less distinct and role-related, and male homosexuality was part of a broader sexual underworld; as such its 'chief continuity' was 'with male heterosexual values',[69] evident in patterns of class and gender relations. This scene was dominated by prostitution: 'The excitement of meeting people from another class was . . . an aspect of the whole male ethos'[70] but the homosexual subculture which emerged from it continued to exhibit a 'common interest among many early twentieth-century, middle-class, self-defined homosexuals with the male working class', giving rise to 'the idealisation of working-class youth'.[71]

Coming from a heterosexual environment, gender difference was mapped on to the class difference, and, as such, sexual relationships conformed to a heterosexual pattern, with the working-class prostitute taking the role of the authentic man, leaving the upper-class effeminate by implication. Even when homosexuals were aware of this gendered structure of their desire, it seems they found it difficult to think beyond these ideological constraints. Edward Carpenter and the novelist E. M. Forster 'shared the structure of feeling characteristic of upper-class homosexuality in the period, a cross-class structure of desire in which what is at stake is the virility embodied in the working-class man'.[72] Carpenter's socialism informed his goal of a new masculinity (men who could be feminine without being effeminate), but his own identity was inevitably compromised by his status as an intellectual, which placed him in opposition to the authentic masculinity of the non-intellectual proletariat. This class divide was inevitably gendered.

Thus the posh queen could get off with a common piece of rough: the latter was rewarded financially, the former rewarded with the pleasure of sex with a 'real' man, a man who was not homosexual. It served the interests of the employer that such partners could not identify as anything other than heterosexual: the low-Other working-class man was idealized as the bearer of authentic, uncultured masculinity. It is this same alignment of heterosexuality, physicality, authenticity and working-class identity which skinheads are reasserting. It also served the purposes of a heterosexualizing society to keep things this way: posh soft queers were conspicuous and preserved a cross-gender erotic structure. Michael Bronski has noted the prevalence of this structure in culture on both sides of the Atlantic:

> In porn, or in the mainstream novels that dealt with homosexuality before Stonewall, there is a clear pattern. The typical gay man desires 'straight trade': hustlers or young boys. Anyone but another gay man. (Of course, real gay men did have lovers, sex with other gay men, and gay male friends – but there was little literary recognition of this in reality.)[73]

In fact there were effeminate working-class homosexuals. Whereas effeminacy in the aristocracy and the upper-middle classes could still be written off as part of class identity even into the 1950s, in working-class men it signalled only one thing: queerness. Martin P. Levine identifies the camp queen as a tactic of *minstrelization*, one of three strategies for neutralizing the stigma of homosexuality in the pre-'Liberation' era. It would seem to be the best-suited to identities existing within the subculture, as the other two ways of articulating an identity around homosexual desire would not allow for any positive self-identification: *passing* involved a double-life with the heterosexual personae dominating, and *capitulation* resulted in a sense of shame that would disallow any participation within the subculture.[74]   Participants in both British and American homosexual subcultures from this time would seem to support this: 'Before 1969, gay men were "not men", that is, "sissies" or "nellies" or "fairies".'[75] The scene was apparently populated by effeminate men identifying as deviants and masculine men who identified as 'normal': 'It was not unusual, for example, for homosexual men to distinguish between "homosexuals" and "men" . . . it was sometimes [self-identified homosexuals'] proud boast that their most frequent encounters were with "men" rather than "homosexuals".'[76]

In the post-war period the most apparent gay identities (that we know of) are the cultured gent and the nelly queen. However, the emergence in the late 1960s of the counter-culturally-inspired gay activist heralded the disassociation of homosexuality from effeminacy. This had implications on the way gay men were to think about themselves in terms of their masculinity, their class, their self-esteem and what they wore.

The masculinization of gay culture

Most accounts of the emergence of masculine gay identities credit this to increased assertiveness, politicization inspired by other rights movements, and the buoyancy of the victory of homosexual rights groups in securing the partial decriminalization of homosexuality in 1967. There was also a very strong American influence; the uprising of drag queens, rent boys and other homosexuals against homophobic police brutality in New York's Stonewall bar in 1969 is seen as the birth of the modern gay rights moment, giving further momentum to urban gay scenes which were already well established.

There are many comprehensive sociological accounts of the masculinization of American gay subculture that occurred at this time, and it is usually assumed that British subculture followed a few years behind. Certainly gay men in Britain are aware of a strong American influence in the area of hard gay masculinity. An effeminate 1960s' gay man (now significantly a macho queen) recalls the influence gay porn had on expectations of behaviour and sexual practice: 'America had a big influence, originally' because the British macho scene emerged 'about the time American porn became more easily available':

> I remember this tremendous skinhead who I got to know who had this porn film – it was all on Super-8 film in those days – from the States and it had fisting. It was the first time we'd ever seen fisting – for months we virtually walked around with a rubber glove on. Throughout the seventies it was becoming more easily available, plus macho magazines were being set up over here, like *MCM* by Brian Derbyshire.

Chesebro and Klenk's consideration of changes on the American gay scene claims that 'Since the Stonewall riots in New York in June 1969 – which gave rise to the gay liberation movement – some gay males have claimed and sought to obtain societal support for an alternative conception of their identity and meanings associated with same-sex relationships.'[77]

This was manifest in the emergence of masculine codes within parts of the subculture. In a climate of

> counter-cultural challenges . . . to the style and content of the male role, a gay liberation movement grew which presented a positive identity concept . . . it is remarkable that in recent years the shift away from images of gender inversion has been so great that there is now a positive identification amongst many male homosexuals . . . with masculine style and demeanour. The cult of machismo has arrived, interestingly, at the same time as the further relaxation of traditional masculine style within the young heterosexual male population.[78]

A new 'liberated' out gay identity was being formed which for John Marshall 'presented a new image at last . . . And perhaps more important, it presented a positive identity concept to those who, in other circumstances, might never have come to regard themselves as being "homosexual".'[79] Not only were the ways in which gay men might conceive themselves expanded, but the number of men who might identify as gay was also increased, as this new masculine gay identity was available to a broader range of men.

> The greater number of participants in the scene encouraged homosexuals increasingly to seek sexual partners *among other identified homosexuals*. This activity may indeed have become more necessary: the strengthening of the male heterosexual identity tended to mean that *fewer* 'normal' men would have occasional and casual gay sex, since this now more clearly carried the stigma of being a queer.[80]

In redefining the territory of 'gay', the divide between homo and hetero became wider, as *all* men who frequented the scene were now gay: no more inverts lusting after real men. So, to those who had access to the scene, there was a possibility of identifying oneself as both masculine and gay. 'The increase in sexual relations among homosexuals meant that *homosexuals became not just the desirers but the desired*.'[81] As such, gay men could start to dress as what they desired. This marked an end to oppositional erotics of gender and class difference which had previously dominated models of homosexual relationships, and an introduction of the erotics of sameness and (quite literal) uniformity in certain areas of the diversified subculture. As such, perhaps this vestimentary foregrounded loss of gender difference signified the first formation of a truly *homo*sexual identity. The idealization of working-class youth in Carpenter's day was still in operation, and the masculine dress codes adopted were inspired by the workwear (and, later, youth cultures) of the working class, due both to middle-class queens getting up in working-class drag, and the increased number of working-class gay men who found access to the scene.

Clones and skinheads

The clone uniform was never really designed as a whole, but collectively invented as an exact replication of a 'butch' male icon at a time – shortly after the first flowering of gay liberation – when male homosexuals were able and eager to assert the reality of their masculinity.[82]

Where geographically there was a larger concentration of gay men, and subsequently the subculture was more complex and diverse, a specialized identity grew around the erotics of masculine codes. Because its urban scenes were already better established, this occurred in the United States before it did in Britain. Martin P. Levine traces the emergence of the clone (so-called because of a uniform consensus within the subculture as to the specifics of masculine codes) to 'the mid-1970s in the "gay ghettos" of America's largest cities'.[83] 'Presentational strategies were typically "butch" . . . clones dressed in such a way as to highlight male erotic features and availability. For example, these men frequently wore form-fitting T-shirts and Levis that outlined their musculature, genitals and buttocks.'[84] British gay subculture was subject to the transformation too, importing this new language of gay eroticism from the United States. Soon British gay macho identity also diversified to

> other more specialist images: the leatherman/biker, the construction worker, the squaddy, the skinhead, the biker. Many, though not all, of these styles of clothing mimic those of occupations and pursuits which are strong male preserves . . . the prescribed forms of masculinity extend beyond dress to gestures and 'body language' . . . to ways of speaking . . . to language.[85]

Within the context of shifts in the dominant culture, the masculinization of gay men is due to a post-liberation radical political critique of the effeminate stereotype, and also the erotic demands of a more visible, diverse and accessible commercial gay scene.

If this new 'butch' culture was about dressing up like real men, then skinhead codes were perfect for appropriation. The skinhead look had already assembled the fetishes of working-class masculinity:

> The adoption by Skinheads of boots and short jeans and shaved hair was 'meaningful' in terms of the sub-culture only because these external manifestations resonated with and articulated Skinhead conceptions of masculinity, 'hardness' and 'workingclassness'.[86]

The identity was concerned with maleness, working-classness and youth, the three idealized aspects within gay subculture. It was also the dominant form of rough masculinity at the emergence of the clone look and, fixed for many years as the most masculine and aggressive youth cult, continued to remain so.

The skinhead image operates as an erotic code within gay subculture, but as a street style, unlike clone (or cowboy or leather) codes, it can be worn safely beyond the physical confines of the subcultural leisure environment: in the street, gay skinheads will pass as straight to the heterosexual imperative while advertising an erotic interest in masculinity to informed readers (other gay men).

In conclusion

Constructs of masculinity and class are interdependent. Dominant attitudes of queers as effeminate and posh, inherited from nineteenth-century notions of effeminacy as a signifier of class, are so central to concepts of masculinity and so pervasive that they have probably blinded analysts to erotic structures which do not conform to this pattern. Available data therefore supports these assumptions, although there are obvious gaps in the material which beg speculation and require further research.

Skinheads operated within and physically enforced conservative social divisions and definitions; subsequently they could not be gay because of their (mutually justifying) working-classness and foregrounded masculinity, qualities which defined themselves directly against homosexuality. As such, however, they fulfilled the erotic ideal of masculinity operating within the class/gender differential which dominated homosexual desire in the subculture for most of the twentieth century.

However, following the masculinization of gay culture (an aspect of the liberal interrogation of societal definitions against which skinheads were reacting), the number of men who could identify as gay increased across class, and gay men could incorporate erotic aspects of masculinity into their own identity which had previously been reserved for the Other: working-class men had access to the scene and middle-class men dressed in working-class-derived styles. Skinhead styles operated perfectly in areas of the subculture where there was a specific identity centred on excessively masculine codes.

Notes

1. George Marshall, *Spirit of '69: A Skinhead Bible* (Dunoon, Scotland: Skinhead Times Publishing, 1991), p. 35.
2. *New Socialist*, Issue 1 (September/October 1981), p. 40.
3. Stanley Cohen, *Folk Devils and Moral Panics* (Oxford: Martin Roberston, 1980), p. ii.
4. Phil Cohen, 'Subcultural conflict and working class community', in *Working Papers in Cultural Studies,*

No. 2 (Spring), p. 23.
5. John Clarke and Tony Jefferson, 'Working Class Youth Cultures', in Geoff Mungham and Geoff Pearson (eds), *Working Class Youth Culture* (London: Routledge and Kegan Paul, 1976), p. 142.
6. Susie Daniel and Pete McGuire, *The Painthouse: Words from an East End Gang* (Harmondsworth: Penguin, 1972), p. 73.
7. Ian Taylor and Dave Wall, 'Beyond the Skinheads: Comments on the emergence and significance of the Glamrock Cult', in Mungham and Pearson, *Working Class Youth Culture*, p. 121.
8. *Ibid.*, p. 117.
9. Clarke and Jefferson, 'Working Class Youth Cultures', p. 152.
10. Daniel and McGuire, *The Painthouse*, p. 19.
11. *Ibid.*, p. 20.
12. *New Socialist*, Issue 1 (September/October 1981), p. 40.
13. Daniel and McGuire, *The Painthouse*, p. 69.
14. *Ibid.*, p. 71.
15. George Marshall, *Spirit of '69*, p. 36.
16. *Sun*, 27 April 1970, p. 14.
17. J. Philippe Rushton and Anthony E. Bogaert, 'Race versus Social Class Difference in Sexual Behaviour: A Follow-up Test of the r/K Dimension', *Journals of Research in Personality* 22 (1988), p. 259.
18. Richard Fung, 'Looking for My Penis: The Eroticized Asian in Gay Video Porn', in Bad Object-choices (ed.), *How Do I Look?* (Seattle: Bay Press, 1991), pp. 145–6.
19. Les Black, 'The "White Negro" revisited', in Andrea Cornwall and Nancy Lindisfarent (eds), *Dislocating Masculinity* (London: Routledge, 1993), p. 181.
20. Clarke and Jefferson, 'Working Class Youth Cultures', p. 155.
21. Ted Polhemus, *Streetstyle: from*

Sidewalk to Catwalk (London: Thames and Hudson, 1994), p. 58.
22. *Ibid.*, p. 60.
23. *Ibid.*, p. 70.
24. Black, 'The "White Negro" revisited', p. 176.
25. 'Why I'm a Skin, by the Brother', *Square Peg* 12 (London, 1986), p. 16.
26. George Marshall, *Spirit of '69*, p. 36.
27. Stanley Cohen, *Folk Devils and Moral Panics*, p. xii.
28. Jeremy Bugler, 'Puritans in boots', *New Society*, 13 November 1969, pp. 761–2.
29. Nick Knight, *Skinhead* (London: Omnibus Press, 1982), p. 30.
30. P. Fowler, 'Skins Rule', in Charlie Gillet (ed.), *Rock File* (London: Pictorial Publications, 1972), p. 19.
31. George Marshall, *Spirit of '69*, p. 8.
32. *Ibid.*, p. 34.
33. Daniel and McGuire, *The Painthouse*, p. 72.
34. *Ibid.*, p. 83.
35. Clarke and Jefferson, 'Working Class Youth Cultures', p. 149.
36. George Marshall, *Spirit of '69*, pp. 10–13.
37. Daniel and McGuire, *The Painthouse*, p. 83.
38. *Ibid.*, p. 84.
39. Knight, *Skinhead*, p. 29.
40. John Clarke, 'Football Hooliganism and the Skinheads', *Sub and Popular Culture Series No 42* (Centre for Contemporary Cultural Studies, University of Birmingham, 1973), pp. 2–3.
41. George Marshall, *Spirit of '69*, p. 34.
42. Clarke and Jefferson, 'Working Class Youth Cultures', p. 156.
43. Daniel and McGuire, *The Painthouse*, p. 32.
44. George Marshall, *Spirit of '69*, p. 31.
45. Clarke, 'Football Hooliganism and the Skinheads', pp. 2–3.
46. Daniel and McGuire, *The Painthouse*, p. 84.
47. *Ibid.*, p. 32.

48. *Ibid.*, p. 25.
49. George Marshall, *Spirit of '69*, p. 27.
50. Richard North, 'The brain beneath the bristle', *The Times*, 22 July 1981.
51. Clarke and Jefferson, 'Working Class Youth Cultures', p. 179.
52. Clarke, 'Football Hooliganism and the Skinheads', p. 9.
53. Knight, *Skinhead*, p. 20.
54. George Marshall, *Spirit of '69*, p. 51.
55. Clarke, 'Football Hooliganism and the Skinheads', pp. 18–19.
56. George Marshall, *Spirit of '69*, p. 38.
57. *Ibid.*, p. 38.
58. Polhemus, *Streetstyle*, p. 70.
59. George Marshall, *Spirit of '69*, p. 55.
60. *Ibid.*, p. 51.
61. Clarke, 'Football Hooliganism and the Skinheads', p. 14.
62. Cohen, *Folk Devils and Moral Panics*, p. 200.
63. Jeffrey Weeks, *Coming Out: Homosexual Politics in Britain* (London: Quartet, 1977), p. 187.
64. Weeks, *Coming Out*, p. 191.
65. Gregg Blachford, 'Male Dominance and the Gay World', in Kenneth Plummer (ed.), *The Making of the Modern Homosexual* (New Jersey: Barnes and Noble, 1981), p. 187.
66. John Marshall, 'Pansies, Perverts and Macho Men', in Plummer, *The Making of the Modern Homosexual*, p. 146.
67. Eve Kosofsky Sedgwick, *Between Men: English Literature and Male Homosocial Desire* (New York: Columbia University Press, 1985), p. 93.
68. Alan Sinfield, *Effeminacy: Some Parameters* (paper presented at Queory seminar, Sussex University, Spring 1994).
69. Weeks, *Coming Out*, p. 39.
70. *Ibid.*, p. 43.
71. Jeffrey Weeks, 'Discourse, Desire and Sexual Deviance', in Plummer, *The Making of the Modern Homosexual*, p. 105.
72. John Fletcher, 'Forster's self-erasure: *Maurice* and the scene of masculine love', in Joseph Bristow (ed.), *Sexual Sameness: textual differences in lesbian and gay writing* (London: Routledge, 1992), p. 73.
73. Michael Bronski, *Culture Clash: The Making of a Gay Sensibility* (Boston: South End Press, 1984), p. 170.
74. Martin P. Levine, 'The Life and Death of Gay Clones', in G. Herdt (ed.), *Gay Culture in America: Essays from the Field* (Boston: Beacon Print, 1992), p. 73.
75. Andrew Kopkind, 'Dressing Up', *Village Voice*, 30 April 1979, p. 34.
76. Weeks, 'Discourse, Desire and Sexual Deviance', p. 146.
77. James Chesebro and Kenneth Klenk, 'Gay Masculinity in the Gay Disco', in James Chesebro (ed.), *Gayspeak: Gay Male and Lesbian Communication* (New York: Pilgrim Press, 1981), p. 88.
78. John Marshall, 'Pansies, Perverts and Macho Men', pp. 153–4.
79. *Ibid.*, p. 152.
80. Jamie Gough, 'Theories of Sexual Identity and the Masculinisation of the Gay Man', in Simon Shepherd and Mick Wallis (eds), *Coming On Strong: Gay Politics and Culture* (London: Unwin Hyman, 1989), p. 129.
81. Gough, 'Theories of sexual identity', p. 131.
82. Kopkind, 'Dressing Up', p. 34.
83. Levine, 'The Life and Death of Gay Clones', pp. 76–7.
84. *Ibid.*, p. 77.
85. Gough, 'Theories of sexual identity', p. 119.
86. Stuart Hall and Tony Jefferson (eds), *Resistance Through Rituals* (London: Hutchinson, 1976), p. 56.

4

'I am what I want'

As it is documented, the masculinization of gay subculture first manifested itself on the diversifying scene in American cities, and then began to make its influence known in Britain through the clone. This would lead to a tidy explanation of how gay skins came to be: queens turned macho; gay men became clones; clones became skinheads. There are two problems with this. Firstly, this still upholds the heterosexist assumption inherent in the phrase 'gay skinhead' – that the genuine article was straight, with queens with an inclination for a bit of rough coming along later and colonizing the look when it was no longer fashionable, adapting it to the established worship of masculinity on the clone scene. Secondly, gay skinheads could not then have emerged as a distinct group until the end of the 1970s. Of course, some gay men arrived at a skinhead identity in the late 1970s by this route.

But my critique of the heterosexualizing accounts of working-class youth subcultures opens the way for gay involvement in the very evolution of the skinhead: young men could find space in these 'delinquent' cultures to articulate a sense of identity around their homosexual desire that did not fit the contemporary organization of sexualities.

Youth subculture did indeed provide more appropriate answers to the problems of sexual self-identification that some young working-class men were experiencing at this time. One working-class lad, David Scoular, found that the masculinity embodied in being a mod made more sense of his desire and identity than the limited identities available on London's gay scene at the time which, waking up to legalization, politicization and commercialization, was still dominated by a pre-'Liberation' cultured gent identity.

I kind of knew there were gay bars in Earls Court; I'm not quite sure how I knew. So all I could do was go down to Earls Court and ask people in the street, 'Are there are any gay bars near here?'; there was no other way I could find out. Interestingly enough, I did not get a negative reaction; I never have had. So I was sent to the Coleherne. That was my first gay bar. I walked in looking like some freak . . . naff, you'd say now, a real naff person from a small town. I was twenty-one. These days, you're twenty-one and you've done it all! But not then.

It wasn't my scene; I was interested in Mods – I was a Mod then, shirts, cravats – I had a scooter. There was nobody like me there. They were mainly middle class, old . . . actually, they were mostly in their thirties, but in those days, thirty was almost ancient, 'cos they had bald heads and wore sports jackets. We were the first generation to wear jeans, don't forget; there were big changes going on, and it wasn't just about being gay. There was a whole sartorial and psychological revolution pushing through, not just in lifestyles, but in everything.

The historical coincidence of gay liberation with the evolution of the skinhead predisposed this particular youth culture to gay men more than any other. Some men who fancied men growing up in the late 1960s were finding that joining a skinhead gang did more to articulate that desire than taking up the still limited identities available on the slowly evolving gay scene. Their eventual emergence on the scene had a transformative effect, the evolution of a gay skinhead subculture enabling a diversification which made space for the macho scene. This was well before the American clone image was imported. The gay skinhead did not conform to the clone pattern so much as constitute it, preparing the subculture for its emergence. 'Many remember with affection those heady and exciting days', wrote Mike Dow in his recollection of the emergence of the gay skinhead. 'It was the first time a "macho" street culture had openly emerged on the scene. Clones were more than a decade away and the young man who didn't fancy the predominantly camp style which was rampant among young queens at the time could make a strong stand against traditional ideas.' Even if they missed out on the gay skinhead, existing analyses of the scene in the late 1960s were right at least to underline the influence that political developments had had on homosexual assertiveness: being a gay skinhead 'was in the real spirit of gay lib'.[1]

Points of identification

For most of the gay men I interviewed who were skinheads in the 1960s, their attraction to the cult was initially motivated by erotic fascination. But it was more than a simple matter of dressing up: many belonged to predominantly straight skinhead gangs. But neither were they skinheads who just happened to be homosexual. Their sexuality and skinhead identity were in fact closely linked, allowing them to voice a dissatisfaction with contemporary ideas about homosexuality and articulate alternatives which made more sense.

Mitchum-born Michael Dover became a skinhead

when I met my first big affair I wasn't a skinhead at all at that time, I had long hair, I was very . . . trendy I suppose is the word. I was on the underground one day and there was this skinhead guy leant on the carriage door in really tight jeans, quite high up his legs, big boots, huge great bulge in his crotch and short hair; and I just sort of stood there gazing at him, thinking, 'My God, you're gorgeous.' And I followed him off the tube and it ended up, well, I left home for him. I was living with my parents, I was sixteen at the time, it was 1966. I moved into a flat with him, well, a room, £17–7–6d it was, between two of us. And the first thing he said to me was, 'Oh your hair's awful.' I said, 'Well, I'll cut it.' I just really fell for him and I'd have done anything for him. Within about week he'd got my hair shaved off, he'd gone out and bought the boots and jeans and everything to go with it.

Although Michael hadn't previously mixed with skinheads to any great degree, through Peter he became part of a skinhead gang.

We virtually never went to gay pubs and clubs at all; we actually had mainly straight friends. There was this huge gang of friends who were straight and I got accepted into that through Peter. The Clapham Mob, they used to call us. I was living in Balham with Peter, and all this crowd lived in Clapham on the Notre Dame Estate, which was quite a rough estate. We spent our whole time with this crew, going to all the straight places. It was a very strange group because they weren't homophobic at all – I don't think that word was around then – they were very accepting. After a while it did dawn on us that they actually knew about me and Peter, because one of the girls said something one day and it was obvious that she knew. We said to her, 'Oh, you know?' and she said, 'We *all* know.'

But they didn't care about it at all, it was really good. It didn't matter to them. We had a flat, which none of them did, they all lived with their families, so we were the focus – they'd all come round and get drunk and we were very open house. We actually got a lot of very good friends that way. There was one guy who was a total closet – he was going round having sex with Peter. And there was only one other guy in the gang, who we dabbled with, and there was a further one who actually left the group and went to live up north somewhere with another guy. We never found out whether he was gay or not, but we were pretty sure. He suddenly disappeared and everyone talked about it, there were strange rumblings about it. Nothing anti, though.

There was this shop in Oxford Street, right by Oxford Circus; we'd go there to nick our Ben Shermans on Saturdays. I did it, I have to admit, only once, but the bolder ones would come out with two or three Ben Shermans stuffed up their jumpers – you didn't have electronic tagging in those days! We never bought them. And Fred Perrys – my mum used to be able to get loads for next to nothing, so I had one of every colour, and I'd sell them to my mates.

And we even went to football, which before that hadn't interested me at all. [Chelsea was their team, although neither Michael nor Peter was really into the game.] Peter was just there to look at the guys. There are so many nice-looking guys at football matches. Quite often I thought I'd like to be standing on these terraces facing the opposite way just to look at them all. But no, we weren't really into football at all, we were just there 'cos there were so many nice guys there. You could actually . . . it sounds like cottaging, but you could go to the loo and see all these really horny skinheads standing there pissing. Straights, for some reason, they don't huddle up close and hide themselves, they tend to stand back. That alone was worth the 2s–6d to get in.

As a mod out of place on a scene populated by homosexual gents, David Scoular too found a solution in skinhead subculture, which he discovered when he arrived in East London in autumn 1967.

For me, the whole skinhead thing started with these straight guys before they were called skinheads, straight guys in Hackney. In October, I got to know the family who ran Sunny Stores near my flat in Dalston. They had a son of seventeen, Barry; absolutely beautiful, he was. He had cropped hair, mohair suits, brogues; he knew I was gay, the whole family did, I made it quite clear to them I was gay. I've always done that. I don't wear a pink triangle and scream in the street, but if anybody asks me, I tell them; I even introduce it when nobody wants me to, just to be awkward.

Barry was very protective towards me and introduced me to all his friends, who were all skinheads, except they weren't called skinheads in those days, they were just East End kids with cropped hair and Ben Sherman shirts. He said, 'You must come out with my mates some time', so I did. We went down the pub and on the way home his mate said, 'Why don't you get your hair cropped short? Just 'cause you're gay, so what? It doesn't matter; we don't care; why don't you join us?' So I did. I got my hair cut short in a place called Ryan's, which is where all the cropped heads got their hair cut. It was on the shopping parade by the bridge next to Hackney Down Station. They used to back-comb and scissor-cut it, before they used clippers. So I had my hair cut short.

I went to a shop in the Kingsland Road, just south of Dalston junction, that sold Ben Sherman shirts. And I got Levis near by, tight-fitting with a zip; I forget what type. And I got some short-sleeved V-neck sweaters and a denim jacket. At the time, these guys used to wear Monkey boots, not Doctor Martens. You used to get them from Blackwells in Shoreditch. But anyway, I went to get these boots, but this guy said to me, 'Don't get those, get these': he showed me brown Doc Martens with a little tan trim round the top, like Timberlands have now. So I got these boots. And all the lads said, 'Where did you get those from?' because they were new at the time. So they all went down and bought them. I was the only gay person in this whole group.

The skinhead subculture extended its influence well beyond its East End birthplace. Chris Clive, who ran the Gay Skinhead Group from 1992 till his death in 1995, became a skinhead in the north of England, in 1969.

It was when they'd just started, in fact, there weren't any really before that; there were a few mods and rockers around, but there weren't any skinheads till '69. I was eighteen; I'd just finished school, I was living with my parents, sporting a Beatles mop. I was walking along the road and I saw two guys with short hair and boots on the other side of the road and I just liked the look of them. I just walked over and started to chat to them. From that day on, that was it. I got involved with them.

Like many teenagers growing up with a sense of homosexual desire, Chris had spent his teenage years feeling 'different'. This meeting with Pete and Tony, who called themselves 'skinheads', had a huge impact on his sense of identity. 'I had never felt so good in all my life,' he wrote in an account published in the GSG fanzine *Skinhead Nation*. 'I had just met two boys with whom I had something in common. I felt a huge expansion inside my jeans and suddenly realised, what if they find out I'm queer? Will they beat me up?' Skinhead identity was a focus of identification and desire, but safely incompatible with the common understanding of queerness. When Chris later revealed his new look, 'Dad was pleased, because he couldn't relate a lad with boots and cropped hair as being queer, which I think he was worried about.'

The following day Chris travelled to Bradford, where he had his hair clippered down to a number one and paid £5–19s–11d for a pair of DMs from the market, 'brown boots with eight sets of eyelets for the laces (they were all that were available in those days)'. Back home, he cut down his tight button-fly Levis and went to work on the brown boots with a tin of Kiwi Ox Blood polish as the market trader had instructed him.

That evening he met up with the skinheads again, when it became apparent that identity was more than just costume: 'I knew I would have to learn their jargon . . . to be fully accepted, or I would be suspected of being "posh" and not a skinhead'. 'Pete was 18 and worked on a building site, and Tony was 19 and worked in a DIY store, and I just assumed that they lived near to each other with their parents.' In fact, the two shared a flat in Dewsbury, claiming their parents lived 'down south'.

Chris went back to their flat with them that night. 'The conversation got round to asking about girlfriends, to which I was quick to say that I didn't have any at the moment. "How about you?" I asked. "No", said Tony, "we're not into girls. Get all our fun together and sometimes with another skin."' That night, the first of many as it turned out, the three of them shared a bed, where they had sex. Although this account could be accused of playing to its audience, Chris was insistent on its accuracy.

Likewise, David soon found that a skinhead identity was an access route to masculine homosexual sex.

After about ten weeks of being a skinhead – it was the spring of '68 – I did my usual Sunday walk along the dock and there was this huge 15,000 ton freighter going past. I sat down and this guy on the freighter wolf-whistled at me. I looked up – it was the first time a non-camp guy had come on to me. I shouted, 'Where do you go?' 'The Cubitt Arms', he said, 'on the Isle of Dogs.'

So that night I got the 277 to the docks. Extraordinary it was, narrow terraced streets dwarfed by huge great ships at the end. I found the Cubitt Arms – as you opened the door, there was the stage, where they used to have appalling drag acts on, dockers in dish-cloth wigs. And there was this gay skinhead. *Another guy who was a skinhead who was gay!* He wasn't great-looking, I didn't really fancy him, but I thought, My God . . . and I went to bed with him. He'd smuggle me in. The pub would close at eleven o'clock, on a Saturday night, and we'd walk up and down the street outside his house till his dad, who was a docker, went to bed; when the light went out, we'd creep in.

We had a mad session that first time, all those years of repression and fantasies coming out. It was amazing. I can still see his face in front of me. I didn't really fancy him, though. He was cute, but not really beddable. He didn't want to fuck; we didn't do that, he wasn't 'gay'. It was very refreshing, because all the gay guys who'd approached me in the gay bars, which I'd ceased going to long, long since, wanted to be like a woman with me, which I didn't want. I'm not criticizing them; it just wasn't me.

So anyway, I'd be smuggled down at three in the morning – we didn't dare fall asleep. He'd never seen another guy who looked like me. I used to go down there probably no more than once every month. He was always there when I went down every month and he never had anybody with him. He'd be like, 'Oh good, are you coming home with me then?' I was never under pressure to see him again, but he was always very pleased when he saw me. It would be the same routine, waiting for the light to go out, coming out at three in the morning, cold, frosty mornings, with the ship swaying, the 277 would come, dockers would get on board.

Notice in this account, the difficulty around the word 'gay' – it can be ascribed objectively according to behaviour, or identified with subjectively. Though obviously homosexual activity was actively sought in these early experiences for Chris and David, it did not necessarily entail questions of identity. David says of the docker's son that 'He either got married or committed suicide or something – he could never accept he was gay.' The words like 'gay' and 'queer' did not describe Chris' skinhead mates, despite what they got up to. Chris claims,

> Back in the early days I wasn't out myself, I was just another one of the lads, another skin out on the street. Originally, the skinhead was a straight thing, totally. But because they're what they are, they did play around a bit. They probably wouldn't admit it, but get one of them on their own, and a few beers, and it's surprising what they'd do.

But he eventually found, like Michael, that 1960s skinhead culture was surprisingly unhomophobic. When he eventually came out to his straight skinhead mates, 'it didn't make any difference. I never had any aggro from them anyway.' David went on to find his homosexual relationships warmly accepted by his straight skinhead gang. 'One guy I was seeing, he'd come out with my straight skinhead mates, and they were all really pleased that I'd found someone who was gay. Isn't that interesting? "Who's your mate?" they'd ask. "Is he gay?"'

The gay skin scene

Admittedly, these instances are individual experiences and could easily be dismissed as exceptional rather than indicative of any cultural change. Michael, for example, was accepted with a skinhead gang *despite* being gay; his induction into skinhead life was inspired by erotic attraction, but being skinhead was not a particularly gay thing, as the predominance of straight-identified skinheads proved. But it seems that so many gay men experienced a simultaneous attraction to skinhead culture that there slowly emerged a gay skinhead scene. According to David,

> A lot of disparate people did it at the same time spontaneously. I believe there's a collective consciousness of some kind. Society throws things up; the whole gay thing was life throwing something up. And I think you're quite right, I'd never thought of this before – all modern gay images are variations on the skinhead theme. I think it threw up something different. It had to happen. So all these guys were doing it independently of each other, all probably for different individual reasons, but we all fancied straight guys.

Mike Dow, then a sales assistant in a casual menswear shop in Cardiff, became a skinhead after he had become a regular on the local gay scene, where boots and braces were a not uncommon sight.

> Oddly enough I didn't see their appearance, which was what appealed to me, as exclusively heterosexual. I just thought, this is a good look. A few of my contemporaries must have thought the same thing because a few gay skinheads just started to emerge, around about the same time as the

straight skinheads were hitting the headlines. Round about Cardiff and south Wales at the time there were a few as well on the gay scene. There weren't many. There weren't may venues to chose from. In those days the scene was not as divided at all as it is today, no specific types of clubs for dress codes or types of music.

Mike moved in exclusively gay skinhead circles, where class identity was less of a deciding factor.

I think on the gay scene the skinhead ran across all types of class. One of my closest friends who was a skinhead at the time was a conductor with the English National Opera, Sadlers Wells opera; he would turn up to conduct an opera with a shaved head and the suit and I'd meet him afterwards and he'd change into his gear and we'd go off. All types were doing it, from conductors right through to working-class lads. On the gay scene certainly there was no class barriers. It was a sexually oriented look. Perhaps it was partly a reaction to the alternative, to become a screaming queen basically. There was a lot more camp about in those days.

The gay skinheads tended to favour the bars where masculine gay identities were already becoming established in the late 1960s. 'You really only had the Coleherne and the Boltons in those days', remembers one regular, 'you didn't have anything like the venues you've got these days.' Skinheads found the Coleherne in Earls Court particularly accommodating at the time, because gay men who had an interest in a previous youth culture – bikers – had already carved a niche for themselves there. 'The Coleherne was the bar that men in biker gear went to. There was a corner that was leather – the rest of the bar was queens, straights, rent boys, you name it.' It's important to remember that in 1968 masculine gay identities were still something of a curiosity: one gay man, heavily invested in an effeminate identity, remembers his first revelatory visit to the Coleherne:

I never really noticed macho queens until I went to the Coleherne for the first time, by mistake, and was absolutely terrified. It was full of men in leather – I thought, My God, I've walked into a Hell's Angels' pub, this really is the end. I turned up there wearing a petrol purple mohair sweater and a pair of white flares – I thought I was the business.

David recalls,

Round about June '68 I went to the Coleherne, because I always had this thing that I didn't want lovey-dovey sex, and I thought that was the place to go. So I used to hang around there sometimes in my brown Doc Martens, red table-cloth Ben Sherman and black sweater and rolled-up Levis. And no one would speak to me in the bar. I never had that effect in the street, mind you. But one night this guy in a leather jacket came over and tried to chat me up: 'I really fancy you', he said, 'I've always wanted to go with a skinhead.' I thought, it's working!

This fellow gay skin introduced David to a popular Soho gay members' club called Le Ducé, at 22 Poland Street. 'Nothing much happened there. I went there from late spring 1968. It was a curious place. There'd be about fifty guys who we'd now call skinheads, gay guys – or whatever.'

David's ambiguity on the subject of these skinheads' sexual identity reveals how the gay skin was something of a novelty and had yet to be accepted as a gay type. Skinheads were strongly identified with straight masculinity, and the macho scene was still in its infancy. A lot of gay skinheads stuck to straight social networks, initially feeling a greater allegiance to their skinhead, rather than gay, identity, and didn't feel welcome on the gay scene. 'There were quite a lot of gay skinheads around', says Michael, 'but most of them were going to straight pubs. Boyfriends were in the closet, just with each other having sex, but acting straight when they went out. I mean, I did with Peter: our regular was this straight pub on the Old Kent Road in 1968.'

But as more skinheads congregated on the gay scene, however warily, they could identify as gay with more confidence. Unlike David's first skinhead partner, the docker's son, the two skinhead boyfriends who followed 'were definitely gay. Although I'm not sure how useful that term is; it's a sliding scale. We still didn't feel part of the gay scene . . . People tended to keep away from you in the bars. Not surprising, looking the way I did – I looked quite threatening.'

'Oh no, they never mixed with the rest of the scene', recalls Daffyd Jenkins, now manager of the Anvil, a south London leather/uniform club, who was a 'screaming Mary' in those days. He was terrified when he first saw a gang of gay skinheads enter the Union Tavern, a gay pub on Camberwell New Road in South London, in the late 1960s. 'I don't know if that was through design or necessity, because when they originally came on to the scene everybody was terrified of them.' Nevertheless, the gay scene of the late 1960s was growing to accommodate this dissident gay identity. With the masculinization of British gay subculture under way, skinheads tended to be drawn towards the venues that were beginning to cater for a specialized interest in leather. As David had discovered, the Coleherne was an early example of such a bar, a logical place to start looking for other skins, so it was only a matter of time before isolated gay skins started to congregate there. As Daffyd observed, 'It was one of the few places where they didn't get turned out or shunned.'

Finding a precarious foothold in the existing network, the phenomenon of the gay skinhead began to transform the club scene. In 1969 a Bromley skin called Terry convinced the manager of the Union Tavern to rent the venue out to him on a Tuesday night. Dubbing himself 'The Prince of

Peace', he played reggae and attracted a skinhead following. One regular called Terry, quoted in Mike Dow's 'Skins', recalls:

> It was fantastic in those days. Tuesday night was skinhead night and you could walk into the pub and there'd be a sea of crops. Fantastic! And everyone was gay! We'd dance to reggae all night, you know, the real Jamaican stuff, and all in rows, strict step. It was a real sight seeing all those skins dancing in rows. The atmosphere was electric.

'It was only open pub hours, it shut at eleven, like most places did', Michael recalls, 'but all these skinheads started coming to it, more and more, ones you'd never seen. Peter and I, before we met people, we'd give new faces nicknames, "Nice Ears", silly things. But eventually you got to know everyone. We formed our own gang; it lasted quite a long while. We used to have fantastic Tuesday evenings. Bethnal Green, Tottenham – they came a long way, because they wanted to be with other skinheads, and it was a good night.'

Indeed, such was the reputation that the night would lure people from even further afield than Tottenham. 'I was at art college in Newport doing Graphic Design', says Mike Dow.

> I had a little Ford Anglia 100E and on Tuesday nights I used to drive all the way to London just to go to that skinhead night at the Union Tavern in Camberwell. It closed at eleven o'clock and then I'd have to drive all the way back again, but it was worth it because it was such a brilliant night, the whole club was full of skinheads, *gay* skinheads. The atmosphere was magic.
>
> Sunday night at the Union Tavern was a particularly strange phenomenon because all the skinheads would dress up, and that would mean two-tone tonic trousers and the tassled loafers or brogues, white socks (showing), the shirts, the braces, the Crombie with the silk handkerchief and the tie-pin; and the porkpie hat, very often. You had to have it all absolutely right. And they'd dance in lines, stomp in lines, and that was very precise as well. Many records had their own steps.
>
> The Union Tavern was a very working-class, even rather seedy type of pub; down there in Camberwell, it was pretty rough round there in those days, but people would pour out into the street after closing time and hang about for a while, and I don't remember there ever being any trouble. The locals weren't funny about it at all. It had this enormous great big floor in the middle, which on cabaret nights would be full of tables and chairs; for disco nights, skinheads nights, would be all cleaned away and become a dancefloor. It was actually a gay pub – in those days, most gay pubs were in working-class areas – but before it opened, there would be things like boxing practice and where the dancefloor was they

would have a ring and all the local kids would be there knocking hell out of each other until about six o'clock, and then they'd all go out, they'd take the ring down, and the pub would be open for business.

Mike feels that the existence of a specifically skinhead gay night was a breakthrough for the London scene.

There wasn't nearly the number of clubs there are now, so all clubs were gay clubs and that was it, you'd get all ages, all types in the one venue. So the emergence of gay skinheads with their own venue goes hand in hand with the development of the scene as a whole. I think that perhaps forced the pace a bit, because here were guys who were not interested in drag acts and camping up, they wanted a particular atmosphere, a particular ambience. Maybe that helped make way for the leather scene and later the more American-style cruisiest macho bar.

Other venues tried to compete with their own skinhead nights, but the market was limited; the Union Tavern, which could hold up to four hundred at a squeeze, was tremendously popular and there were only so many gay skinheads to go round.

So it was always the same people who you saw at these places. They tried to start a night at what is the Black Cap now, which was not so smart then, and this Terry set up a skinhead night there, a disco night. But the first thing they did was tell us all we weren't allowed to dance, 'cos we were all into reggae, moonstomping, so that didn't last very long. And then the pub went on to become more famous when the drag came along.

The gay skinhead gangs which grouped at the Union Tavern tended to favour straight venues and gay pubs whose clientele was gravitating towards specializing in machismo. 'We'd have places where we'd meet', says Michael. 'We used to go to the Vauxhall Tavern on a Friday night, some of us. And there was a pub in Tottenham called the Flowerpot, a lot of gay skinheads from the Tottenham area would meet there, ten or twelve of us, we'd go there every week. It was a straight pub, but it was a good night.'

Centrefold skins

The gay skinhead was not only transforming the scene; the skinhead was also being recruited into an expanding range of gay sex symbols. Gay men's fantasies were changing too, and the expanding British gay publishing industry was growing to reflect this. The trendy, glossy Carnaby Street-based gay magazine *Jeremy* ran its first skinhead sequence in February 1970: three full-page pictures by Johnny Clamp of a very cocky, very young skin in a white button-collared shirt, braces, and tight jeans rolled to expose socks and ankle-high work boots, photographed against an anonymous derelict urban landscape of crumbling brickwork and timber. Interest in skinheads was strong enough to warrant a profile of the youth culture two issues later. Trevor Richard's article challenged the public image:

> To the general public they are most famous and feared for 'aggro' but to imagine that all skinheads are aggressive is to judge solely by appearances and to believe all that the popular dailies say . . . Most skinheads are out for a good time. Their real enthusiasms are harmless enough – football, clothes, girls (not always), music.

So even within gay subculture, 'skinhead' still meant straight, although 'not always': featured with the text was a picture of DJ Terry, 'The Prince of Peace' on the decks, and the three pages of pictures by Hunter Reid that followed the piece were of Michael Dover, his boyfriend Peter and Terry photographed on street corners around the Union Tavern.

The photographer Anthony Burls was at this time setting up business as a specialist in male studies. His personal dissatisfaction with the identities on the scene led him to discover and later create alternative types. This had a significant transformative effect on the range of types available to gay men not only as fantasies but identities.

> I first started getting involved in the scene when I came out of the army. It was back in the fifties; I was living with mum and dad in Mitchum, and I had no idea where to go if you were gay. There isn't a manual – well, there is now, with the gay press, but in those days there wasn't, and even if there had been, you wouldn't have known where to look for it.
>
> I was working in a factory. I was a plumber and there was a carpenter there who I thought was very tasty. He turned out to be gay; we had it off in the Managing Director's Office one Saturday morning. We got together purely by accident, but we turned it to our advantage. He introduced me to the London scene, started to take me round the scene, some of the clubs. They were all very smart piss-elegant places and I didn't ever meet anybody there that I really liked.
>
> But he and his boyfriend used to go to Hyde Park near Speakers Corner and I noticed there were a lot of people up there with leather jackets, looking as though they had motorbikes. All the motorcycle boys used to gather there, and I saw people there I liked. But my parents' influence was still very strong in the way I dressed, it would be very smart-casual, tweed trousers, yellow sweaters, suede jackets. I realized I wasn't going to get anywhere dressed like that. So jeans and a T-shirt were immediately to hand.

Youth subcultures were having a direct influence on the way some gay men dressed: 'Skinheads came much later – first you had rockers. Skinheads were the first masculine gay style after leather.' But Tony does not think many found access to a gay identity via those youth subcultures; it was more a case of adopting their codes to disguise a sexual interest in the fetishistic elements of the clothes. 'Some of these gay men into leather might have got into it growing up as rockers, but I don't think many. Put it this way – there were a lot more people with jeans and leather jackets than there were bikes; there were a lot more people with full leather than there were with bikes.' Class identity also separated many individuals from the youth culture they resembled. 'These motorcycle people were always reasonably well off; the gay ones always came from a rather posher background.' These were what the biker gang in *The Leather Boys* referred to as 'leather Johnnies'.

The dominance of effeminate identities on the more established scene alienated Tony. 'It was all very prissy – camp dancers, hairdressers, reeking of Aramis, things like that, not at all natural.' As far as he was concerned, effeminacy broadcast homosexuality all too conspicuously.

I never enjoyed being in the company of screaming queens because I never liked being identified with being gay when I was young – I lived at home, I couldn't afford it. And I still like men to be men. This is what I liked about the leather crowd, because generally they weren't like that. They were very butch, they were opposite to the camp ones. I liked them because seemingly they were men.

Leather identity was a narrowcast advertisement of homosexuality: 'Not a lot of people knew about leather on the gay scene back then, so it helped me, being with a crowd who were all gay but it wasn't obvious to people who weren't in the know.'

The discovery that masculinity and homosexuality were not necessarily mutually exclusive led Tony to establish this new erotic on print, where this developing interest was having little impact. In the early 1960s, gay men's pornography was largely imported from the United States, with glossy titles such as *Athletic Models Guild* and *Physique Pictorial* disguising themselves as fitness magazines. Homosexuality was a dirty sickness; these publications disavowed the shadow of such suspicion by an overinvestment in the idea of health, often purporting to be body-building magazines, showing over-styled, over-oiled physiques of uncommon muscular perfection. British magazines tended to ape this American style.

There used to be magazines called *Male Classics, Modern Adonis, Ser Gee, Body Beautiful*. They were all published by a guy in Kensington. He was straight: when he was putting magazines together, he was hopeless, he didn't have a clue what gays liked, so he always had a gay person do the layouts. These magazines had incredibly good-looking people with immaculate hair, dressed in pouches, shot in classic poses. But there was a photographer around called Scott, who did all this masculine thing, bikers, and that was the theme I started on and developed.

The idea was to take pictures of the boy next door. Originally I never started with anyone who was gay in these photos. They were definitely straight.

Working under the name of Cain of London, Tony would shoot photographs either on location in parks or in a garage in the Oval which served as a studio. He regularly published catalogues of his work, mainly distributed by mail order, although a few brave London newsagent sold them too. 'There was the Adelaide book shop up in Leicester Square in this alleyway down the side of the Garrick Theatre. I think there were a couple of newsstands around. But a gay bookshop as such was a nonsense in those days.' Starting out as *The Londoners*, and later developing into other series such as *The Young Londoners* and *Cain's Leather Boys*, these acted as erotic magazines in their own right. But their function was to encourage the reader to buy a full set of prints, of which the magazines only ever showed a few. 'The magazines didn't make much money; I was a photographer, after all, and my job was to sell photos.'

'Initially in the first three or four magazines I did, didn't have a gay person in them. All the models were definitely straight.' Working-class straight men were quite literally recruited into the gay scene's new-style collective fantasy, with a friend acting as an unofficial but highly productive talent scout.

He used to get a lot of these models for me because he knew the kind of person I wanted, so he'd be cruising around, either at work or whatever, building sites, looking for manual workers, anything like that. He really was quite outrageous in his manner, he'd call people down off four flights of scaffolding, with all the other workers taking the mickey. It wouldn't worry him; he'd approach them and tell them that I was looking for models, you know, 'Call this number, any questions answered', etc. He got a lorry driver out of his lorry at Hyde Park Corner one night for me: 'Oi you! Get out of your lorry, I want to have a look at you.' I used to say, 'Aren't you worried they might get a bit aggressive?' He was the campest thing on two legs. 'Ooh no', he'd say, 'I'd be quite happy if they laid into me.' He was very much into SM and being kicked and gobbed on and abused.

'To be honest, I only photographed people that turned me on. Photography was a great sexual release.' The photographer becomes the arbiter and consolidator of attractive masculinity. 'There was this fitter I was besotted with. I just thought to myself, if I am besotted with him, then lots of other people will be besotted with him as well. And I wasn't wrong because he did sell very well.' Clothed models were paid £6 a session. 'I always gave a reasonable fee. Most photographers in those days only gave around two quid. If I did a second session then it was because they were popular and I would put the fee up.'

I always used to tell these straight models I was doing a magazine about Londoners – and that wasn't a lie. In the early days everyone used to have a false name, and we used to have these little stories about what they did, a little profile. 'Ken is twenty, his hobbies are motor-racing' – he didn't even own a bike! But there was nothing there that suggested these people were gay. So I felt that I wasn't distorting the truth too much. Quite often I did find that when I photographed somebody I felt that they got a sense that there might be more in this than just photos. How they handled that, we'll never know. But if I'd asked them to pose nude, then of course it would have been different. Why are they nude if they're not for gay people? But by the time I started doing nudes, I'd discovered a lot of gay models. Once you've got established, people write to you and contact you and then gay people started to be on the scene. And if they were good enough and I could make them look the part then I'd use them. The primary difference between photographing straight models and gay models was: if you say, 'Give us a sexy pose', the straight person will puff up his chest, the gay fella will push his crotch forward.

The invisible progress from straight to gay models is significant. Michael Bronski has written of the emergence of macho gay porn on both sides of the Atlantic at this time:

In the fifties, the predominant stereotype of a gay man was the limp-wristed swish . . . Most of the sexual iconography from this early period was an attempt to break away from, or modify, sexual stereotypes of gay men . . . Homosexual attraction to muscle magazines like *Iron Man* or *Strength and Health* was partially the simple appeal of uncovered bodies. But these publications were also appropriate sexual objects for gay men because they were clearly *unlike* the standard gay stereotype.

What motivated this expansion of gay subculture's pornographic *dramatis personae* to straight boys next door was a fantasy projection: wanting the one you could never have. But the invisible transition from straight to gay models communicated new notions of gay masculinity to the readers of *Young Londoners*. Certain types of maleness, which had previously been seen as the preserve of heterosexuality, became available to more gay men through such magazines, inviting readers not just to fantasize about them but to identify with them too.

This transition from fantasy projection to identification was quite literally embodied in what Tony called his 'biggest ever challenge'. For diplomatic reasons, he was coerced into shooting a model he had not recruited himself.

> When he turned up – well, I thought it was a woman standing there: dark green trousers that were more like slacks, shirt more like a blouse, silk chiffon scarf and a white shoulder bag. And I thought, this is *not* what *Young Londoners* is all about! It was a hairy moment, but I managed to fit him out in a pair of jeans and a leather jacket, and I really did succeed in making this fella look quite butch. It was so successful that I actually put him on the cover of one of the magazines.

The once-effeminate model went on to live out this new fantasy identity: 'He was over the moon about the name and actually changed his name to Steve Board by deed poll. He worked down this Chelsea gay club called the Catacombs and readers were interested in him; he became very popular.'

Volume 3 of *The Young Londoners* from 1969 featured a sequence called 'Skinheads': shots of Michael, Peter, the skinhead model Wolf and a mate called Terry in various urban landscapes, as well as studies of Michael (under the name Gary) in his skinhead gear. The following issue was skin-dominated, with sequences of two more skinheads identified as Mark and Joe Ellis, as well as further pictures of 'Gary' (this time in various stages of undress) and a picture of a skinhead gang in a park. The front cover sported a close-up of a pair of 12-hole Doc Marten boots and rolled up Sta-Press.

> This cover I regard as my most successful cover, basically because it said everything, really. Skinheads were still very much in in those days, and if you were on the scene, those boots just said so much: the menace of the boot because it could kick you, things like that. This wasn't a detail blown up – I deliberately photographed just the boots. I thought to myself that will make an excellent cover because that says it all. This is the thing with magazines, you've got to make impact with your cover; but it had to be a cover that could be put in a window without causing objections. So you've always got these worries about what you can show.

Skinheads' Doc Martens were cast as an inconspicuous, narrowcast image of gay significance because of their all-male sadomasochistic function.

'The skinhead pictures were very popular. They were sexy by nature. I've always liked short hair so I found them really attractive. Perhaps they would have been even more so if I'd done some nudes. But then I wasn't interested in nudes, that doesn't interest me at all. It's the clothes they're wearing.' Whereas previously gay porn had been pushing towards total nudity, excused by either a quasi-classical styling or the socially abstract setting of an art class life study, the Cain of London *oeuvre* traded on the erotic connotations of socially contextual masculinities: for the readers, the clothes that signified working-class male identities were at least as erotic as the bodies they threatened to reveal. 'The skinhead is more than just short hair, isn't it? They were always very smart: Sta-press, Ben Shermans . . . It's the boots, the jeans, the braces – it's the clothes people go for. If you take all that away, you're not left with anything other than a short-haired nude, and the image is gone.'

The model Wolf, the *Sun*'s 'Mystery Man in Leather', came to be a popular figure in gay magazines and a well-loved regular on the gay skinhead scene. 'He was an enigma', remembers Tony.

He was a lovely fella. I got really attached to Wolf. He was initially a skinhead, and when we got talking, I found he was interested in leather as well. So we did a lot of photos. When he ended it all, it really screwed me up. I'd just finished a book that featured him throughout. He ended it all just before it was published and I couldn't cope with it when it came out, so I just got shot of the lot; I sold every copy off to an agent.

Wolf was one of those people who was quite professional and where he was staying in digs, if I phoned up for him and he wasn't there, I could leave a message and he would always contact me.

But when a four days passed without a message being returned, Tony called the police.

I'd heard they'd found a body in the Thames, and I got a phone call asking if I'd go to Tower Bridge Police Station. They actually sent a car all the way to Streatham to pick me up. And it was quite a nasty experience to see the jacket that I'd photographed him in and to realize that he was no longer around.

The important transition from straight to gay models in Tony Burls's studies was of course invisible, although implicit in the gay models' willingness to pose nude for a male photographer. If that didn't get the message across, Burls's next innovation afforded *Young Londoners* readers the opportunity of meeting these sex gods in the flesh and finding out for themselves that the straight boy next door was not so straight after all. With the encouragement of Michael Dover, Tony took over the lease of a gay club in the Kings Road which he opened as The Young Londoner in 1970.

It was originally the Dorian in Chelsea and Mickey [Dover] knew the owner. It had a dubious background – it was originally something to do with the Kray brothers back when the Krays were doing their thing. The photography and the name the Londoners seemed to lend to being a club, and having a magazine was a good vehicle to advertise the club. The Dorian was being run down because the people who owned it were involved in other ventures elsewhere and didn't have the time to keep it going.

The idea was to get the readers along. It started in the winter of the year we went decimal, 1970. The scene wasn't big enough for a club to specialize solely in one type, but it was very popular with skins thanks to Mickey's efforts – he was a great ambassador. Obviously the customers would recognize him from his pictures in the magazine, and he even DJ'd a few nights. I was quite surprised at who came. I always imagined my readers would be old men, but many were only eighteen or nineteen.

But complaints from local residents about noise and inadequate fire escapes caused licensing problems with the Kensington council, and Tony did not enjoy the unsocial work hours that club management demanded. 'Basically the club needed a lot of money spending on it and I wasn't going to spend money until I had it in writing that it was mine to spend money on. So after about seven months, I gave it the elbow.' But, due to Michael's input and influence, the venue was popular with gay skins, and afforded *Young Londoners* readers, many of whom were isolated in terms of access to and knowledge of the scene, a chance to mix in a gay environment and discover that their masculine icons were in fact gay.

The transition of *Young Londoners* from a magazine to a club, although short-lived, marked an important stage in the transformation of identities on the scene. The magazine encouraged the establishment of familiar, 'ordinary' men as object choices. The models started out as straight, but ended up being gay, as the readers could discover for themselves, in person. The invitation to desire through the photographs became an invitation to identify at the club: masculine sex idols went from being sited in an ambiguously heterosexual distance to an avowedly gay presence.

Public reactions

Skinhead aggro would guarantee skinheads news coverage, which served to broaden the subculture's constituency. John Byrne, now famous for his skinhead photographs, became a skin just after leaving school in 1970. 'I used to see them on the TV. I thought it was a really good fashion; I thought, I'll be one.' Although he mixed with a local straight skin gang, the Castle Square mob, his aversion to violence caused him to keep some distance. 'I didn't really like violence at all. I think I was fairly typical of other skinheads, really. The other gay skinheads in the 1970s, I don't think any of them liked violence.'

However, mixing in straight skinhead circles meant that aggro was sometimes inevitable: he recalls an incident during a regular skinhead night at Brighton's Top Rank Suite nightclub in August 1971.

One night I was there and some of the Castle Square Mob had a visit from skinheads from Guildford. And the DJ was a woman called Sherry Ann, she used to play skinhead reggae and Motown. One of the Guildford gang got up on stage and wrenched the arm off the record. There was a big fight, all these chairs and tables over the balcony on to the circular dancefloor they used to have, and one of the Castle Square skins called George, he got a bottle in his head. It bled a lot, I think he was knocked out.

The very sober coverage of the incident in the local newspaper, the *Evening Argus*, reported that six members of the Guildford gang were charged with unlawful fighting and making an affray, and three also charged with malicious wounding.

Reports of such incidents ensured continued fear of skinheads among the general public. Mike remembers:

I was listening to *Woman's Hour* one afternoon for some reason. They were talking about security: a woman said she had a guard dog, and if it saw a skinhead coming it would attack them immediately. So I wrote and said 'Why would she automatically assume they meant trouble?' At the time I was running my own business, I wasn't a troublemaker, although I always wore all the gear. So I wrote them a letter and it was read out on *Woman's Hour*. I was quite incensed to think that a skinhead automatically was violent and aggressive.

But this was exactly the common perception of skinheads that some straight skins were all too ready to reinforce. Gay skinheads were indistinguishable from their straight mates and were therefore subjected to the same mistrust from others. 'No one would look at you in the street', recalls David. 'On the streets, there were occasions when people crossed over to the other side of the road.'

But in this initial skinhead period, inflammatory news coverage did not seem to cause them trouble. Although his appearance was perceived as aggressive, 'at the time, it didn't seem to matter', recalls Chris. 'They called us "bovver boys", but the press didn't really turn on skinheads until the revival in the late seventies. I certainly didn't have any trouble at work. The job I was doing didn't really bring me into contact with customers so it didn't really matter.' Mike remembers when

the skinheads were just making their first appearance in the news and the media, always derogatory; it was always about violence. I was working for a clothes shop in Cardiff, selling smart suits and casual wear, in my gear, boots and braces. The Manager accepted it. He obviously didn't think it was doing the shop any harm.

Similarly, Michael found that his skinhead image didn't compromise his employment prospects. 'I started working at Apple records then, so there was no trouble at work with the way I looked. I grew my hair a bit to get the job, but that didn't last long.' When he went to work for the Beatles in Saville Row, the Managing Director of Apple Records used to refer to him as 'the camp skinhead', much to his annoyance. 'He was very well-spoken, like a Colonel, and he'd ring down and say, "Is the Camp Skinhead there?"' Indeed, John Lennon famously joked in an interview that Michael had beaten someone up to get the job. 'John Lennon was a very witty person, so he obviously used that line as a joke. It was quoted by the press at large and I was quite proud, actually, of him talking about me.'

But beyond the fairly liberal environment of a fashionable record label's offices, reactions were different.

The funniest reaction I ever got in those days was on my twenty-first. A friend of mine who was very well off, a very nice person, very well-spoken and all that, he offered me a choice of presents for my birthday. I chose this Tchaikovsky concert at the Albert Hall 'cos I'd never listened to classical music really, and I just thought I'd try it. So he took me along to this classical concert. Four of us went, and me and my boyfriend turned up in rolled-up jeans and boots and braces and T-shirts and the reaction we got was really strange. Immediately we went in, we were asked, 'Can I help you?' They obviously thought, what are they doing here, why are skinheads coming to a Tchaikovsky concert? I was really aware of it at the time, I was being looked at as if I shouldn't have been there, which made me all the more determined to enjoy it. And I did enjoy it, actually.

If reaction from the general public was not hostile, skinheads certainly aroused the suspicion of the police. Michael recalls a case of police harassment on the way back from a pub.

It was the first time we got arrested, and I'm there with my boyfriend and we came back on the bus, we got to Elephant and Castle and got arrested for using obscene and offensive language and ended up in court. I was innocent I must add, the copper stood up and lied, but they simply picked on us 'cause we were skinheads. All three of us who were arrested, we were all gay, but I don't think anyone realized that.

Similar cases followed: groundless arrest, trumped-up charges, acquittal.

Although being a skinhead aroused the suspicion of the police, negative press coverage did little to arouse public hostility towards them, and involvement in aggro seemed rare. 'There used to be a lot of press coverage in the time of the Bank Holiday things', recalls Michael, 'huge massive coverage for that, but it wasn't an ongoing thing, not that I was aware of.'

The only hassle we really used to get was when we went down to Brighton on the Bank Holidays, along with everybody else. But that was a good day out. There was aggro around, but you didn't have to get involved.

The police were very, very heavy-handed. They used tactics like they'd let you walk along the prom and you'd see a huge crowd of skinheads; you'd get in with them and then they'd block you from coming back, hem you in and keep you there all day, so you didn't go anywhere and cause trouble. They'd take away your boot laces as you came out of the station. We weren't there to cause trouble, we were there for a day out and a laugh.

And in fact, over the years – I went there for a few years running – when we eventually got to know more and more gay skinheads, we'd go down as a gay skinhead group. It culminated one year with twenty-four of us going down, and everyone of us was gay. And every one of them, apart from two of them, were actual skinheads, the other two were just camp guys who were just there, and we were having really great fun, you know. In fact it turned into a camping up day, everyone would be really camp and outrageous, just to shock people I think, 'cos they'd be thinking, 'Oh god, a gang of skinheads' and this little queen who was with us would mince ahead. I remember him going up to this policeman who was trying to break us up into smaller groups, and this John, he'd say to the policeman, 'But we're peaceful pilgrims, dear, *peaceful* pilgrims.'

But sporting an image that unintentionally inspired terror had its compensations: 'No one dared call you queer,' recalls Michael. 'They wouldn't say anything to you. I didn't feel I was obviously gay and we didn't act obviously gay. And for other skinheads, it was enough that you were part of the gang.'

If skinhead gear also served its wearer in allowing him to pass as straight, this was not always protection enough from homophobic violence. Michael's first skinhead boyfriend Peter was murdered on his way out of a gay club in July 1977. 'He went to The Rainbow Rooms by Manor House station', says Michael. 'The only problem we used to get was, when you fancied someone, you used to stare at them really intently, and when you're in a straight crowd, and you're staring at a guy, they think you're after trouble.' There were straight men in the Rainbow Rooms, 'even though it was a gay club. The people he was with say he was really staring at these guys, cruising them, and eventually when they came out of the club, they went after him. They chased him down the road and he unfortunately ran down a cul-de-sac and he was battered to death with chair-legs bound in sacking.' He was rushed to hospital where he died without regaining consciousness. 'They turned his machine off the next day.' The attack was homophobically motivated. A report in the *Sun* the following day, '"GAY

NIGHT OUT" MAN BATTERED TO DEATH'[2] stated that 'Detectives are satisfied that the gang, all aged between 17 and 25, went out to find homosexuals to attack.' Scotland Yard's appeal for witnesses led to the imprisonment of three men. 'According to the court case', says Michael, 'they'd gone there specifically looking for someone to beat up.'

Gay skinheads from this time seem confident that straights assumed they were straight on sight. Whether or not gay skinheads signalled to other gay skinheads was another matter. 'In a gay club it obviously wasn't a problem and that's when you'd do most of your meeting', says Mike.

On the streets I think you would probably assume skinheads were probably not gay, certainly in the early days. But then gay skinheads were very very precise in the way they put their clothes together, in what they chose and how they wore it and the details, so precise in a way that straight skinheads weren't – they were a lot sloppier.

Tony agrees:

You could never tell by looking at them on the street whether they were gay or not, because the gay skinheads were acting stroppy and butch. So sometimes if you saw some coming towards you in the street, you couldn't tell whether they were going to get out of your way or do you in or get off with you. The Young Londoner Club was in a rough area of Chelsea. I remember one night two skinhead customers had been queerbashed on the way in. It was in a rough area, so we had to have bouncers on the door to keep people out. So these skins came in, and they'd been beaten up and were crying – it wasn't very good for the image.

Those initial skinheads had a short life, I think, just a few years. It was a good, clean image, all too short-lived. There were some die-hard skins who stuck at it.

The decline of the skinhead saw Tony increasingly disillusioned with his work as dominant masculine modes became more feminine. 'After the skinheads disappeared, it was all long hair, which I hated, it was a dreadful tacky era; there was nothing sexy about that. It ruined my photography really, because there wasn't much you could do with it.' Instead, he set up a very successful amateur football team, where three of his players eventually agreed to be photographed. It was called Cain FC.

The decline

Although the number of straight skinheads started to dwindle in the early 1970s, many gay men still had enough erotic investment in the most masculine youth cult to keep faithful to their skinhead identity. 'It didn't fade away', says Mike. 'I always kept the dress style, or something very similar. And it never seemed to disappear completely on the gay scene at all, whereas on the straight scene it did. It was always a part of gay culture, there were always gay skinheads around.' The continued existence of gay skinheads ensured that, according to Michael, 'in the early seventies, there was a great time when virtually all the skinheads you used to see were gay; you didn't see that many straight skinheads for a long, long time in the early seventies.' However, with macho queens still a subcultural secret, and the dominant expectation that queers were effeminate, this still did not signal to straights. This made the skinhead look all the more attractive to gay men; not only was it sexy, it publicly advertised one's sexuality to other gay men without alerting the interest (and, most likely, derision) of straights. On the contrary: with the community of knowledge so limited, it protected the wearer from accusations of homosexuality.

'Then with the emergence of the leather scene, things get slightly confused', says Mike. 'There was some overlap and I suppose I drifted then towards that.' The skinheads continued to form and inform the macho scene it had helped to emerge.

One leather venue which seems to have had a particular appeal to gay skinheads in the early 1970s was the Ship and Whale in Rotherhithe, taken over by the landlady of the Cubitt Arms and luring its macho gay crowd. According to Daffyd Jenkins,

> There was an unofficial group that was made up of skinheads and leather guys in the early seventies called the South East London Leather, SELL, that met there. Pam [the landlady] wouldn't allow it to be an official group. Everybody used to meet up at Lewisham Baths on a Sunday at eleven o'clock, swim for an hour and then over to the Ship and Whale. She used to refer to it as the Ship and Whale Underwater Formation Cocksucking Team.

Gay skins continued to find refuge on the leather scene throughout the decade. When work brought Chris Clive from Newcastle to Earls Court in 1977, he became a regular at the Coleherne.

> I met a skinhead there one Sunday lunchtime who rode a Suzuki motorbike. He was a member of the élite London Bikers, which had only eleven members, with their club room at Charing Cross in a railway arch down Hungerford Lane . . . I was later to become the twelfth and last member to join the club. Anyone who can remember the weekly parties/orgies we had there, usually with about fifty visitors, will bemoan its closure.

This came about when the News of the World ran a characteristically sensationalist front-page exposé about the club.

This period in history marked the transition from the desirers to both the desirers and the desired. Previously the prevalence of the effeminate model seemed so secure that, as one put it, 'if you were gay, you had to be a screaming Mary. There was no two ways about it, you couldn't be gay and macho.' But machismo was precisely what was prized: 'At the same time, I found anybody who was exceptionally macho-looking attractive. He could've been Quasimodo – as long as he looked butch, I'd have fancied him.' So the hostility experienced by some early gay skins from queens on the scene was motivated by more than fear: it was also reverence. 'It was like fancying a film star – you could go to the cinema and see him but you couldn't throw your arms around him. Nobody I knew ever tried to get off with them.'

This older attitude marked a divide between identification and desire, a gendered, heterosexual paradigm of sexual attraction. Gay skins heralded something new, says Mike:

> The people I speak to now who were around then, speak very passionately, very fondly of that time. I suppose maybe because we were a lot younger and you look back to your youth with affection. But being a gay skinhead at that time, you were part of a group within a group, you felt a very strong camaraderie with other gay skinheads. There was a very strong bond, and it was good. You did feel it was something new, something slightly odd even, because society saw skinheads both as not being gay at all, and as something not to be looked up to. So you were pushing the boundaries on two levels, a) because you were gay, coming out and being yourself, and b) because you were addressing the world in a uniform that was uniformally despised. So you were challenging the world on two levels, on your gayness and on your role in society. It didn't appear to take guts at the time, you just did it because you wanted to. But it was a confrontation.

The gay skinheads represented a convergence of masculine identification and desire. 'From the day I met Peter on the tube I just looked at him', remembers Michael, 'and thought: *That's what I want to be, that's what I want to look like, that's what I want.*' But this was more than simply asserting that masculinity was not at odds with male homosexuality; men were adopting a more masculine identity as part of the process of identifying as gay.

Notes

1. Mike Dow, 'Skins', *Out* (April 1985), p. 20.   2. *Sun*, 25 July 1977, p. 11.

5

Cult Fiction

Newspaper reports were only one aspect of the manufacture of the myth of the skinhead. Television, gossip, local rumour and fiction also played on social fears and fantasies which had been circulating about the nature of working-class youth and its extended leisure time well before the appearance of bovver boys.

Published in 1962, Anthony Burgess' *A Clockwork Orange* projected contemporary fears about male gang culture into a near-future sci-fi setting and envisaged a society menaced by seemingly mindless thugs. On the run from the law for a string of violent attacks, fifteen-year-old Alex is eventually caught and subjected to reconditioning, 'Ludovico's Technique', a literal and violent enactment of the manufacture of consent, where aversion therapy is used to alter his psychopathic behaviour. Although science fiction (the cover of the 1972 edition questioned the text's own generic status: 'Horror farce? Social prophecy? Penetrating study of human choice between good and evil?') it shared many of the elements of the teen schlock novel genre from which it drew and to which it contributed (*The Leather Boys* is a similarly marginal member). This included the detailed description of the subculture's clothes. When Stanley Kubrick translated the novel into film in Britain in 1971, most elements of this description were ignored, the designers instead turning to contemporary youth culture. In all but their Smoothie hair, Alex and his 'droogs' were realized as skinheads in their suedehead incarnation, dressed in Sta-press-like rolled-up trousers hitched up with braces, accessorized with bowler hats and walking sticks. One element from Burgess' original text remained: 'flip horrorshow boots for kicking',[1] 14-hole Doctor Marten boots.

A Clockwork Orange's prophecy of unsocialized youth, its terror of unsocialized working-class masculinity and sexuality, is fulfilled in the skinhead. In the introduction to *Suedehead*, Richard Allen writes, 'Youth has always had its "fling" but never more blatantly, more unconcerned with averse publicity than today.'[2] Boys have always been boys but it was never this bad in the good old days.

Richard Allen wrote seventeen books about violent youth gangs, beginning with the publication of *Skinhead* in 1970. Later titles went on to concentrate on other youth movements, but *Skinhead* was the most popular, selling over a million copies in the early 1970s and securing three more outings for the hero Joe Hawkins: *Suedehead* (1971), *Skinhead Escapes* (1972) and *Skinhead Farewell* (1974). Hawkins' eventual demise (a plane crash in Indonesia) was apparently inspired by the character's increasing identification with the National Front, who were urging Allen to sign the character up to the organization. Despite the far right content of the social commentary in his work, Allen was unhappy with this. 'This was not on', he later said in a very rare, written interview published in *Scootering Magazine* in May 1992. 'Joe was a patriot, not a political idiot.' Apparently he was prevented from writing other skinhead novels because his publishers did not want to be seen to be supporting skinheads.

A 1992 profile of Allen's work in the *Guardian* claimed that Allen 'did much to popularise the early skinheads'; his works 'made the skinhead – for all his violence and unpleasantness – into an almost noble figure'. According to Steven Wells in the *NME*, the influence of the *Skinhead* series was widespread: 'For any kid attending a comprehensive school between 1971 and 1977, Richard Allen's books were required reading . . . If you had a smidgen of cool . . . then it was the *New English Library's Skinhead* wot provided your sex'n'violence education.'[3]

In his *Skinhead* books, Allen exploited and elaborated pre-existent anxieties and fantasies about skinhead violence in his readership inspired by the contemporary journalistic accounts. As the blurb on the jacket of the first title boasted, '*Skinhead* is a story straight from today's headlines'. As such, it was a representation perfectly in accordance with the expectations and assumptions about delinquent white working-class masculinity in circulation elsewhere in popular culture. But as these books were only likely to have been read by those already sympathizing to some degree with the cult, the books contributed to a climate of gritty glamour which a negotiated interpretation of news coverage had already afforded the skinhead cult. The *Skinhead* series acted as a recruitment advertisement, constructing subjects in the image of Joe Hawkins, an access point for those beyond the geographic spread of the skinhead. The books functioned as a fantastic amplification of the news, as if Allen had cut out a series of random press cuttings, exaggerated them and reinscribed them within a single narrative. This fictionalizing process nevertheless resulted in an account which seems somehow to be more credible, more real than the news reports. Unifying these various, familiar events by centring them within the deeds of a single character lent the violence a causality that would make them somehow more feasible than journalistic accounts of inexplicable, sporadic, localized aggression.

Indeed, in his introductions to each new addition to the series, the author himself claimed that his works were more authentic than the sensationalist articles which inspired them. Allen, like the skinheads he wrote about, seemed excessively taken with the notion of authenticity, and used his

Mike Dow, 1969.

Left to right: Michael, Wolf, Peter and Terry. (Photo: Anthony Burls.)

Michael Dover, photographed by Anthony Burls for his magazine *The Young Londoners*, 1969.

Michael and Peter on Queen's Road, Brighton, 1969.

David Scouler (right) photographed on Brighton's Palace Pier, 1969.

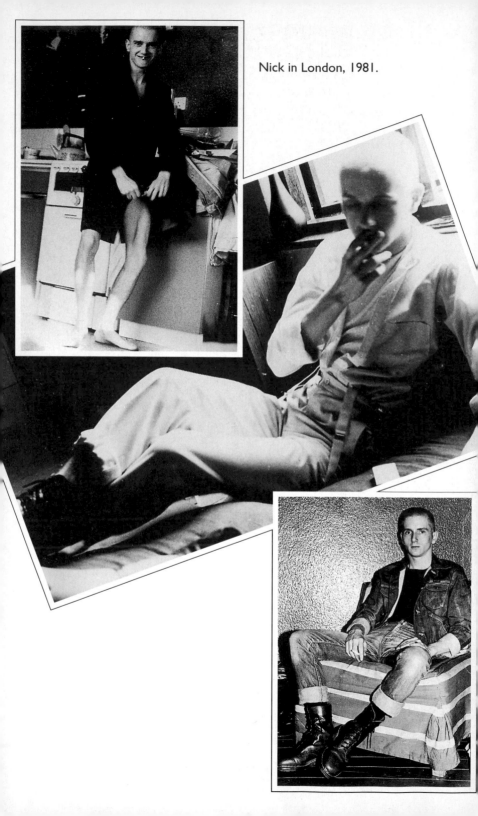

Nick in London, 1981.

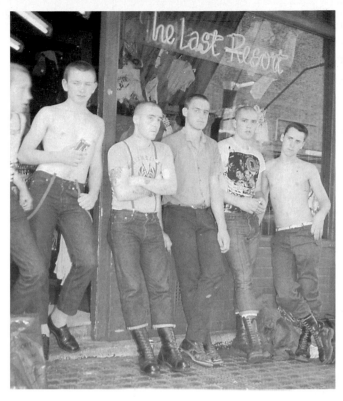

Outside the skinhead shop The Last Resort in London's East End. c.1985. (Photo: John G. Byrne.)

Skin photographer John G. Byrne and mates in Brighton, 1986. (Photo: John G. Byrne.)

Richard, manager of gay skin night Silks 95.
(Photo: Richard Maude.)

Soft porn image of skinhead and Union Jack.
(Photo: Cactus Studios (01273) 623525.)

Brighton skins, 1984.
(Photos: John G. Byrne.)

prefaces to argue that his books are the only authoritative account of the subculture. In the introduction to *Sorts*, he wrote of his *Skinhead* books: 'according to letters received from countless thousand fans, the consensus of opinion is that they – *and they alone* – present skinheads, suedeheads, bootboys and now smooths as they really are'. He considered the *Skinhead* series to be 'representative of our modern society and a source of reference for future students of our violent era'.

Allen used this authenticating discourse to defend his work against public outrage at his books. He repeatedly used his introductions to each new title to counter accusations that he was championing a menace to society, and making violence not only acceptable but attractive to his readers, with the claim that he had a moral duty to record the truth. He plays the card of social responsibility and argues that it was his duty as an honest writer to reflect reality:

> *Skinhead* looked at the cult, took note of everything that the average skinhead did in the course of his anti-social duties and faithfully represented Joe Hawkins as the epitome of society's menace. . . . Those who would demand controls on what we, the public, read, seem bent on denying us the opportunity of learning about life as it's lived in the raw. Where would their value be if every 'terrace terror' spoke and acted like an undergraduate of a theological college?[4]

His libertarian argument against censorship, articulated in the name of liberal democracy and exercised through the use of rousing words like 'the public', 'consensus' and, indeed, 'democracy', is conspicuously incongruous given his calls for the state to exercise greater controls over the people to an almost totalitarian degree. Not so much a case of fact being stranger than fiction as fiction being more real than fact.

Allen's self-appointed (and, if we are to believe him, skinhead-supported) claim to be the custodian of the first flare of the subculture should not necessarily be casually dismissed as high-handed hype. The press and sociology departments are not the guardians of truth, after all: in the 1960s journalism, like academia, was a middle-class profession not well suited to accommodating and appropriately representing working-class subjectivity, regardless of the class background and status of the individuals involved. Certainly few readers now fail to question the nature of 'the truth' that the press once claimed to accurately and objectively represent.

But if Allen thought his books were a true sign of the times, some contemporary skinhead readers thought otherwise. The photographer John Byrne grew up with the books after he became a skinhead in 1970 and is a proud owner of the complete set of Richard Allen original editions. He believes they were pure fiction. I didn't know any skinheads anything like Joe Hawkins. I'm sure Allen knew very little about skinheads; he just did a bit of research and turned out this book – which I thought was very good; I really enjoyed it, but it wasn't at all realistic. He discovered he'd hit on something, and he wrote more, but they weren't as good.

Of course, Allen's motives in writing what amounts to just another (albeit extended) sensationalist account of youth violence are just as questionable as those of any journalist. Although his works have been celebrated or condemned as mere teen schlock horror, pulp fiction or dangerous celebrations of violence, his texts betray a fairly explicit far-right agenda which warrants examination, as they account for the ambiguous status of Joe Hawkins as the hero/demon constructed through and (occasionally and unconvincingly) condemned by them.

Allen has pronouncements, mostly conservative and racist, to make on contemporary social change. The violent incidents, which are usually considered to be the primary purpose of the books, and were certainly a primary motivation for their purchase in many cases, are in fact a string of parables populated by various social stereotypes, one of whom the author will invariably side with, to act out some concern he has with modern culture. For example, in *Skinhead*, Joe and his gang assault a man on a tube train. The police officer called to the scene 'didn't believe in countering violence with more violence. He believed, as his superiors had taught him to believe, in the British policeman's duty to temper violence with understanding . . .' The explication of his thoughts provide another occasion for Allen to break in with his opinion:

. . . and therein lay is problem. He could not reason that consideration for these thugs gave them a feeling of confidence. He could not see where tolerance was taking him and the public. He could not see that the teenage hoodlums needed strict measures and stricter punishment when caught in the act. (p. 30)

The author counters his characters' thoughts or statements with his own approval or disapproval, made explicit by his own interruption with an unambiguous statement of his beliefs. He plays epistemological games with his characters, countering their thoughts with that which exceeds their limited knowledge: for example, Joe looking from the window of a train on the crumbling remains of warehouses leads to a broader sociological consideration for Allen: 'the brainwashed mind could not see further than his own betterment. It couldn't accept that all of this slumland had to be cleared and kept free from decay.' Joe is 'ignorant of historical heritage, believed in modern sterile skyscrapers as the ultimate construction', so he sees 'Nelson's Column as a roosting place for dropping-birds and not the heroic valour that had made his homeland great' and this train of thought allows Allen to list further tributes to the Empire.

This tactic then allows for a clear distinction between the characters' personal ignorance and Allen's universal truth – a fairly literal use of the authorial mode sometimes referred to as the voice of God. Allen's own thoughts aren't subject to the same scrutiny as those of his characters; his words do not constitute an analysis, they are solid fact. Obviously much is left beyond this authoritative closure which the text does not allow, but as an example of the rhetoric of propaganda it is very effective, as it allows space only for the reader's acceptance or rejection, but not critique, of that which is proposed.

Some characters' sentiments receive no comment from Allen, which, given the heavy-handedness of his usual tactic, would seem to suggest that they voice his opinion, particularly as some of them are prone to contextually incongruous outbursts. For example, James Mowat is championed for refusing to be one of 'the masses unwilling to share their responsibility for putting teenage hoodlums in their place' (p. 28), in standing up to Joe and his gang's intimidation on a tube train. Although he is assaulted as the other passengers watch silently, further functioning as a heroic contrast to their cowardice, he is conspicuously less concerned with his injuries than with the ideology of welfare capitalism: he shouts at the police officer called to the incident, 'You'll not lift a finger to apprehend the thugs and, even supposing you catch 'em – what'll they get? Ten pounds' fine and the Social Security pays for it from my taxes? Hell, man – can't you see what this bloody Welfare State is costing Britain?'

A later scene, when Sergeant Snow calls Dr MacConaghy to the police station to examine an old man seriously wounded by a skinhead attack, functions as a debate on social policy. The sergeant's proposed reforms ('Stricter controls over demonstrators, over students who forgot that the public paid for their right to education, over skinheads at football matches and on "special" trains were definitely required. Stiffer penalties would help, too') (pp. 96–7) are countered with the doctor's. Blaming the environment, MacConaghy says 'I'd like to see what a dictator could do in this country. Slums wiped out, harsh measures to curb the grab-all boys, savage sentences for injury to persons, hanging for child rapists and cop-killers, the birch for young offenders like these skinheads' (p. 97). Not so much character amplification as a manifesto; only the police sergeant's views receive any qualification from Allen.

The skinhead functions for Allen as a test of the state's ability to control its subjects. 'Skinheads! My God – can't our society control even them?' Doctor MacConaghy exclaims, and it is this verdict that allows the author to articulate conservative anxieties about the nature of cultural change.

This is ironic given that the skinhead was a conservative project of identity reclamation, and the irony is not lost on Allen. In the Author's Note which opened *Suedehead*, he twice refers to Joe as the 'hero' of *Skinhead* in scare quotes. He explicitly states: 'At no time did the author attempt to glorify Joe Hawkins.' Instead he 'faithfully represented Joe Hawkins as the epitome of society's menace'. And yet he admits with some satisfaction the fact that the character had 'aroused a *national* following and made the paperback a best-seller is, indeed, gratifying to an author'.

'This conflict between the young and the state was, in fact, all-out war' (p. 28), writes Allen in one of the authorial comments that punctuate *Skinhead*, 'A war threatening the authority that a country needed to keep it stable.' But the character of Joe threatens to destabilize the seemingly concrete ideology of the text because Allen cannot place himself in opposition to the embodiment of skinheadism that Joe Hawkins represents. So the book functions as a sensationalist exposé and a condemnation of, and (most of all) an apology for, the antisocial activities of skinheads.

When it came to writing a new introduction for the reprint of his books in 1992, however, Allen was far less disingenuous; the nature of the 'heroism' of his character was far less ambivalent.

Joe Hawkins and his ilk were, essentially, patriots fighting for a heritage. The battle was lost, though, when many in high places yielded to pressures from beyond our shores. And these wishy-washy types celebrated what they believed was the end of a bothersome cult. As in every war, when the overpowering might of an enemy appeared to have crushed the opposing force, underground armies regrouped and prepared to regain their rightful place in a homeland they had never relinquished.[5]

Joe is revealed as always having been the romantic warrior-hero for a British nationalist ideology.

Ultra-violence

But, undeniably, it is the violence which gained the *Skinhead* series its reputation. It is literally excessive, providing the texts with an ideological excess with which Allen enticed and seduced his readership and with which he himself was fascinated. It also stops the series from being a dull 'state of the nation' complaint as it contests Allen's understanding of society – a fairly hydraulic model – which cannot accommodate Joe Hawkins' aggression.

Allen is caught in the nature/nurture trap: he teeters between environmental explanations for violence and the common belief that violence is a natural attribute of the working-class man. 'Violence was a *natural* part of life as a docker saw it' he writes in *Skinhead* (p. 10, my emphasis). It is written into the very structure of male working-class society: Ed Black, the dockers' union representative, walks around 'with four of his special cronies trailing behind like bodyguards, ready to prevent physical harm to their adored leader' (p. 8). 'He could count on certain "heavies" to protect him during a strike' (p. 9). It is a cultural expectation. But skinhead violence is a deviation from this 'natural pattern', as Ed's thoughts tell us: 'the style of brutality these kids employed frightened him silly . . . one man was no match for a bunch of savage little bastards ready to tear an individual apart just for fun'. If working-class men embody natural masculinity, then skinheads are the terrifying excess, hypermasculine.

So Allen has to concede that Joe's propensity for violence is beyond environmental explanation and makes recourse to 'the natural'. This is expounded at length in *Skinhead*, and the main points of this passage are repeated in the books that followed:

> Basically, Joe had a 'feeling' for violence. It was an integral part of his make-up. Some do-gooders trying to explain his attachment to the skinhead cult would, no doubt, stress his environmental background . . . They would gleefully assign all manner of reasons for Joe being what he was without ever touching on the most important factor of all – his character weakness for brutality. It wasn't something that had grown inside him because of surrounding blights. It was him; he was one of those incurables – one of those born to be hard, mean, savage. Nothing had made Joe this . . . Joe Hawkins was one of nature's misfits; one of her habitual criminals. (p. 50)

Violent skinheads are born, not made; they are *essentially* aggressive. However, the cultural materialist tendencies in Allen's claim to reflect reality still pull towards an environmental explanation, and the resulting contradiction is manifest in his description of gang violence: the natural (instinctive, genetic, biological) and the artificial (learned, programmed, societal) confusingly converge and contrast in Joe's mob, who are described as 'clockwork soldiers', 'a pack of wolves', 'ants swarming over a tasty morsel' and 'automatons'. But Joe characterizes a different understanding of violence.

Ultra-violence, a term borrowed from *A Clockwork Orange*, is perfectly appropriate. It was originally used by Alex to refer to the nature of his attacks, but, by extension, came to refer to the fictional representations of spectacularized excessive violence used by writers and directors to ensure guarantee markets. It characterized the teen schlock novel genre and a strain of action movies to which both the novel and film versions of *A Clockwork Orange* contributed and, arguably, belonged.

The film's violent content guaranteed it controversy even before its release, and many local councils would not allow it to be shown in their cinemas. Although initially defending his work, Kubrick's later decision to ban his own movie shows the ambivalent status of his representations of violence. Although the intention, apparently, was to inspire horror in cinema audiences at both the activities of Alex's gang and society's counter-measures, the sci-fi skinhead's transition from aggressor to victim does seem to make him the hero, resulting in a troubling slide between disapproval and celebration of his actions. And, after all, it was the promise of sex and violence which pulled the crowds in the first place. The spectacle of violence – road-side accidents, boxing – is guaranteed to draw an audience.

In the 1980s the term 'ultra-violence' entered common media-speak to refer to the phenomenon of graphic violence in films and TV programmes which was attractive (certainly in terms of audience figures) precisely because it was so excessive. This trend was interpreted in two ways: the excessive nature rendered it camp, referring only to the cinematic stylistic device of 'violence' and not to 'real' violence. On the other hand, more conservative commentators and viewers' groups (in Britain dominated by the National Viewers and Listeners' Association), who recognized no such distinction, interpreted any rise in representations of violence as likely to increase its acceptance.

Ultra-violence became the 'natural' expression of hypermasculinity: the term was often used with reference to the Rambo movies, which featured a ridiculously over-pumped hypermasculine hero killing thousands at a time when, in what could be considered a conspicuous effort to promote and naturalize *laissez-faire* capitalism, dominant Western ideologies were valorizing competitiveness and ruthless aggression.

Like his mates, Joe's violent impulses are bestial: he is described as naturally 'foxy clever' and possessing 'native fox-cunning'. But, as the central character, he is afforded a greater degree of agency, and this natural drive is countered not with the 'clockwork' mindlessness of the artificial but the diabolic fiendishness of the supernatural. The hypermasculine qualities with which Allen endows him exceed even the 'natural', so 'explanation', which becomes tantamount to mystification, requires recourse to the language of magic. In an encounter with a liberal vicar, Joe is described as representing 'uncontestable evil; Lucifer in clip-on braces and wearing devilish boots'. In this mythologizing, the skinhead is literally demonized. If working-class men are 'naturally' violent, then hypermasculine Joe Hawkins is supernaturally ultra-violent.

Allen writes of skinheads in the very language of the sensationalist reports that he condemns. His belief that skinhead violence is an expression of individual evil amounts to the same refusal to interrogate that characterizes those very news reports that he condemned. Equally, this shows how close the condemnatory reports are to celebration.

Although he slams sociologists, Allen concords with many of their findings. The generic requirement, a passage showing the hero assembling the elements of his subcultural style before the mirror, explains those elements in the same way as the academic studies explain an articulation of working-class identity: 'Union shirt – collarless and identical with those thousand others worn by his kind throughout the country; army trousers and braces; and boots! The boots were the most important item. Without his boots, he was part of the common-herd – like his dad, a working man devoid of identity.' The boots are the symbol of difference, of individualization.

Working-class identity asserts itself through the persecution of the middle-class kids:

> One thing Joe really detested was a hippie . . . He had to work . . . But not the hippies! . . . The bleedin' Welfare State took care of them – grants if they were students (and that was a big laugh!), handouts from Social Security to pay for fines for demonstrating and pot-taking . . . Christ, what a rotten way to treat tax-payers! he thought. (p. 40)

The lack of any contradiction from Allen would seem to signal his approval of these thoughts and, sure enough, when hippies appear in the text, they conform to Joe's prejudices, because they concord with Allen's factuality. Cherry 'had been arrested sixteen times for obstructing and disturbing the peace and, always and without exception, had the Welfare State pay her fine. She had had two abortions on the State, been in receipt of a student grant . . .' (p. 58).

Skinhead attacks are seen as a defence of territory: 'The Cockney had lost control of his London . . . the old Cockney thug was slowly being confined' as other social groups staked their claim on the capital, so areas have become 'enemy territory' (p. 13). These enemies are identified in terms of ethnicity: 'Like most East End skinheads – and for that matter, population – Joe detested the influx of immigrants into what had always been a pure Cockney stronghold. It wasn't so much the colour of the skins that annoyed him. Any intruder would have been subject to the same treatment' (p. 20).

In accord with the tabloid coverage, Joe's gang actively seeks out non-working-class and non-white targets to victimize. Indeed, within the text, the press is afforded a role in the mythologizing of the skinhead. Joe, hungry for fame, meditates on his reputation as a skinhead: 'he had a name, but it was too local, too limited. He hadn't done "porridge" and he hadn't been written up in the papers as an "outstanding" example of skinhead terrorism. He'd have to do something drastic to make the grade' (p. 39). This motivates an attack on an Asian student through whom Allen further reminds the reader of the role the press has to play in writing the fantasy of the skinhead: 'he didn't have to be reminded of the last exploit involving one of his fellow-students and a skinhead mob – it had made headline news in the Barking paper'. Joe feminizes the race- and class-Other when he laughs, 'Ain't he pretty . . .' before offering to take his books in a mock show of gentlemanly behaviour to a lady.

Sexy Joe

'I'm not a bloody virgin but I do want respect,' she snapped.
'And?' he asked the pertinent query with his eyes.
'That too! Nothing queer, mind you . . .'
'The normal way is fab!'[6]

Joe is straight – it goes without saying. There is nothing queer in *Skinhead* – no queens, not even any queerbashings. But as he is hypermasculine, Joe has to be shown to be excessively sexual. In fact, the only point of pleasure in the grim tales of Joe Hawkins is his penis. Allen betrays a conspicuous phallic obsession in his work: as a letter in response to the *NME*'s résumé of Allen's works pointed out, *Mod Rule* (1980), which the article had overlooked, contains 'in one memorable passage, no less than fourteen euphemisms for the hero's virile member'.[7]

Allen presents skinheads as undeniably sexy, which, given that the author is a man, *queers* them. Presumably Allen envisaged his readership to be young and male, and the descriptions of Joe's sexual prowess are supposed to invite approval, admiration and . . . ?

Jack Shamash wrote in a consideration of the series in the *Guardian* that 'Allen is obsessed by the sexuality of his male characters. Sex is always groping and mechanical. Women forever admire the swelling jeans of their men folk.'[8] The queerness of his male-admiring authorship is neutralized through female third parties who distance that admiration. Certainly in Allen's early works, where the male teenagers are the focus, women have only one function: to bear witness to the desirability of the young men. In *Skinhead*, the gang's appearance is eroticized by the barmaid Mary Sommers. 'She couldn't take her eyes off Billy . . . she thought about how wonderful it had been pressed against his hard young body. Looking at Joe and the others she even wished Billy would waylay her tonight and share her with his mates tonight' (p. 17). For Joe, looking at least three years older than his sixteen years, 'wasn't a bad-looking youth . . . at a fleeting glance, many a young girl's heart would flutter when he appeared on the scene' (p. 14).

Allen's descriptions of Joe's sexual encounters cast the skinhead in the role of a porn star. Just about every woman he meets seems to want to bed him. The description of his regular Tuesday afternoon session with fourteen-year-old Sally Morris reveals an endless capacity for immediate post-orgasmic erections and centres on her pleasure at the sight of his penis, 'shuddering as she saw his nudity'. Even her distraught mother, who catches them in the act, 'could not quite prevent herself from peeping to see what he had to offer' (p. 75). When he strips for his old friend Flo in *Skinhead Escapes*,

> She eyed his nakedness and grunted.
> 'That's terrific!' she exclaimed.
> 'It'll fit,' he said with a nonchalance she loathed.

Unsurprisingly, the essentialist patriarchal discourse of masculinity – that male libido is an uncontrollable natural drive requiring expression, frequently still used by male institutions to excuse sexual violence (towards women at least) – requires Joe to be a rapist. The rape of Lottie Newman in *Skinhead Escapes* is written in the language of male pornographic fantasy, the scene opening with the 'pretty' twenty-three-year-old 'naked and available' at her window: 'The Pill was a boom when the mood for intercourse filled her being with uncontrollable longing. Like now!' Allen uses Joe to voice the usual excuses: 'You teasing bitch . . . you've asked for this' (p. 202).

Curiously, the first and only hint of queer desire in *Skinhead* comes towards the end of the book, in an exchange between Joe and his father, whose lenience, Allen suggests, is partly responsible for his son's criminal nature. Sergeant Snow, knowing that Joe has been involved in a fatal shooting incident, has called at the Hawkins' house:

> Joe laughed. 'You don't take that cunt seriously, do you?'
> Roy's hand flashed knocking Joe to his bed. 'I like Desmond Snow,' he said.
> 'Then take 'im to bed!' his son screamed.
> Roy smiled easily. He didn't believe in violence, nor sadism. But, tonight, he would teach Joe a late lesson. His hand lashed out again . . . and again . . . More than once he hoped Joe's manhood would assert itself and force the boy to hit back. It never did – and the beating continued until Joe lolled around on the bed in a semi-conscious state. Only then did Roy Hawkins stop. He only hoped his wife had not heard the beating.' (p. 107)

This punishment is sexualized, given the physical environment of the bed, Roy's uncharacteristic, smiling sadism, the presence of Allen's most common penile euphemism, 'manhood', and the sarcastic accusation of queerness that first prompted the scene. It may indeed be homosexual panic caused by the accusation that prompts this show of masculine authority – after all, the presence of the law has, as far as the author is concerned, shown the father to be failing in his duties as a man. With his insistence that characters like Joe need stricter punishment, Allen makes sure Joe gets what he's been asking for throughout the book.

The stylistic difference between *Skinhead* and *Suedehead* is stark. With an espousal of totalitarian politics and an ideologically totalizing prose style, the Joe Hawkins of the structurally rigid *Skinhead* is socially fixed. Allen's moralizing interruptions are suspended in *Suedehead* to give a far more open text where Joe's identity becomes more fluid. (Allen instead voices his far-right political agenda in *Demo* which was published in the interval between the two *Skinhead* books.)

The Joe Hawkins who emerges from prison in *Suedehead* is far queerer. Indeed, Joe's appearance is queered from the outset: during his spell in jail 'he discovered he was the special target of every queer in The Scrubs', who did not conform to his stereotyped vision of the effeminate queen: 'small, dancing men with carefully manicured hands, lisps and a walk that signposted their aversion to women. He had found they did not belong to any such tight limitation. Some of the ones who had tried to lure him into their cells were big, strong, typical "heavy-types"' (p. 10).

Just as the queers had refused to be confined to their social expectations, the new Joe rejects the solidity of his previous skinhead persona: 'The old days of outright slaughter had vanished as surely as bovver boots were a dying symbol of a passing phase' (p. 76). The new Joe is far more slippery. He uses the skills he learned inside to find a well-paid job in accountancy and lets his hair grow 'to suede' for 'that was his new image. Suedehead – a smoothie, one of the elite now' (p. 27). Where once he operated as part of a gang, Joe is now a 'hate-filled individual', the romantic outsider ('A genuine suedehead had neither creed nor association'), dangerous in his social mobility and fluidity, but still possessing the same propensity for violence. Indeed, it is Joe's chameleon-like abilities that lead him to believe he can escape from justice at the end of the novel, because police records cannot keep up with his changing appearance.

In fact, with his newfound ability to slip between the company and the impersonation of various social types, Joe learns to 'do' queer – but only in order to gain easy access to the homes of rich gay men. In one episode Joe, now eighteen, is travelling home on the tube, wearing a suit and a Crombie, his attractive appearance attracting the attention of women – and sometimes men too. As one cruising male commuter eyes him up, Joe suppresses his immediate violent impulse. 'As a skinhead he would have kicked the bastard in the balls' but now as a 'neophyte suedehead' his tactics are different; he flirts with his admirer expertly (Allen fails to explain how he came to learn what he refers to as the 'standard procedure'), rubbing knees and following him off the tube.

> On the station platform the man took Joe's hand and squeezed.
> 'Do you . . . ?'
> 'Anything,' Joe replied with a return squeeze.

'Ohhhh!' The man's hand jellied as emotions ran riot through his soft, queer frame. (p. 40)

The homosexual is an effeminate stereotype ('The queer *giggled* girlishly'), who lives with 'Auntie' in a tastefully decorated, antique-littered guest-house on the Bayswater Road. Joe's homophobia is merely temporarily suspended, and soon assaults 'the pathetic creature . . . All the fury, all the hatred went into those vicious fists' before stealing his money and valuables.

Cruising queens and cottaging have become favourite activities for Joe, of which he has expert knowledge and for which he has a particular aptitude. Later on he decides to

walk down to Regent Street into Leicester Square and pick-up a queer. They still hung out there, like they always had. If he went to the toilet – the public one in the square – he was sure to be accosted. He'd play the 'game' and nobble the bastard once they reached where the queer lived . . . None of those fast masturbations in a locked toilet, either. He wanted money – not homosexual thrills.

Allen has to disavow any shadow of homosexuality in Joe, but in this far more open, dangerously slippery text, the direct disavowal is immediately problematized by a curious interior exchange between Joe and his reflection in the mirror: '"God, what the hell kick do the bastards get out of men?" he asked his conscience. "We like girls, don't we?" His little man in the chest cavity did not answer.' And only a few lines later he explodes, 'Shit on girls' (p. 84).

And his queerbashing in the hotel on Bayswater Road only serves to sexualize his subsequent, curiously hungry search in Soho: 'Joe wanted companionship. Not womanship. He wanted to find his own . . . Looking for one sign. Searching for another who felt exactly as he did' (p. 46). He follows a youth towards Leicester Square.

A queer minced into sight, blond(e) locks flying in a slight breeze, perfume wafting from his floral shirt in waves. If he wasn't in such an exposed position I'd kick his sexy-ass, Joe though delightedly. Queer-bashing was not on the cards tonight, though. Some other time he could vent his hatred and capitalise from the pleasure. (p. 47)

This strange encounter happens directly before Joe chats up his youth with 'I'm Joe Hawkins . . . mind if I join you?'

Skinhead with its straight, closed narrative cannot contain the romantic excess of Joe Hawkins. *Suedehead* allows this excess, the fascination with the 'hero' to spill over into its converse, creating a free-floating, potentially quasi-queer character.

This potential was realized some twenty years later by the appropriation of Allen's style and favourite youth cult in the novels of the semiotically subversive, Situationist-inspired skinhead writer Stewart Home. In 1990 his first novel, *Pure Mania*, was published. 'As is the case with all my writing, plagiarism plays a major role in the process of composition.' he said. 'In *Pure Mania* I take Richard Allen's *Skinhead* books as a role model for my prose style and narrative technique.' 'In the tradition of *Skinhead*, *Suedehead* and *Boot Boys*', shouts the front cover of *Pure Mania*'s follow-up, *No Pity*. Home subjects the pulp fiction of the New English Library to the same kind of postmodern reconfiguration for which Quentin Tarantino has become famous; both politically ironic but earnestly celebratory of their source in their gleefully cliché-ridden descriptions of sex and ultra-violence, Home's novels are populated by neo-Nazis, marxists, anarchists, vegan vigilantes, and oversexed queer skinheads. The hero of *Pure Mania*, Terry Blake, was a fully queered Joe Hawkins whom *Gay Times* described as a 'skinhead hero of sexual excess'. The 'Positive Plagiarism' followed with three more novels; the most recent, *Red London* (1994) follows the movements of the Skinhead Squad, a semi-mystical brotherhood of queer anarchist 'Satanists in Sta-Press' (as they come to be dubbed in the press) whose initiation ceremony involves the kind of group sex that only exists in the world of gloriously cheap porn. Their leader Fellatio Jones, we discover, is an avid Richard Allen fan:

> Jones led the girl down to his ground floor bedroom. His pride and joy was an old New English Library display case which he'd found at the back of the Roman Road Woolworths. Every inch of its shelf-space was packed with NEL classics. Naturally, there were all the Richard Allen books neatly stacked alongside the Peter Cave, Alex R Stuart, Mick Norman and Thom Ryder hell's angels novels . . . Fellatio had been reading the NEL canon since he was a 12-year-old schoolboy.[9]

Could Allen have envisaged queer skins among his readership? Going by the number of gay men who used his texts as sexual fantasy-fodder, it would seem that the questionable sexuality of his 'heroes' guaranteed their presence among his cult following. But the anarchist London of Home's novels, the queer activities of his skin heroes, and a culture where such appropriations are not so much feasible as inevitable, hardly constitute the kind of tradition Allen would have wanted the conservative political vision of his books to inspire.

Notes

1. Anthony Burgess, *A Clockwork Orange* (Harmondsworth: Penguin, 1961), p. 6.
2. Richard Allen, *Suedehead* (London: New English Library, 1971), p. 5.
3. Steven Wells, 'Bovver Books', *New Musical Express*, 11 February 1988.
4. Richard Allen, Introduction to *Sorts*, in *The Complete Richard Allen: Volume 2* (Dunoon: ST Publishing, 1993), p. 95.
5. Richard Allen, *The Complete Richard Allen: Volume 1* (Dunoon: ST Publishing, 1992), p. 5.
6. Richard Allen, *Skinhead Escapes*, in *The Complete Richard Allen: Volume 2*, p. 242.
7. *New Musical Express*, 27 February 1988.
8. Jack Shamash, 'Bovver Books', *Weekend Guardian*, 27 June 1992, p. 14.
9. Stewart Home, *Red London* (London: AK Press, 1994), p. 94.

Fetishizing Masculinity

SKINHEAD DISCO SUCCESS CAUSES ROW AT LESBIAN AND GAY CENTRE
The huge success of the country's first gay skinhead disco has been
dampened by the reaction of a group of lesbians at London's Gay Centre
during the Moonstomp disco organised by the Gay Skinhead Movement
when a cry went out from the women for assistance to defend the centre
from invasion. The Centre's Management Committee received a letter
complaining that some of them had been angered, intimidated and
frightened by the presence of the group. The letter states formally, 'By
most people's standards, skinheads are fascists.'[1]

This confrontation between radical lesbians and gay skinheads in 1985
marked an ongoing dialogue between the left-radical political and
masculinist scene-based areas of lesbian and gay culture. Although initially
it might have seemed a radical move in the face of dominant expectations of
effeminacy, the masculinization of gay culture was soon condemned by
homosexual activist groups such as the Gay Liberation Front as a process
which introduced patriarchal oppression to the very backbone of gay
subculture: the 'scene'. Desire for 'real men', they argued, involves condoning accepted 'masculine' qualities: violence, strength, aggression, and
sexist oppression. The wholesale incorporation of the dominant definition
of masculinity is politically problematic for a group of people who have
been oppressed by that definition, and interest in leather, uniforms and
sadomasochism was condemned for fetishistically reproducing that oppression. Claims that macho identities are self-oppressive and even fascistic in
their valorization of male power have continued ever since. The controversy
climaxed with the gay skinheads' second rise to prominence in the mid-
1980s because, in the wake of many post-punk skins' highly publicized
recruitment to far-right organizations, the skinhead had come to signify
fascism far more directly than any other macho type.

Liberating masculinity

The Gay Liberation Front was formed in London in 1970, an out and proud
successor to the cautious homophile organizations of the 1960s. It was part
of a larger radical-left political revolution that had emerged from campuses

in Europe and North America in the late 1960s and which included Women's Liberation and black rights movements. Like those on the burgeoning masculinized commercial scene, the GLF's participants were attempting to smash the homosexual stereotypes which had formerly oppressed them with an unapologetic, politically aggressive attitude. But they defined themselves as political radicals in alignment with other oppressed 'Movement' groups in direct opposition to dominant patriarchal power. So they could not simply displace the old effeminate model with oppressive masculinism; new ways of being men, of being gay men, had to be created. So, informed by feminism, part of their project was to create a liberated maleness through consciousness-raising, making themselves aware of the invisible ways dominant ideology oppressed them and how, as men, they might be agents of that oppression to themselves and others. Radical drag was one attempt: whereas drag traditionally had involved either passing as a woman (female impersonation or transvestism) or exaggeratingly parodying female attire, this was about men in frocks in an attempt to expose the ridiculousness of gendered social roles. However, it was difficult to communicate that radicalism: to most straight passers-by, radical drag queens were unproblematically identifiable as screaming queens.

Attempting to contest dominant expectations of effeminacy whilst avoiding recourse to masculinism was a difficult, ambitious project. With homosexual men's exile to the prison house of effeminacy apparently at an end, how should gay men relate to 'masculinity'? Patriarchy had them in a double bind. Any attempt to redefine masculinity is difficult, as the strength of gender binarism, the ease with which society labels attributes as masculine and feminine, means that anything not immediately identifiable as masculine in men is immediately dismissed as feminine. Any new modes of masculinity that might emerge from such a project simply re-create new versions of the effeminate homosexual. On the other hand, an uninterrogated reclamation of, and an unquestioning conformity to, the dominant definition of 'real man' is problematic, as heterosexuality is a primary requirement in this definition and homosexual visibility evaporates.

The GLF were more concerned by the prospect of self-oppression, of capitulating to the very oppression they were trying to fight as gay men, than the prospect of being seen as effeminate. But elsewhere in the subculture – predominantly the commercial scene – there was less anxiety about the uninterrogated redeployment of dominant masculine codes, as many British gay men joyfully shed the cashmere sweater image and slipped into something more uncomfortable. Ever since, gay men politicized in the radical-left tradition have criticized the masculinist discourse invoked by the predominance of macho dress codes on the scene. Indeed, most of the studies of the masculinization of gay culture come from writers directly involved with the GLF or inspired by its legacy, which is why so many accounts tend to be critical.

Gregg Blachford in 1980 looked back at the changes in the way gay men dressed in the preceding decade: from urban subcultural 'extremes' of military uniforms to 'certain watered-down elements such as denim', these changes were politically suspect because of their celebratory signification of 'toughness, virility, aggression, strength, potency – essentially, masculinity and its associated machismo'.[2] These new codes gave rise to a specialized gay masculine identity in urban areas which employed fetishes of accepted masculinity and, associated with this, a sadomasochistic subcultural practice. As such they were in direct conflict with the liberated masculinity as outlined in the Gay Liberation Manifesto:

> Self-Oppression: we become the enemy of our own liberation: . . . when we persist in identification with fascist war-game metaphors such as cops and robbers . . . when we persist in identifying with the master class.[3]

Thus antagonism existed between political-activist and commercial approaches to masculinity on the gay scene at this time. Both energies derived from the recent legislative changes with regard to homosexuality and counter-cultural gender challenges which allowed for a questioning of what it meant to be, among other things, a male homosexual. But the new macho gay role seemed to be more an interrogation of 'homosexual' than 'male' and as such was repudiated by liberationists as capitulation to the dominant: it was a symptom of self-oppression and desire for assimilation. What seemed to them a real chance to radically redefine masculinity was being given up for a reassertion of conservative definitions. This was manifest in three areas of objection that the radicals had to the new macho gay identity.

Firstly, these codes operated within a capitalist-sanctioned ghetto of commercial clubs which was itself questionable. 'In essence, the commercial gay scene represents not so much the liberation of the homosexual as his co-option into consumerist society . . . it represents the triumph of the capitalist entrepreneur over traditional morality.'[4]

Secondly, the codes did not challenge dominant masculinity, heterosexism and all. Machismo on the gay scene merely reproduces the dominant notion of 'masculine' within the subculture and is therefore assimilationist. Even considered within the specific context of gay subculture, Blanchford asserted that 'the oppositional force of showing that homosexuals can be as manly as heterosexuals is limited in that it hardly threatens the overall social order'. The 'new' gay role is in fact an old one, 'the role of the very source of oppression that homosexuals suffer: masculine gender roles . . . it is to the uniforms of the oppressor that the oppressed run to in the hope of safety'.[5] In other words, passing. This tactic, described specifically in relation to gay skinheads, has since been similarly, but far more ambivalently, described as 'protect[ing] yourself . . . by identifying with the oppressor in order to survive'.[6] The liberationist reception of gay men's failure to exhibit radical visibility was less understanding: Seymour Kleinberg, writing of the rising profile of macho queens on the scene in the 1970s, called it a 'perversity of imitating their oppressors . . . to Nazis, Jews are Jews, sidelocks or not. Welcoming the enemy does not appease him.'[7]

And thirdly, the homophobia and misogyny of the uninterrogated masculinity survived this subcultural appropriation. This was manifest in the desire of many macho queens to disassociate themselves from the effeminate model through the ridicule of nelly queens. Gregg Blachford saw the adoption of masculine behavioural and dress codes as an attempt at 'differentiation between oneself, who becomes a "real man" through these outfits, and the absurd, condemned and ridiculed role of other homosexuals'.[8] They 'distance themselves as far as possible from the stereotyped role of the homosexual which they have internalised as negative and undesirable.' 'Effeminate homosexuals are going to be stigmatised by the more "normal" homosexuals – gays within the subculture persecute each other for failing the dominant's conditions.'[9] This was supported by the reactions of gay men in a New York men-only macho bar recorded by Chesebro and Klenk in 1981: one commented, 'I find it very relaxing. Mainly because I go with a lot of other men, and not with a lot of screaming queens, and I'm not with a lot of women.'[10] Again, similar attitudes continue to persist on the gay skinhead scene: Bob, interviewed at a Gay Skinhead Night at the Anvil in 1992, said, 'I come here because it's a chance to get away from the disco-dollies.'[11]

Of course, with the understandable cultural impetus to consign the effeminate type to history, it wasn't just scene queens who were guilty of this effeminaphobia. The conservative predecessors of the GLF also bought into dominant masculinity to afford their cause respectability in the eyes of those they sought to appease. In 1976 Mike Brake interviewed a pipe-puffing member of a 'respectable homophile organisation (notoriously anti-drag)' who had been barred from an anti-gay pub: 'They said I was effeminately dressed. I was furious.' His indignant defence was, 'I may be a queer, but at least I am a man.'[12]

Fetishism

The 1960s skin was an accumulation of fetishes of working-class (authentic, utilitarian, violent) masculinity. Certain elements – denim, collarless Union shirt, very short hair – were overburdened with a sense of working-classness and criminality for the wearer, whose confidence that those understandings would be shared by those who saw him was confirmed by the fear he inspired. The post-punk reworking of the image is a further exaggeration of this already fetishized masculinity. So any gay man who has adopted a skinhead identity since 1980 is consciously eroticizing an already doubly fetishized hard-manliness.

'The look is so obvious a queer thing', agrees gay skin Jamie Crofts, 'a thing that gay men got into, because everything about the look originally was sexy, and then got more so.'

Take everything bit by bit. The idea of wearing big boots and showing them off is a major part of the look, and has got more so: in the older photos, it's smaller DM boots and just a bit of roll up, and it seems like the eighties' look is much bigger boots and highly polished and all that. Everybody argues over whether you're supposed to have your boots really sharp or whether you're supposed to get all your mates to trample on them; it depends on what you want to look like, I suppose. The tight jeans: it's obvious, show off your boots, show off your bum, show off your, er, equipment. And your braces – either you have them under your bum to show off your bum, or you have them up to pull the whole lot up around your stuff – and still show off your bum. The bomber jacket, I think that's sexy anyway, it exaggerates your shoulders and the broadness of your back. And those Levis jackets, tight, make you look really good; Fred Perrys to show off your tattoos.

I've always though short hair was sexy anyway. When I grew up, my teen years were all in the seventies, and long hair didn't turn me on at all – I didn't have any friends with short hair, so it was a weird time to grow up! I suppose it's a natural thing you get into, the shorter the better.

And that's the look.

The masculine codes that became an accepted part of gay subculture in the 1970s are consciously acknowledged by those who enjoy them as fetishes. Boots, denim, muscularity, shaved head; all these are sexy in themselves because they signify masculinity. As one gay skinhead explained:

There's a skinhead who I've had sex with quite a lot who only has sex with all his gear on, he never takes his clothes off. In fact he slept in his boots and his jeans, 'cause he didn't want to take them off. That's the kind of pervert I am, I really enjoyed that, you're into the gear, the jeans on somebody's arse, it's not to do with skin on skin. You can have sex with some skins who are really into the gear, it's nothing to do with violence or associations of it, it's to do with all the clothes. It's a fetishist thing.

Freud's original definition of fetishism warrants reconsideration with regard to its function in the macho gay scene: it is a sexual overvaluation of a substitute for the sexual object, connected with an abandonment of the sexual aim. Setting fetishism within the context of heterosexual sex from the point of view of a man (as Freud habitually does), this means allowing something to compete with the woman as the focus of his sexual desire, affecting his readiness to have sex with her. As such, he admits that 'a certain degree of fetishism is . . . habitually present in normal love',[13] where the sexual object is required to fulfil a fetishistic condition if the sexual aim is to be attained. Freud distinguishes such overinvestment as a fetish when this is no longer a condition attached to the sexual object and substitutes for it instead.

The function of the fetish for the boy child is to safeguard his marker of gender difference through the disavowal of the castration of the mother, which implies his own impending castration. Freud therefore believed that it was usually influenced or inspired by the last item seen before the first viewing of female (phallus-less, castrated) genitals which inspired this castration anxiety. The fetish reinstates the phallus, 'a token of triumph over the threat of castration and a protection against it. It also saves the fetishist from becoming a homosexual'[14] because the boy child will only require that a phallus, and not necessarily a penis, will be present during sex in later life.

But given its centrality to the macho scene, what is the function of fetishism in sex for gay men? With both the self and other(s) possessing a penis, where does the threat of castration come from? Historically, the clone scene emerges as a dominant subcultural identity precisely at a time when the subculture is reacting against the (castrated) feminizing discourse of inversion theory. Therefore, even from a cultural materialist perspective, it would seem fairly likely that an erotic overinvestment in male-related symbols should take place. Clone culture fetishes (which include muscularity, moustache, hairiness, genital size) are all directly derived from male iconography and phallicism. Psychoanalytically, the fervent extremes of the masculine signifiers used may be seen as a symptom of traumatic amnesia: an attempt to forget that queers are not real men. Where one is the same as one's sexual partner, the partner's castration would infer one's own, so the femininity of both must be denied through fetish. The penis alone is not protection enough; the phallic fetishes guard against castration inherent in earlier homosexual identities, reinstating them as real men.

This may explain the preference some skins profess for keeping their clothes on during sex. Exposing their nudity would strip them of the phallic symbolism which rendered them sexy as skinheads in the first place. As Richard Dyer pointed out on his critique of male pin-ups,[15] the penis isn't a patch on the phallus. This concords with photographer Tony Burls' attitude to nudity in relation to representing the sexiness of the male:

I wasn't interested in nudes, that doesn't interest me at all. It's the clothes they're wearing. The skinhead is more than just short hair, isn't it? It's the boots, the jeans, the braces – it's the clothes people go for. If you take all that away, you're not left with anything other than a short-haired nude, and the image is gone.

Fetishes are what makes the skinhead simultaneously sexy and powerful, and this phallic power is revealed in a more practical, less sexual way when they are recontextualized in the heterosexual mainstream, where they operate socially as a protection against the castration ritual of queerbashing in allowing gay men to pass as 'real men'.

This investment in masculine codes cannot therefore be separated from the male social contexts that give them meaning, and all the oppressive patriarchal privilege that entails. Playing with male symbols is a power game; fetishes are power tools. Left-radical considerations of fetishism equate the redeployment male symbols with the reinforcement of phallic law. Gough and Macnair, for example, believe that fetishism is experienced as a compulsive urge because sexuality is 'exercised for alien social needs'[16] – in other words, dominant, heterosexual hegemony swamps the individual's agency through the power of the fetish, allowing dominant patriarchal ideology to take over even in the marginalized context of homosexual sex. This fetishistic power is not restricted to the strict Freudian definition (the compulsive need for the involvement of particular objects in sexual activity). It extends beyond particular sexual acts to the more common overinvestment in socially approved male features (for example, male body, now a requirement of the scene), and is seen by them as limiting sexual capacity to the fixed gender roles in the dominant culture.

But perhaps object fetishism is not enough to safeguard against castration anxiety. The phallus is powerful as a signifier of difference. Luce Irigaray suggests that, in homosexual sex, the phallus is disempowered as it is no longer a signifier of difference but sameness.[17] This might explain the over-compensatory stockpiling of masculine fetishes that characterizes gay macho presentational codes, in a strenuous effort to disavow the powerless phallus. This would seem to concord with Freud's theories on the double nature of the fetish: as a disavowal of the fear of castration, it is always shadowed by the memory of the acknowledgement of the mother's castration.[18] If Irigaray is correct and it is only difference that will re-empower the phallus, then this hyperaccumulation is doomed to failure as it leads only to a uniform extreme masculinity. It is no accident that the masculinized subculture came to be christened the 'clone' scene, with everyone expected to wield the same phallic symbols, and uniformity still rules in its subsequent permutations. Difference – signifiers of femininity – is often forcibly disallowed, with door policies at these clubs barring women and drag queens, and ensuring that uniform codes are strictly adhered to by clubbers.

Given that sameness still characterizes this scene, the evolution of the hanky code within it is therefore particularly significant. According to the sociological accounts, by the late 1970s American clones were advertising their preference for a particular sexual practice through the colour of a handkerchief they wore. This code is still common in clubs and in particular personal ads, where explicit statements of sexual intent are illegal. But there was a significant second dimension to this code: the positioning of the hanky from the left or right back pocket signalled whether the wearer wanted to do it or have it done to him. It unambiguously signalled the binaric identity of active/passive, which is perhaps the last vestige of the gendered role play of previous erotic structures. As both partners are 'real men' this difference of role is no longer consciously gendered; that the roles of active/passive are pushed to the extremes of master/slave (or oppressor/oppressed) may be an attempt to overcome the evaporation of phallic difference which occurs in a truly homo context. So the phallus is reinstated not only through symbols but also the introduction of difference and hierarchy into sexual activity: sadomasochism.

The simultaneous acknowledgement and disavowal of castration embodied in the fetish results in a divided attitude: hostility and affection in the treatment of the fetish, and resultant rituals of symbolic castration and phallic reinstatement. Freud cites the example of 'the Chinese custom of mutilating the female foot and then revering it like a fetish after it has been mutilated'.[18] This is a sadomasochistic ritual. It is no accident that in areas of the scene where the emphasis is on uniform masculinity, SM is an institutionalized subcultural practice: a ritual castration and phallic reinstatement, investing partner(s) with and stripping them of the phallic power.

Sadomasochism

People say you must be into the idea of having your head kicked in by a butch skinhead, the people you have sex with must be into this fantasy of violence; well, yeah, some people are, but some aren't. The thing that attracts me to SM sex with skinheads is that it's not generally to do with the master and slave thing, role-playing. Although you do see a lot of ads for those, I haven't come across skins into role-play of that type. I'm attracted to it partly because I can get into SM sex and I can dictate what I want to happen. SM sex of whatever type, role-play or physical sensations, you can do much more easily as a skinhead because you get into much more heavy physical stuff without being stuck in a single role. Skinheads seem much more into that idea. In other SM scenes, it's about whether you're a top or a bottom. Someone once said to me, 'You're wearing your braces up, that means you're a top.' Does it bollocks! It's got nothing to do with that! That's another thing I'd say wasn't a skinhead thing.

The thing I associate with real skinhead sex is that you can do all those SM things and it's much more mutual, two-way, without having to piss around with pretending you're doing something else. There's this ludicrous thing in SM sex where you can't just do things to each other, someone has to play at being someone else, it seems daft to me. Skinhead sex I've had has been much more open to the idea of, you do this and now why don't you do that – although you don't say it just like that; it just seems much more a two-way thing, because, both being skinheads, you go into it as equals.

By no means does a skinhead identity always necessarily declare an interest in SM, although it is no accident that gay skinheads in the early 1970s quickly found their niche in those areas of the scene where SM was popular. But the sexiness of the skinhead, somewhere along the line, trades on a reputation for violence. 'The implication of violence cannot be ruled out of the attraction', wrote gay skin Mike Dow in his 1985 feature, 'Skins'.[20] 'The fetishism centred on the boots is merely part of the inevitable fact that the connection between sex and violence is part of the human psyche.' The DM boot at some level signifies the masculinity of the worker, but its fetishistic function more likely derives from its usefulness on the football terraces as an effective weapon (hence the preference for steel toe-caps). Posing a physical threat, it has a specifically sadomasochistic significance in its fetishization. The reverence with which the DM boot is treated as a fetish can be witnessed at skinhead venues where boot-shining services are available. This ritual echoes the popular gay skin SM practice of boot-licking, the prone skin demonstrating his subservience before his booted master, whose dominance is secured by the phallic power of his boots. What makes skinheads particularly suitable subjects for homosexual sadomasochistic fantasy, of course, is their association with queerbashing.

Sadomasochism features in the sexual experiences, expectations and fantasies of many gay skinheads. This can be anything from 'hard sex' and laddy wrestling to worship and humiliation and more sophisticated sub-dom games. Ads that appear in the skinhead contacts section 'Boots & Braces' in the gay freesheet *Boyz*, for example, tend to stress the ability of the sought partner to engage in specific sadomasochistic practices:

● Rough but friendly, uncut, East End thug wanted by likeable 39 year old. Your mean attitude is my dream. Make it reality. Come and frighten me into submission with your anger, please.

● Me: 6', horny, active skin, 36, WE, into CP, BD, WS, looking for guys, in 20s, who will slave and serve.

● Very slim, smooth, boyish-physique, master, 38, looking for sub skins/ slaves, 21–28, into beige, red, yellow, brown, CP, BD.[21]

The continuity with clone culture is signalled by the use of known acronyms and colour codes.

In the late 1970s, sadomasochism became an urgent debate for radical feminist lesbians, who considered it to be a patriarchal eroticization of violence and therefore alien to female sexuality. The all-female context of lesbian sex should ensure the absence of such patriarchal sexuality, but SM was becoming a seemingly popular sexual activity amongst lesbians, accompanied by an increasing visibility of SM paraphernalia in lesbian bars. *Take Back the Night* and *Against Sadomasochism: A Radical Feminist Analysis*, both published in the early 1980s, argued against this trend. The latter was produced by a lesbian separatist feminist collective in an urgent attempt to alert fellow lesbians to the dangers of what was being considered harmless bedroom fun. Talking of 'scenarios of submission and humiliation, dominance and control', Rose Mason says, 'I can't help but think that's very male.'[22] That socially oppressive power roles are recontextualized for the express purpose of sexual *pleasure* is no defence, as radical lesbian feminism sees no discontinuity between the bedroom and the street: Judy Butler condemns SM scenarios for ignoring the historic and social context of their origin in separating 'private/public' and 'sexual/social'.[23] It merely reinforces patriarchy, even in an all-female environment.

That those involved in sadomasochistic sex *actively seek* to dominate or be dominated is usually given as a refution of the accusation that such activities are oppressive. This rests on the notion of consent which is informed by liberal discourses around choice and individual freedom. In opposition, those who object to sadomasochism argue that liberal ideology blinds participants to the construction of choice which is predetermined by the social order. Karen Rian argues 'since our sexuality has been for the most part constructed through social structures over which we have no control, we *all* "consent" to sexual desires and activities which are alienating to at least some degree'.[24] As such, consent is illusory, manufactured, an unwitting collusion with the dominant, an instance of false consciousness (hence the title of Judy Butler's article in *Against Sadomasochism*: 'Lesbian S&M: The Politics of Dis-illusion'). Indeed, the sentencing of sadomasochists arrested by the British police in a sexual crackdown they called Operation Spanner in 1992 proved, literally and perversely, that consent does not protect individuals from the power of the law.

Scene-based, commercially sanctioned homosexual practices which rest on gendered or power role-play are seen by radicals as inhibiting the challenge to dominant patriarchy which such marginalized sexualities should provide. Karen Rian believes that SM 'is a mode of sexual satisfaction which has been learned in an alienating social context which remains satisfying as long as its social context remains unchallenged . . . we cannot simply wish it away . . .

we have to get rid of the *conditions that require* and engender dominance and submission'.[25] The rise of SM amongst lesbians was a rally cry to redouble radical feminism's efforts to transform society through overturning the patriarchal organization of sex/power. Similarly, gay male radicals opposed to gender-play looked to a socialist revolution of the society which continued to create such gender roles in the first place: 'Distinct fetishised individual sexualities are a product of the contradiction, inherent in capitalism, between the social institutions of the family and the market'[26] – socialist societal reorganization would entail the disappearance of these institutions and their contradictions, and, indeed, sexualities.

Such arguments suggest that there exists some non-alienating, non-contradictory utopia of the real self beyond the social. A Foucaultian analysis would argue that there is no self beyond that which is socially constructed and restricted. If sadomasochism is alienating, it is not a case of alien outer societal demands imposing themselves on the needs of the real inner self, it is merely an awareness of the contradictions in one's subject position and broader ideologies of identity. It may well be that fore-grounding these contradictions will at least expose them, if not help to undermine them, as leaping completely free of inherited identity-positions is not possible: one cannot exist beyond the power network. Such arguments have been used in support of sadomasochism and there is a tendency among those against it to be highly dismissive of Foucaultian theory: 'Foucault's view reflects a resignation and political passivity which succeeds only in reinforcing the sexual status quo. This tone of resignation and disillusion marks the majority of SM literature and discourse that I have heard.'[27] But as all social and sexual roles, including those of gay and lesbian, are constructed by a patriarchal society, then *all* sexual activity must be equally alienating. Similarly, the radical arguments refuting consent in SM scenarios lead to the conclusion that consent to *any* activity may be patriarchally sanctioned behaviour even if it claims to be opposed to patriarchy. Whose perception is so ideologically undetermined that they can detect which consciousnesses are false?

Many gay radicals recognize that political action is restricted to received structures but nevertheless condemn role-based sex games and identities. Michael Brake says of masculine codes on the gay scene that 'the infiltration of false consciousness is to be found in gay men and women's imitation of the straight world . . . These are reflections of the worst elements of male hegemony, but society with its present dichotomous roles leaves them little choice.'[28] The socialist gay writer Jamie Gough sees the 'category masculine' as 'a wholly reactionary one. The fact that no individual can choose to live outside the social system of gender, and that all of us therefore participate in masculinity/femininity, does not remove this reactionary content. The styles therefore present a real political problem . . . the new styles are in many ways oppressive to women and to gay men themselves.'[29] Such appropriation is oppressive because 'it uses the idea of gender roles that exist in society already'.[30]

But where else are any symbols to be taken from? The heterosexual masculinity that initially informed clone codes is arguably heterosexist and homophobic, but that is not to say that gay men cannot, or should not, try to change that order, nor play with that symbolism. After all, homosexual sadomasochism usually operates in a context of homo uniformity where there is no gender difference. Opponents of SM would argue that the masochist in such a scenario is always inherently, if not consciously, gendered feminine. But the belief that active/passive is fixedly mapped on to male/female (and vice versa) smacks more of 'resignation and political passivity . . . reinforcing the sexual status quo' than the recognition and dramatization of power dynamics in relationships.

Queerbashing fantasies acted out by gay skins provide an appropriately complex illustration of these debates. Queerbashing in the street, on an unwilling subject, is a patriarchal punishment for being homosexual. For left-radicals, sadomasochism ensures the continued deployment of that patriarchal, homophobic project, the pleasure being illusory, derived from a concordance with the dominant's 'alien social needs'. Although considering homosexual sadomasochism as a form of self-punishment for being queer is often derided as a simplistic pop psychology explanation which refuses to acknowledge the complexity of desire, it would be unwise to dismiss the opinions of those participants who voice that opinion. One gay skinhead recalls his sexual experiences with other skins in the 1960s: 'They were into CP games; it was a symbolic way of being punished, although I didn't know that at the time.'

Equally simplistic is the counter-argument that the sadomasochistic reappropriation of this scenario in the bedroom (or wherever) radically reclaims it in the name of homosexual pleasure. This approach would have us believe that the socially ordained roles of queerbasher and queer victim are in fact free-floating identities up for grabs, where the power differences can be exploited for a sexual purpose. So the violent act of a (straight) queerbasher punishing a (queer) victim becomes a sexual act between two queers. But this analysis stumbles on a problem common to theories of appropriation: it places the gay SM scenario as a secondary redress to the primary act of queerbashing, threatening to reinforce the hierarchy of hetero, with all the authority of the origin, over homo. In fact, it is often felt by queers that the two scenarios are never that distinct: that the straight 'origin' of the act of violence is sexual in nature, implicating the straight queerbasher. Nick's experience as a skinhead in the early 1980s articulates a common belief about skinhead queerbashers – that they were in fact gay, with queerbashing acting as a ritual of disavowal:

Being gay challenged your masculinity. So what they'd do is take on a really masculine thing and go, I'm not gay, I'm not gay, and go queerbashing, 'cause they were fighting themselves, some of them. Some of the worst skinheads were gay, 'cause that was their fear, looking at what they were, so beating them up was a way of dealing with it.

The contra-definitional terms of appropriation and origin, of sex and violence, of homo and hetero dissolve into each other, exposing their constructedness. And queer/postmodern accounts of sexuality champion SM queerbashing scenes as radically deconstructive in the way they expose the instability of these terms. Whereas the social violence imposed on identified groups attempts to fix them within their definition, consensual sexual activity between individuals freely adopting those roles is supposed to expose the free-floating nature of social categories.

But once the elements of the field are thus unfixed, the implications can work both ways: there is a disturbing converse conclusion to draw from this celebratory argument. If there really is no difference between sex and violence, gay and straight, then queerbashing (on the streets, executed by straights) was always/already a queer act that could be enjoyed sexually by both the unwilling queer victim and the queered agressor in the same way as a gay bedroom scenario.

This was the conclusion of one prominent gay skinhead on the contemporary scene who mixed with fascist skins. When I asked him about their association with queerbashing, he responded:

It's not an association with queerbashing, it's an association with sadomasochism. It's a turn on to kick the shit out of somebody. That is something that we like to do. To each other, or *preferably to someone who doesn't actually want the shit kicked out of them*. So the skinheads who go around and kick the shit out of queers are in fact satisfying their own sexual pleasures by kicking people. It is a sexual thing: that's why they're doing it; that's why they're doing it in the gear; that's why they're doing it with the closeness of their friends. So if they can get someone who's gay, that's probably even better. And I think given half a chance, they'd then bend that bloke over and shove their dick up his arse. With the social barriers in place, they can't go that far; but they'd bloody well like to.

For this gay skinhead, primary and secondary scenarios do not swap places, they are indistinguishable. The hierarchy of social/sexual violence is not so much inverted as completely ripped apart. He does not differentiate between queers and queerbashers, sadism and sadomasochism, sex and violence – they are the same thing. The categories of gay/straight, aggressor/victim, violence/sex are so dangerously unstable that they need to be violently reimposed. SM is not a matter of consensus and free-floating identity in a violent power-play, it's a matter of getting off on imposing violence on an unwilling victim. The reciprocity of sadomasochism, the dynamic of desire which assures its consensual nature in the consideration of liberals, is undermined by his extension of the category of sadomasochism to encompass what by common understanding amount to purely sadistic acts. It is more than disregarding the consent of the masochist participant – the unwillingness of the victim is a specified requirement. This would seem to substantiate the criticism that separating 'private/public' and 'sexual/social' is a false step.

Fascist symbolism and recontextualization

The argument that utilizing power symbols and roles in homo sex may not so much expose them as reinforce them is therefore a strong one, which is given credence by the prevalence of Nazi imagery on the scene, as Mike Macnair has warned: 'Legitimacy of SM may legitimize more traditional conservative ideologies of acceptance of the social order . . . The reality of this danger is evidenced by things like the casual use of Nazi insignia by SM people.'[31] The most extreme social metaphor of domination and control is that of fascism and its related symbolism.

Gough observes that 'some gay masculine styles imply, and to some extent must encourage, admiration for, or condoning of militarism and fascism',[32] and clone culture's interest in masculinity led to the appearance of fascist symbols in some venues. By the late 1970s Greg Blanchford could write of dress codes in macho bars exhibiting 'extremes' of uniform which use 'images of sexual violence and dominance, including neo-Nazi adornments' as well as styles of 'masculine working class labouring occupations'.[33] Indeed, these were well-established macho scene practices. As Kenneth Anger's films (most notably *Scorpio Rising*) attest, flirtation with Nazi fantasies and the use of fascist iconography were not uncommon on the urban American homosexual underground leather scene of the 1950s.

The gay skinhead identity is so popular and so controversial precisely because it is a site of convergence of debates around, and provides proof of the continuity of, eroticized masculinity, fetishism and sadomasochism. Fascism contains elements of all three aspects of the pre-existent erotic structure identified here. This is also why it is particularly controversial: debates over sadomasochism's eroticization of patriarchal power and fascism converge in the skinhead.

Certainly the use of the British national flag has been so successfully appropriated by British nationalists that by the early 1980s it had come to signify fascism to many people. Its use is common among gay skinheads as an authenticating element of the skinhead costume. For all the protestations that skinheads should not be considered as fascists, nearly every gay skin I spoke to referred to the skinhead as 'a British invention' and said that the British flag was merely an aspect of this.

Jamie Crofts, who wears a Union Jack as part of his skinhead gear, finds that some people object.

> It's mainly liberals. I think that's important; I don't think there's anything wrong with having that as an image. There's nothing about that that says fascist to me, but it seems to to a lot of people. OK, saying I identify with a particular country, but then I live here – so what? Obviously if you're waving flags about and goosestepping all over the place, well that's dodgy for me.

He acknowledges the ability of the Union Jack to signify fascism but sought to disrupt this through his adoption of the symbol as an anti-fascist: 'The flag, that's just a look, a position, *a thing to be played about with*.'

This is a contest over signification; whether a symbol 'really' means something, and how this delimits who can lay claim to it. 'I can't understand why [fascists] haven't got a swastika', objects John Byrne, citing a common argument. 'During the war, I thought we were fighting Nazis. So people who are Nazis nowadays must be the enemy of British people.'

The gay skinhead artist Andrew Heard championed the reappropriation of the Union Jack from far-right groups in his work and in his appearance (he proudly sported a Union Jack tattoo on his left arm); stars of post-war popular culture, World War II skylines and skinheads featured in much of his work, which evoked a nostalgic *Carry On*/Ealing comedy Englishness. In an interview in the gay arts magazine *Square Peg* he complained that the flag is 'interpreted as National Front and that's one of the things that's gone wrong, unfortunately, that kind of ridiculous association that anyone that uses the union jack is in any kind of way associated with the N.F. I absolutely loathe that idea.' The artist and writer David Robilliard added, 'The union jack has been given the same status as the swastika.'[34]

But given that that is the case, is it responsible to try to reclaim it through wearing it? Punk played similar games of appropriation with that unambivalent signifier of fascism – the swastika. The early Sanskrit symbol was claimed by the German nationalists in the late nineteenth century and now, fifty years after the fall of the German nation state, still powerfully seems, eternally and essentially, to stand for fascism. Yet its initial appropriation was highly problematic. Malcolm Quinn writes of the way the swastika was originally dismissed in 1880 as a potential symbol for German nationalism because 'its wide spatial distribution rendered it useless for the determination of time'. Yet by 1893 this 'migratory image with no link to geographic place or historical time' came to be successfully appropriated as the national symbol of Germany.[35]

In his book, *The Swastika: Constructing the Symbol*, Quinn identifies the process by which such a seemingly impossible appropriation was achieved. It is an exercise in semiotic tautology: by 'forcing it to exchange itself for itself', the swastika, which was previously so free-floating, previously open to so many cross-cultural interpretations as to be meaningless, becomes rigidly grounded in a specific context and closed to a specific meaning so strongly that it blots out the memory of its previous circulations. It becomes, as Quinn calls it, 'pseudo-absolute'.

> In a potentially infinite system of economy and exchange, tautology remains one of the few ways of exhausting sign exchange and marking out its symbolic limit . . . the tautology is productive, not of meaning, but of self-representation . . . The symbol is absolute, self-identical and above all nonexchangeable, which is why Goebbels' laws for the protection of the swastika were introduced to prevent the Nazi 'national symbol' becoming a sign which could be used to mirror the value of mass-produced objects such as a hairbrush or a pair of cuff-links.[36]

The swastika was resignified, its previous ubiquity undone through the restriction of its circulation to particular contexts, usually in monumental representations. These contexts had to be safely observed; it was for this reason that Goebbels drew up *Laws for the Protection of National Symbols* which specifically condemned 'pictures of artistically low value, with self-illuminating swastikas'. Inappropriate contextualizations threatened to reduce the transcendental nature of the swastika to kitsch.

As with masculine codes and sadomasochism, it might be argued that the use of fascist-related symbolism in such a homo environment is a conscious or even ironic recontextualization which causes them to be read differently. Certainly punk's initial use of the swastika (along with other international tautologous symbols of political and religious value) was part of a project to undo the reverence afforded it by breaking its restricted circulation and exposing it as kitsch. While punk's anarchic games with signification were celebrated by liberal commentators, the swastika presented a particular problem of bad taste which led to some fairly desperate exercises in redemption. Tricia Henry in her consideration of punk and its legacy, *Break All Rules*, concluded that swastikas 'were not worn to indicate that punk was in agreement with fascist philosophy, but rather to remind society of the atrocities it permits'.[37] Dick Hebdidge in *Subculture: the Meaning of Style*, concludes that bad taste was the whole point. Also denying any particular allegiance between punk and the far right, he claims that 'the swastika was worn because it was guaranteed to shock', or as one punk put it, 'Punks just like to be hated.'

This represented more than a simple inversion or inflection of the ordinary meanings attached to an object. The signifier (swastika) had been wilfully detached from the context (Nazism) it conventionally signified, and although it had been repositioned . . . within an alternative subcultural context, its primary value and appeal derived precisely from its lack of meaning: from its potential for deceit. It was exploited as an empty effect. We are forced to the conclusion that the central value 'held and reflected' in the swastika was the communicated absence of any such identifiable values.[38]

Such tactics of tasteless appropriation achieved the results that 'meaning itself evaporates', and Hebdidge and many others have read punk as a project of de-signifying the socially intelligible. Certainly this was one of the goals of the Situationists, the semiotically subversive movement that sought political revolution through popular culture, who informed the aesthetic and ideology of the art-school mode of early punk.

But for those who continue to claim it in the name of fascism, those who are terrorized by it, and the majority of people who (according to such sophisticated, semiotic analyses) 'mis'-read it as being 'really' fascistic, the swastika cannot afford to be considered an empty symbol. Stanley Cohen makes this point when highlighting the inadequacies of what he sees as Dick Hebdidge's extremes of semiotic decoding:

Displaying a swastika . . . shows how symbols are stripped from their natural context . . . it is *really* being employed in a metalanguage: the wearers are ironically distancing themselves from the very message that the symbol is usually intended to convey . . . But how are we to know this? . . . In the end, there is no basis whatsoever for choosing between this particular sort of interpretation and any others.

Someone may not be wearing a swastika for ironic effect but for reasons of 'simple conformity, blind ignorance or knee-jerk racism'.[39] As a question of interpretation, some cannot afford the risk of misreading the swastika as an ironic recontextualization only to discover the encoder (i.e. 'wearer') is a fascist. In fact it could be argued that punk's sign-play with the swastika made it easier for the post-punk skinhead revival to recontextualize it within the rising far-right movements.

Susan Leigh Starr's consideration of the recontextualization of the swastika within sadomasochism concretizes these abstract theoretical debates within the very personal, very real discourse of her own survival. She finds that her social survival instincts informed by personal experience (what she calls her 'street sense') render theory-based semiotics invalid and possibly dangerous. She is sensitive to the free-floating *potential* of signifiers, but the association of the swastika with the Third Reich is

very strong . . . They trouble my street sense . . . the connection with a direct threat to my physical well-being is recent in history . . . I could try to remember that the swastika was once a Sanskrit symbol of peace, and that what has changed once can change again. Or that sadomasochists are using it in another context, one that doesn't concern me.[40]

But intellectual theories of appropriation and cultural change cannot override her instinctive street sense of things as they are: the physically enforced association of the swastika with genocide and personal injury. Starr then cannot afford the luxury of objective idealism and its ahistoric tendencies. Arguing from a left-radical perspective, she underlines its continuity with those theories of appropriation that vindicate sadomasochism: that 'when you set the rules of the context, it's OK to use any symbol within that context (or for that matter to perform any activity). When sadomasochism is consensual, the symbolic level changes because the context changes.' She instead argues for a material realism which does not ignore history: 'For any theory or explanation I ask, what is its grounding in material reality? . . . one cannot specify the context of a psychological experience at will. One must be accountable to the historical and material consequences in describing psychological experiences of any kind.'[41] The control necessary for resignification through recontextualization can only work if 'one has power over a wide social context and is willing to enforce the reinterpretation of the symbols over the scale of their usage'[42] – which, in the case of specialized sexual activity within a marginalized minority subculture, is not the case.

Commercial masculinized gay subculture stood accused of patriarchal oppression, covert fascism and the indirect encouragement of the parading of fascist regalia by the radical-left. These ideological arguments seemed to be literalized in the early 1980s when, just as the skinhead was becoming a neo-Nazi stormtrooper in the popular consciousness, the macho scene was welcoming a rising number of gay skins.

Notes

1. *Out*, August 1985, p. 1. For the debates about identity and oppression that crystallized around the London Lesbian and Gay Centre, see Sue Aardhill and Sue O'Sullivan, 'Upsetting the Applecart: Difference, Desire and Lesbian Sadomasochism', *Feminist Review*, 23, Summer 1986.

2. Gregg Blachford, 'Male Dominance in the Gay World', in Kenneth Plummer (ed.), *The Making of the Modern Homosexual* (New Jersey: Barnes and Noble, 1981), p. 191.

3. Simon Watney, 'The Ideology of the GLF', in Gay Left Collective (eds), *Homosexuality: Politics and Power*

(London: Allison and Busby, 1980), p. 65.

4. Dennis Altman, 'What Changed in the Seventies?', in Gay Left Collective, *Homosexuality: Politics and Power*, p. 57.

5. Blachford, 'Male Dominance in the Gay World', p. 203.

6. Dinesh Bhugra from the Royal College of Psychiatrists, speaking on 'Skin Complex', *Out*, broadcast on Channel 4, 29 July 1992.

7. Seymour Kleinberg, 'Macho men: or where have all the sissies gone?', *Gay News*, No. 142 (1978).

8. Blachford, 'Male Dominance in the Gay World', p. 191.

9. *Ibid.*, p. 189.

10. James Chesebro and Kenneth Klenek, 'Gay Masculinity in the Gay Disco', in James Chesebro (ed.), *Gayspeak: Gay Male and Lesbian Communication* (New York: Pilgrim Press, 1981), p. 95.

11. Ian Peacock, 'Boot Boyz', *Boyz*, 17 July 1981, p. 14.

12. Mike Brake, 'I may be a queer, but at least I am a man', in Barker and Allen (eds), *Sexual Divisions in Society: Process and Change* (Cambridge: Cambridge University Press, 1976), pp. 186–7.

13. Sigmund Freud, *On Sexuality: Three Essays on the Theory of Sexuality and Other Works*, trans. James Strachey (Harmondsworth: Penguin, 1991), p. 66.

14. *Ibid.*, pp. 353–4.

15. Richard Dyer, 'Don't Look Now: The Male Pin-up', *Screen*, No. 23, 3 April 1982.

16. Jamie Gough and Mike Macnair, *Gay Liberation in the Eighties* (Guernsey: Pluto Press, 1985), p. 193.

17. Luce Irigaray, 'Commodities Among Themselves', in *This Sex Which is Not One*, trans. Catherine Porter (New York: Cornell University Press, 1985), p. 193.

18. Freud, *On Sexuality*, p. 356.

19. *Ibid.*, p. 357.

20. *Out*, April 1985, p. 21.

21. *Boyz*, 3 July 1993.

22. 'Racism and Sadomasochism: A Conversation with Two Black Lesbians', Karen Sims and Rose Mason in conversation with Darlene R. Pagano, in Robin Ruth Linden *et al.* (eds), *Against Sadomasochism: A Radical Feminist Analysis* (San Francisco: Frog in the Well, 1982), p. 102.

23. Judy Butler, 'Lesbian S & M: The Politics of Dis-Illusion', in *Against Sadomasochism*, p. 172.

24. Karen Rian, 'Sadomasochism and the Social Construction of a Desire', in *Against Sadomasochism*, p. 49.

25. *Ibid.*, pp. 46–7.

26. From Gough and Macnair, *Gay Liberation in the Eighties*, quoted by Jamie Gough in 'Theories of Sexual Identity and the Masculinisation of the Gay Man', in Simon Shepherd and Mick Wallis (eds), *Coming On Strong: Gay Politics and Culture* (London: Unwin Hyman, 1989), p. 151.

27. Butler, 'Lesbian S & M', p. 170.

28. Brake, 'I may be queer', pp. 186–7.

29. Gough, 'Theories of Sexual Identity', pp. 121–2.

30. Blachford, 'Male Dominance in the Gay World', p. 191.

31. Macnair, quoted in Shepherd and Wallis, *Coming on Strong*, p. 160.

32. Gough, 'Theories of Sexual Identity', pp. 121–2.

33. Blachford, 'Male Dominance in the Gay World', p. 191.

34. 'So What Sort of Pictures Do You Do?', *Square Peg*, No. 12, August 1986.

35. Malcolm Quinn, *The Swastika: Constructing the Symbol* (London: Routledge, 1994), p. xii.

36. *Ibid.*, p. 137.

37. Tricia Henry, *Break All Rules: Punk Rock and the Meaning of a Style*

(Ann Arbor: UMI Research Press, 1989), p. 80.

38. Dick Hebdidge, *Subculture: The Meaning of Style* (London: Routledge, 1979), p. 117.

39. Stanley Cohen, *Folk Devils and Moral Panics* (Oxford: Martin Robertson, 1980), p. xvii.

40. Susan Leigh Starr, 'Swastikas: the Street and the University', in *Against Sadomasochism*, p. 132.

41. *Ibid.*, p. 133.

42. *Ibid.*, p. 134.

7

Real Men,
Phallicism and Fascism

Never mind whether or not he had a swastika tattooed on his scalp or white power patches sewn on his flying jacket; thanks to the efforts of the British press and British nationalist groups such as Blood and Honour, and despite dedicated campaigning from anti-Nazi skinhead groups, by 1982 the skinhead had become a fascist symbol for many people.

The skinheads' association with fascistic violence is so strong that the same tendencies in other white working-class youth cults is often overlooked or downplayed in comparison. But skins were certainly not the first and only white working-class youth culture to carry out racist and homophobic attacks: previous subcultures were also characterized by such violence. For example, the sociologist Geoff Pearson gives an account of a racist attack which took place in Accrington in 1956 by 'a large gang of about 100–200 white youths and men . . . The appearance suggested that they were "the lads".' But interestingly, Pearson, writing in 1976, has to emphasize that 'these were not skinheads . . . The style of this gang was of the latter-day teddy boy'.[1]

But since the original skinhead movement was an attempt to reassert conservative masculinity in the face of cultural change, skinheads have a particular investment in authenticity, the fixing of identity and the preservation of boundaries, which, in the current sociopolitical organization, lends itself to conservative ideologies and far-right politics. The conscription into neo-Nazi movements did not happen until the late 1970s' revival: the original skinheads did not operate through organized political movements, not even class ones. For most skinheads of voting age 'Labour would no doubt have been the most popular choice',[2] although this is due to class loyalty rather that any socialist leanings; the tendency to the right in skinhead culture is already apparent in the 1960s. The Collingwood gang consider voting conservative an act of treacherous bourgeoisification, but when discussing immigration, say 'That's what we need – a Chinese Enoch Powell' (because 'ya don't see no blacks in China').[3] In the wake of his famous, racist 'rivers of blood' speech, in which he used classical literary allusion to lend authority to his prophesy that many races living in close proximity could only result in mass murder, this far-right conservative was adopted as an unofficial skinhead figurehead. George Marshall claims that 'Many a young skinhead might have claimed old Enoch as a hero' and describes the skinhead contribution to the Great Vietnam Solidarity March of 1968: '30,000 students and related lazy bastards . . . and a few sore heads courtesy of 200 shaven-headed bootboys in Milwall colours, running along behind chanting "Enoch! Enoch!"'[4] And awareness of this extended beyond the confines of the subculture: a *Times* report in 1981, trying to account for the rise of neo-Nazism among skinheads, traces right-wing tendencies among skinheads back to their first incarnation, recalling how 'In 1970 skinheads (not at his behest) formed a guard of honour for Mr Powell when he spoke at Smethwick.' The report attributes his status as a skinhead hero to his being 'a champion of nationalism and tribalism'.[5]

Emerging from the punk scene, the new skinheads inherited the fascist symbolism punk had played with. But post-punk skins were reacting against the intellectual, bourgeois, 'art school' aspects of punk. Marshall states that 'most of the new breed of skinheads started out as little more than bald punks, who had taken shock value two steps further in a bid to distance themselves from the middle class mess punk had become'.[6] So if sporting a swastika had ever been a semiotic experiment with cultural and political symbolism, this was not to be the motivation for many skins. Susan Leigh Star's thesis that the inability of objective idealists to control the circulation and subsequent meaning of symbols will probably lead to their reinscription within the dominant is proven to be true: sporting a swastika as a fashion statement or a semiotic experiment facilitated its subsequent adoption by white working-class youths across various subcultural styles as an expression of their right-wing political allegiances.

In the late 1970s, the British Movement and the National Front sensed a swing to the right in the political climate with the Conservative Party being voted into office on a right-wing agenda in 1979. They began to run fairly high-profile recruitment campaigns for organizations outside the political mainstream, targeting young working-class males across the many youth cultures that had found themselves regenerated in the wake of punk. In 1980 the organizer for Youth National Front, Joe Pearce, boasted in an interview with *New Society* of 'widespread support among heavy metal fans and mods as well as skins'.[7] But the factors which differentiated them from the others – their particular conservatism and boundary fixation, and their status in British social memory as the most violent subculture – did seem to render skinheads predisposed to right-wing affiliation: the article countered Pearce's claim with the fact that a 'recent National Front march in Lewisham was 80 per cent skinhead', and such a spectacle was to recur throughout the 1980s. The skinhead look also appeared the most militaristic: the anti-style dress – particularly the razored hair and boots – functioned as a highly practical fighting uniform. This was perceived at the birth of the style: 1960s skins developed from 'gang mods, hard mods, who changed uniform to fight more easily'.[8] George Marshall consciously acknowledges the function of the dress code as the 'adoption of a uniform'; in order to be 'just like an army, all copied each other in dressing'.[9] The revived uniform underwent a transformation, though, drawing elements from punk and exaggerating elements of the original look. Jeans got tighter, DMs stretched towards the knee, the hair was completely shaved. The result was an even more terrifying appearance and 'gave out the image of an almost robot uniformed army'.[10] And, subjected to political organization, that was just how they functioned:

> In recent years, the new National Front have tried to create a street fighting force . . . Their intention was to set up a group that appeared unconnected with the NF leadership but in reality could have their strings pulled by them. They would be used for street destabilisation, fighting at sports events and keeping up racial attacks.[11]

The visual association of the striking skin image with right-wing demos on the streets and associated activity on the terraces was very strong. According to Peter Evans' report in *The Times*, by the winter of 1980 skinheads 'giving Nazi salutes and chanting racialist slogans' had become a common sight.

Significantly, visible reminders of the skinheads' debt to Jamaican culture were erased with their revival, as the Rude Boy elements disappeared from the skin wardrobe (Rude Boy styles were experiencing a contemporary revival with the formation of Two-Tone); the sharp, expensive tailored tonic jacket was dropped in favour of the cheaper, more practical MA-1 flying jacket. Similarly, Ska and Motown were ditched in favour of a new musical offshoot of punk, Oi! The monosyllabic musical movement was championed (and allegedly christened) in the late 1970s by *Sounds* journalist Garry Bushell, who claimed it celebrated working-classness, authenticity and inarticularity in the face of bourgeois, sophisticated intellectualism:

> Oi! was real punk. Punk had always made a big thing about being from the tower blocks and the working classes having a say. In reality it was all art school kids, posh kids from Bromley like Billy Idol. The real punk, the new punk, the Oi! bands were just working class kids.[12]

In erasing the last influence of black culture, the working-class identity that Oi! purported to celebrate was unequivocally white; the Kent organizer for the British Movement, Nicky Crane, famously starred on the sleeve of an early Oi! compilation.

Subjecting members of minoritized groups then became less a case of random sporadic violence than an aspect of a consistent political project.

The increase in queerbashings was horrifically successful in so far as it popularized homophobia and deterred many people from adopting visible lesbian and gay identities. Tony remembers witnessing a particularly violent attack as a (closeted gay) punk in 1981 on the London underground.

We'd been to a gig; there were three carriages of us. My girlfriend got separated. We pulled up in a station and I heard her screaming, so I went into her carriage and I could see a couple of punk blokes and a couple of skinheads who were kicking the shit out of this bloke. He must have been in his forties or fifties, and he was wearing leather gear, cloney stuff – it was about that time – and they were literally kicking the shit out of him. Of course, my girlfriend was shouting at them to stop, but they wouldn't take any notice.

Obviously, being a punk, you got involved in violence, but I hated violence, and I couldn't go up to them and say to them stop. It certainly made me feel less like coming out as gay. I knew for a fact that one of my so-called best friends, this skinhead, was really, really anti-gay. He used to go round giving out leaflets in pubs, saying, 'I don't want any queer coming up my 8-year-old son's arse.' I think he was messed around with when he was a kid, he had this real chip on his shoulder about gay people. It was like something out of the war, saying, they should all be taken to an island and bombed and tortured, and he was serious, he wasn't just mucking about.

So they were laying into this guy, and basically this guy was hospitalized. And he hadn't done anything to them, he was just sitting on the tube. It wasn't like a whole gang, just two punks, two skinheads.

One gay skinhead of the time recalls,

Straight skinheads were in gangs and everybody knew each other. A lot of them were politically motivated; they were NF, they *did* hate queers and they *did* go queerbashing and have marches and all that stuff. It was something they sensed. Or they'd stop you and say, 'Oi, where are you from then mate?' and you'd be like frightened 'cos they really would headbutt you, they really were hard.

The event which probably cemented the relationship between skinheads and neo-Nazism was the anti-Asian violence at a gig featuring the Business, the Last Resort and the 4-Skins at the Hambrough Tavern in Southall, London in July 1981.

The polarization around the issue of race with Nazi skinheads active in an area with a high immigrant population meant that anyone who resembled a skinhead had to be viewed as a potential racist. Given the rising number of skinheads carrying out racist attacks on black and Asian people, allowing for semiotic ambiguity had become a luxury that people could not afford; this was a matter of survival. One gay man recalls the attention his skinhead appearance earned him in the spring of 1981:

> I was out with this girl and this Indian guy; we'd been to the Hambrough Tavern and we were walking back home when we came across this skinhead lying on the floor with a group of people around him, bleeding from the head. They said that three Indian guys had got out of a car and hit him across the head with an iron bar. Little did I realize that ten minutes later the same thing would happen to me. They smashed me across the head with an iron bar, and while I was lying in the road they smashed me in the face with it, so I lost my front teeth and my top lip was split completely open. I'd been on anti-racist demos and all that, I thought it was so ironic that that should happen to me.

He remembers the burning of the pub:

> It was front-page headlines in the news that weekend. I used to go there regularly 'cause I was living in Hayes, and Southall was the next place, and they used to have really really good punk groups there. They'd give you flyers telling you who was coming on, and I remember thinking, my God, the 4-Skins playing in Southall, that's a bit risky. I wanted to go to the 4-Skins 'cause I knew there'd be lots of skinheads there. But it just turned out that I went to see Siouxsie and the Banshees in Bracknell instead. This girl I knew was in the pub that night, she said that one minute they were just sitting there, the next there were molotov cocktails flying through the window. They had to get out of the toilet window to escape; the whole place was up in flames and was surrounded by local Asian people, who obviously thought they weren't going to have some skinhead group playing in their area, basically.

George Marshall is particularly bitter about the media coverage of this event.[13] The press focus on skins as neo-Nazis turned 'original' skins off the subculture and attracted non-skin right-wingers to the cult. The media created a focus which activated, polarized and fixed its results through deterrence/amplification, turning the post-punk skinhead into a neo-Nazi symbol. 'The effect of the media circus around the white power scene meant that all skinheads were seen as being racist by the general public', says Marshall, who goes to great lengths to blame this on fascist appropriation of the image rather then skinheads' sympathies with right-wing politics: 'The truth was that it wasn't so much skinheads turning to Nazism but Nazis turning into skinheads.'[14] But he concedes that 'maybe a lot of skins were fascist at the time . . . Most kids were NF just because it was fashionable . . . NF mods and BM trendies.'[15] Even today, 'there can be little doubt that Blood and Honour represent a sizeable slice of the Skinhead cake'.[16] Blood and Honour, an umbrella group uniting Oi! groups which together formed 'the independent voice of Rock Against Communism' and which was fronted by Ian Stuart of the neo-Nazi skinhead band Skrewdriver, did much to cement the connection between fascism and skinheads. Blood and Honour gigs proved to be rally points for British nationalists, with far-right literature circulating among audiences of skinheads making Nazi salutes.

In the face of the far right's troublingly successful recruitment of the skinhead as a public image, non-fascist skinheads mobilized resistance. In the early 1980s, the extensive media coverage given to fascist skins belied the fact that there was a diversity of political opinion expressed on the skinhead scene. In 1982, skin group the Redskins formed, originally called No Swastikas, foregrounding their socialist politics; skinheads formed highly visible groupings at Anti-Nazi League demos; and Marshall cites the example of the Marxist comic and writer Alexei Sayle, who was rising to fame at the time, as a famous example of the popularity of the skin image amongst left-wing activists.

This political contest over the image of the skin has continued: as nationalist parties in Europe, Australia and the United States adopted the image through the 1980s, Britain saw the emergence of skin fanzines such as *Bovver Boot*, *Zoot*, and *Spy Kids* which attempted to resite the authenticating origin of the skinhead in terms of apolitical style. Skinheads Against Racist Prejudice (SHARP) formed in 1988, claiming to be the representative voice of skinhead subculture. Jamie Crofts feels that, because the press have played into the far-right's hands by continuing to cement a relationship between skinheads and the far right, the situation is worse now for anti-Nazi skins than it was when fascist skin activity was at its height. 'Anti-racist marches in the early eighties in London used to have lots of skinheads marching with them, and it wasn't seen as odd. If I went to an Anti-Nazi League demo, I'd probably get beaten up by some dickhead people who haven't got two brain-cells to rub together. But back then, it hadn't been seen in that way at all.'

But the press coverage was keen to dress the new fascist as the skinhead. Coverage of the Hambrough Tavern incident made the front page of the *News of the World* on 5 July 1981, describing how the arrival of 'coach-loads of Swastika-decked skinheads' had inflamed racial hatred under Enoch Powell's famous quote, 'BLOOD ON OUR STREETS'. The tabloid seized on the incident to define the parameter of acceptable masculinity, literally centring the law between the poles of anarchy and racial otherness: on the front page, under the title 'The Tide We Must Turn', was the comment, 'Skinheads to the right of them. Sikhs to the left of them. And in the middle – bleeding, battered, bruised, bewildered – the British bobby.'

That summer saw an ongoing interest with political extremes in the *News of the World*'s front-page stories, as if to reconfigure political territory. The following week ran with the headline 'EVIL EDITH', telling of a fifty-year-old teacher who was spreading Nazi propaganda; 'Her latest pupils are skinhead "stormtroopers" in town with large immigrant populations.' Two months later, the front page boasted an exposé of 'CLASSROOM CORRUPTERS' – 'left wing teachers from the Socialist Workers' Party who want to teach about sex with kids and "cottaging" – slang for picking up homosexuals'. So lefties are perverts and fascists are skinheads; with the public distracted by the spectacle of political extremism and its new cast of political types, right-wing movements in the political mainstream could go undetected.

Various newspapers then, although claiming to denounce the intentions of the Nazi skinheads, helped to close the interpretation of skinhead symbolism to one reading. Closure to fixed definitions is itself a strategy of the far right and certainly plays into the hands of neo-Nazi organizations: no doubt they wanted the public at large, and minority groups in particular, to be afraid of their skinhead street army. Claiming the authentic skinhead identity, the subculture's history can then be rewritten and its boundaries strictly defined. Thus Ian Stuart of Blood and Honour would frequently reiterate his belief that skinheads were a white working-class nationalist movement, refuting the subculture's black roots and rejecting any possibility of participation or contribution from gay or black people.

The Real Thing

Claims as to who represents the authentic voice of any group are always heated: the debates on sadomasochism and gay masculinity, for example, rage over the questions of who are the authentic men, the real feminists, the truly liberated gay men, and so on. Controlling the representations of a group by defining the terms of constituency is a problem that has dogged radical-left identity politics, more recently saliently played out over the question of whether male-to-female transgenderists should be allowed in women-only spaces. This concern with border control is paradoxically similar to that of the skinheads. Authenticity is particularly important to skinheads as the subculture arose to preserve what was perceived to be a traditional, authentic identity, and the challenge of skinhead identity ever since as been to make that authenticity apparent. How ironic is the subtitle of George Marshall's book, *Spirit of '69: A Skinhead Bible*? Given the proliferation of myths of the origin in the wake of the politicization and factionalism of skinheads in the early 1980s, the book proposes to set the record straight. It authenticates itself on the grounds that it is an insiders' chronicle of the subculture, and that those insiders are real skins. A similar tactic characterizes the promotional material which accompanied Gavin Watson's book *Skins*, from *Spirit of '69*'s publishers in 1994. 'The photos were taken by a skinhead, Gavin Watson, and not some middle class middle-aged bastard getting his kicks by living his life through others', and those pictures 'say more about the skinhead cult than a thousand books written by social workers will ever say about us.'

Adopting a skinhead identity is still a highly potent way for a gay man to claim (or play with, or undo) notions of authentic masculinity. But just as in other areas of skinhead subculture, exactly who is embraced within the group 'genuine skin' is a controversial matter, and entails a questioning of what constitutes a gay skinhead. Obviously the category 'gay skinhead' encompasses much diversity, as this is no more a homogeneous group than the broader categories of 'gay' and 'skinhead'.

Within gay skinhead subculture, debates about authenticity are usually played out around the opposition between 'real skins' and what are popularly derided as 'fashion skins'; real skinheads stake their claim by highlighting their difference from the others who only 'dress up' or are attracted to the look solely for a specific sexual purpose. This was emphasized in Mike Dow's piece on gay skins which appeared in the gay weekly *Out*, in April 1985:

> The real skin is suspicious of the poseur who is someone that dresses in boots, braces and wears his hair short solely to attract other men with the image. This upsets 'real' skins like Mitch.
> 'It annoys me to see poseur skins dress up to get trade. They're just taking the piss!'[17]

Fear of 'fashion skins' is present in the straight subculture too; 'Out now,' pronounced the publicity for *Skins*, 'and not for sale to trendy wankers.' Trends are about social change; skinheads are supposed to represent an intransigent, timeless essence of masculinity. But the proof of one's authenticity as a skinhead should be apparent on sight: it has to be materialized, and that can only be through one's manner and one's dress. The skinheads' fear of trendiness is motivated by the fear that being a skinhead *is* in fact only a pose, only a look. So, potentially, *anyone* could be a skinhead. This motivates an emphatic disavowal of fashion: 'The skinhead is beyond fashion and cannot be assimilated', writes a skinhead in gay arts magazine *Square Peg* in 1986, 'his clothes are "anti-clothes".' In the *Out* article, Mitch removes the skinhead from the subcultural history: 'Teddy boys and mods have come and gone but they all still look as though they're wearing a fashion. Being a real skinhead has nothing to do with a fashion.'

If being a skinhead is about being authentic, then it has to be more than just dressing up, because fashion is only skin-deep. So this tangible shallowness of the skinhead's surface appearance is counteracted by abstract, deep concepts sited at a mythologized interior. 'You can't wear a feeling', says Mitch, 'that's something only your heart can explain.' Genuine skinhead identity is the expression of something unseen and internal: a sense of real commitment to the essence of skinheadism, rather than the mere donning of a fake, surface fashion. In gay subculture, this requires a commitment to a public, full-time, social street identity as opposed to a private, part-time, sexual leisure identity. 'It's my way of life', says Mitch. 'I can't wear anything else. I'm alive when I'm wearing my gear.' Although preserving the gay skinhead's subversion of the division between homosociality and homosexuality, this criterion of full-time social commitment does position homosociality as primary and the sexual aspects as secondary.

This importance of social over sexual motivation is manifest in Jamie Croft's description of what constitutes authentic skin status.

> If you're just into the look 'cause it can help you pick up in bars, you're letting people down with that, you're not operating as part of a [skinhead] community. Being a skinhead means you can bump into another one anywhere and just start talking to them, it's a cult thing. That's definitely one of the attractions for me.

Being a gay skinhead means being part of a skinhead community as well as a gay one. Many gay skins feel no camaraderie with straight skins,

> and that's what distinguishes the real skinhead from the phony ones. You meet people all the time who are standing round posing in bars. There's one in the bars round here all the time: when I first saw him, I thought great, I'll go and chat to him, but he just stuck his nose in the air and looked off, and that's not what a skinhead's about. It's sexual, yeah, but it's social too.
>
> Some gay skinheads get hassle from straight skinheads, and I reckon that's where it comes from. Say you walk past a straight pub with a group of skinheads hanging round outside, if you walk past with your nose in the air, they're immediately going to start shouting abuse at you, 'cause you're not the real thing. If you take on the look, I believe you've got to take on that side of it as well.

The public, full-time nature of his skinhead identity is far more than a matter of wearing the right clothes: he feels he has what he terms a 'responsibility' to the reputation of skinheads. 'If you just do it as a look, you can see people failing, 'cause they can't confront what it's about.'

Significantly, those who played a prominent part in the Gay Skinhead Group (GSG) emphatically also stressed that their skinhead (social) identity is primary to, and subsequently affects, their sexuality, rather than their sexual preference dictating what they wear. One gay skin who ran GSG in the late 1980s was interviewed for *Skin Complex* in his capacity as a member of Skinheads Against Racial Prejudice, a skinhead group whose primary interest is not with sexual identity. In declaring himself 'a skinhead who just happens to be gay', mixing in predominantly straight (skinhead) circles and distancing himself from the gay 'fashion skins' who have evolved from the clone model, his hierarchy of identification places 'skinhead' above 'gay'. For him, his claim to authentic skinheadism is the primacy of his skinhead allegiance, unlike fashion skins, who only exist within the limits of gay subculture, their skinhead identity being secondary to their sexuality.

The same is true of Chris Clive, who took over the running of the Gay Skinhead Group in 1992. As someone who became a skinhead when he left school in 1969, he also had an advantage in arguments over authenticity, as his skinhead identity preceded his gay identity historically as well as ideologically. He would proudly describe himself as a 'genuine skinhead' rather than a gay man whose interest in men had lead him to fetishize skinhead imagery. Whilst accepting fashion skins into the Gay Skinhead Group, when he spoke to me on the subject, he was keen to insist that 'the members in the group, a lot of them are real skinheads, but they've got no animosity against the ones who just dress up, if you like, the fashion skins. Most of them shave their heads or just copy the image. But they're all welcome.'

'Real' skins are united by their commitment to skinheadism; motivation would seem to be the deciding factor in weeding out the fakes. But given that authentic skinhead status is highly prized amongst gay skinheads, there is much investment in authenticating oneself, and the criteria will change from person to person according to the restrictions of each participant's own identity. For example, one 'genuine' gay skin was adamant that class identity was not a deciding factor; he was middle class. This would explain the anxieties on this matter – a lot of gay men who want to be included in this grouping are afraid of their exclusion. Those who wish to claim an authentic status but are conscious of the skinhead component of their identity as appropriation or drag are likely to assert their authenticity all the more vociferously. In a feature on the gay skinhead scene that appeared in the gay weekly *Boyz*,[18] Ian Peacock, discovering that 'some of these guys are lawyers, doctors and students', satirized their lack of one of the primary markers of the skinhead – working-class identity. Nevertheless, the regulars stressed the authenticity of their skinhead identity: one interviewee said, 'We are *real* skinheads. *We're not just impersonating them*. We're not just fashion queens with cropped hair. A lot of these guys here are *genuine* East End boyz' (my emphasis).

Unsurprisingly, all the gay skinheads I spoke to were unambiguous about their authentic skinhead status. But they were unable to articulate *why* the matter of authenticity warranted so much investment and required so much evidence. My own suspicion is that it centres on a problem around the phantom of heterosexuality that haunts the skinhead even when existing within a homosexual context. Gay skinheads have to assert the authenticity of their skinhead identity all the more strenuously as a disavowal of the suspicion that gay men cannot be skinheads. Some gay skins are conscious of this. 'A friend of mine said that somebody was definitely the real thing', said one, 'and I said, "Well, *I'm* the real thing." He assumed that if you're gay, you're not the real thing. That's very common. That's why I make a point of saying I'm the real thing.'

The anxieties around inauthentic masculinity that characterize straight skins' attitudes to gay skinheads – 'They're not real, they're just copying us' – are reproduced within gay subculture and displaced on to the schism between real skins and gay skins, between those who live it and those who 'imitate' or 'just copy the image'. After all, if we consider the gay skinhead as an appropriation, that concedes that the look did originally belong to someone else – straight lads. Chris Clive maintained that 'the skinhead is not originally a gay bloke at all' and tellingly distinguished the real skinhead members of his group from 'the gay ones', the fashion skins.

Adopting *any* identity is an exercise in self-reinvention to some extent; authenticating that identity entails a disavowal of its inventedness. Although signifiers of class can be adopted or changed, biographical facts are beyond the limits of self-reinvention. As the phrase in the *Boyz* feature, 'genuine East End boyz' suggests, geography comes to displace class as a deciding factor in the criteria of authentic skinhead status, because it has biographical implications. So if you cannot choose the conditions of your upbringing, you can at least choose where you want to live.

The diversity of types of gay skinhead can be traced to the various routes by which one may arrive at a gay skinhead identity. So a working-class gay skin who grew up in a skinhead gang obviously has more credibility as an authentic skin than a middle-class man who got into skinheads after a few years on the scene as a clone. The social holds dominance over the sexual, working class is more real than middle class. But this may lead the middle-class skin to go to greater lengths to authenticate his identity. Among working-class gay skins, those who identified from an early age as queers and were subsequently alienated by and excluded from the hard masculinity represented by skinhead culture, who later reclaim a skin identity by adopting the scene image, are less authentic than those who grew up in a skinhead gang. The latter's continuity bears witness to the social primacy of his motivation: the skinhead identity may dominate, allowing him to continue to mix in the straight skinhead circles he grew up in. As such, this is perhaps the most 'authentic' gay skin identity – those who were always/ already skinheads. In his *Boyz* article, Ian Peacock found one who became a skinhead at thirteen: 'I wasn't out then, so I used to hang out with straight skins. I used to get embarrassed when they said anti-gay things. They didn't like it much when I hit 17 and decided to come out.' Given that the look started to disappear for a second time from the early 1980s, the number of gay lads who can follow this route must be decidedly small and ever-decreasing.

A very small number of gay men, in a desperate attempt to authenticate their skinhead identity, wear swastikas, even while voicing anti-fascist sympathies. The reason for this might lie in one gay man's recollection of being a skinhead in the early 1980s: 'the object was to look as hard as possible, and fascist skinheads, the hard-core skins, were the hardest of the lot'. Notice the conflation of fascist with *hard-core*: this sites the fascist skinhead at the centre of the subculture, marginalizing other variants, authenticated in his phallic solidity. So, even though they are aware of the diversity of political allegiances within skinhead subculture, some gay skins submit to the common conception that 'real' skinheads are neo-Nazis and lay a symbolic claim to that realness.

This is the criterion by which one nationalist gay skin judges the 'Real Thing' when he's out on the scene.

I'll grade people, and if someone's got Nationalist badges or union jacks, that's something. Fashion skins wouldn't wear anything like that. White laces – I know on one level it's superficial, it's all image, but trendy skins, fashion skins go near that. They wouldn't 'stoop that low' as they'd say. So if I see patches, Skrewdriver, Nationalist badges or T-shirt, 20-hole rangers, white laces, there's a pretty good chance they're real, 'cause they're showing a bit more commitment.

Of course, it may well be that the skinhead's association with fascism itself draws some gay men to the image. This fascination may be sexual, suggesting SM fantasies. Or it may be social: the sexualized masculinity of the fascist skinhead may motivate some men to become involved in the politics of the far right.

Gay fascists

Most gay skinheads speak of gay and Nazi skins as unproblematically distinct groupings, often defining them against each other. For example, Nick, who was a member of a gay skinhead gang in London in the early 1980s when fascist skins were on the rise, said, 'Gay skinheads weren't racist. They knew about being a minority', whereas he estimated that over half the straight skinheads of the time were involved to some degree in fascist politics. The separate identities kept to their separate territories, but the shared self-representational codes allowed for some overlap, a particularly useful thing for what this interviewee called 'closet gay skins'. These would be active on the straight scene but also venture on to the gay scene, the two subcultures being separate enough to keep the knowledge from straight homophobic peers. Particular geographic sites acted as points of convergence: The Last Resort, the skinhead shop in Goulston Street, was a popular hang-out for hard-core skins, both straight and secretly gay. The Craven was a similar crossover point on the gay scene. 'It was a gay club and pub near Heaven in Craven Street, upstairs with a camera entry system', remembers John Byrne.

> The skinheads moved in there in the mid-eighties; soon, about 98 per cent were skinheads or skinhead admirers. There were a lot of closet skinheads, especially in a place like the Craven, you used to get a lot of 'straight' ones as well as gay ones, but nobody cared. It only closed when they redeveloped Charing Cross station in the late eighties.

The population of this territorial overlap troubles this simplistic homogeneity of the categories gay, straight and fascist skin: 'Some of the really big fascist skinheads later came out', concedes one.

Nicky Crane, by his own admission a devout Nazi who idolized Hitler, was the organizer and recruiter for the Kent British Movement in the 1980s. At the same time he was a regular at the Craven Club. 'He used to come to Brighton on Bank Holidays too', says John Byrne.

> I think he was interested in the young skinheads. I first got chatting to him in 1984 at the Craven Club. At first, I didn't know he was a Nazi, but even when I found out, I carried on talking to him, 'cause he was very friendly. But most skinheads didn't know he was gay. I had a bit of trouble once on a Bank Holiday, because these skinheads swore blind that he wasn't, 'cause he was more renowned for being a Nazi. They told me I was making it up.

A familiar face at gay skin gatherings, Crane even starred in some gay porn videos in the mid-1980s, where he can be seen ordering other skins to lick his boots whilst shouting racist abuse. Knowledge of Crane's sexuality, if not his political activism, was fairly widespread on the gay skin scene long before he came out on *Skin Complex* in 1992. A secretly gay member of Blood and Honour at the time claims, 'People knew about Nicky Crane for years and he was still active in those circles. I suppose no one dared take it up with him. I remember, years ago, *Searchlight* [the anti-fascist journal] claimed that he could be seen on Thursday nights in Heaven. But everybody knew that.' It seems the British Movement were happy for him to carry on as long as he did not publicly acknowledge it.

In the TV interview he confessed he had long known he was gay but had felt unable to come out, although he claims he avoided involvements in queerbashings. When he finally had sex with a man at twenty-six he 'felt like a hypocrite', although it was some time before he felt enough conflict between his homosexuality and his fascist loyalties to motivate him to leave the BM, denouncing his past and claiming conversion to liberal individualist ideology. Such stories are not uncommon: the March/April 1993 issue of *Skinhead Nation* contains a confession by a former White Power skin and 'deprogrammed Nazi' whose discovery of queer politics at seventeen led him to denounce his fascist loyalties.

These histories see an 'out-gay' identity as incompatible with far-right ideology, to the extent that the ritual of coming out entails an almost mystical ideological conversion. But, although it is a common assumption, one cannot assume gay men to be committed to left-wing politics any more than one can assume that all skinheads are automatically fascists. Being a sexual outlaw does not guarantee an essential commitment to counter-hegemonic ideology, and stigmatized subcultures may in fact intensify dominant forms of oppression, albeit unconsciously, as some claim to be the case in the prevalence of masculine codes on the gay scene.

There are obvious historical reasons why the modern understanding of identity politics sites 'gay' as a left-wing phenomenon. The dominant modern notion of gay identity is informed by the radical-left politics of counter-culture revolutionary movements of the late 1960s, and gay rights issues, like those of other oppressed minorities, have since been championed by the left. The British press, eager to secure the government's Conservative majority after it came to government in 1979, exploited this connection and consolidated it in the public consciousness by simultaneously demonizing the 'loony left' and homosexuals in a reductive tautology: the left are not to be trusted because they are all queer perverts; homosexuals are not to be trusted because they are communist subversives. This is illustrated by the two front-page stories from the *News of the World* quoted above (pp. 127–8).

In fact, despite the vociferously homophobic agenda of all right-wing political parties, homosexual identity may not necessarily be incompatible with far-right ideology. While stressing the ideological, cultural and geographic divisions between gay and neo-Nazi skins, Nick recalls that in the early 1980s

there *were* NF skinheads that were gay, but that didn't come out till much much later, because for a lot of skinheads it was unheard of to be gay. They didn't want to come to terms with being gay and that was the way they hid it, because you could be very aggressive and nobody expected a skinhead to be gay.

There is in fact much anxiety among the far right that their political leaders engage in homosexual acts; Ian Stuart repeatedly emphasized on record that 'the leaders of the National Front were homosexual scum'.[19] In a bid to deter skinheads from conscription to Nazism, the Gonads, an Oi! band fronted by the godfather of Oi! Garry Bushell, exploited this anxiety with the song 'Hitler was an 'Omo':

Hitler was a homo
A snivelling little queer
He never got a round in
He never bought a beer.

The band's own implication in this anxiety was disavowed by the 'humorous' lyrical context of the sentiment: according to Bushell, 'Garry & The Gonads was all joke stuff.'[20]

As these suspicions confirm, homosexuality and neo-Nazism may not be conflicting components of an individual's identity. But it is usually expected that an out-gay *identity* conflicts with far-right ideology. Nicky Crane, after all, claimed that once he had come out, he found his politics to be incompatible with his sexual identity: gay neo-Nazis must therefore be closets and not 'really' gay. Gay fascism is discussed in terms of disavowal and suppression: fascist homosexuals are usually 'revealed' to have gone to great lengths to 'conceal' their sexuality.

But this is not always the case. When asked about skinheads and fascism, one club promoter emphasized that 'it has to be said that a lot of skinheads are fascists. They are, one can't deny that. Not necessarily on the gay scene. Although . . .' After a pause, he continued, 'Er, I know a lot of gay skinheads who are fascists, who go on marches with the BNP. The National Front for example is very much a gay organization. There are lots of gay skinheads who are members of that.'

Regular faces on the local macho scene include the members of a group of neo-Nazi gay skins who live in Earls Court, indistinguishable from other gay skins aside from the occasional sporting of sew-on badges of fascist Oi! bands like Skrewdriver and No Remorse. For them, their homosexuality does not contradict their political ideology: they are famous locally for being aggressively defensive of their sexuality. According to a nearby resident, 'You often hear them shout things like, "Yeah, I'm queer, got a fuckin' problem with that?" at people in the street.' Two were interviewed in the front room of their basement flat in shadow for *Skin Complex*. One, Scott, claimed that there were many gay men in the British National Party, which he felt would eventually have to drop its anti-gay stance because of this. 'I've known a lot of skins who are supporters of the BNP', says a friend of Scott, 'but I know even more who have never been skinheads in their lives who are totally right wing, have been members of the Front, who still support it, who are queens. Some are married, some aren't.' He refuses to see the naturalized opposition of homosexual identity with far-right ideology:

It's just as likely that there are going to be gay people who'll join the SWP as there are others who'll be drawn towards the other end. The idea of the gay community is a load of crap – the idea of the Rainbow Alliance that could be created around any disaffected minority. In other words, I must have something in common with a Rastafarian, and an Asian man must have something in common with an African women, is absolutely crap. And that is something I cannot fucking stand. It's like someone in the Anvil telling me that, as a gay man, I can't wear nationalist patches on my bomber jacket. It's bollocks, because there is no gay community.

He too feels that British nationalist political organizations will have to drop promises to recriminalize homosexuality because of their sizeable gay support:

They obviously can't admit to it, because they're supposed to be for law and order and the family. So they can't put 'We'll allow homosexuality' in print in a manifesto. Their agenda is, they'll look at anything to get votes. So banning poofs, they hope, is an extra vote. So that's why they won't drop it from their manifesto.

But there are loads of queens on the right. And I always got the impression that as long as it wasn't obvious, they weren't worried. They still had your subscription.

Nazism and homosexuality

The fact that homosexuals were one of the persecuted social groups in Germany under the Third Reich is often used to naturalize the current organization of sociopolitics which cites support for homosexuality on the left. Gay rights *is* a left-wing issue, because the discourse of rights belongs to the radical left. But being gay does not automatically predispose one to a socialist ideology. I make this point in order to counter the glib generalization that, somehow, any fascist symbolism appropriated to a gay context magically strips it of its fascist value. Gay fascists do not wear white power insignia because they are being ironic.

It may seem paradoxical that gay men should be involved in homophobic political movements, and those individuals themselves are usually not very good at accounting for their involvement. While they claim that there are many other gay men involved, it seems that they are all closeted: homosexual activity would seem to be rife, but homosexual identity is beyond discussion. The work of Klaus Theweleit may shed some light on understanding why neo-Nazis do not see their sexual identity precluding their political allegiances.[21] His complex consideration of masculinist ideology in Nazi Germany provides an explanation of how a fascist cultural organization in fact *requires* homosexual activity, while ostensibly prohibiting it.

The myth of phallic totality, solidity and closure is central to the absolute and strict imposition of the law which characterizes fascist ideologies, and in Theweleit's psychoanalytic argument, fascism is a cultural project of border-preservation and identity-fixation (not dissimilar to that of the skinheads who police local stomping grounds and football terraces against 'outsiders'). According to Theweleit, fascist ideologies see survival as a matter of maintaining the distinctness of the individual's own identity: the monolithic self has to be clearly delineated to counter the anxiety that the enemy, the other, is similar. This is evident in Nazi propaganda, which reveals a conspicuous effort in emphasizing the difference of targeted groups; that difference becomes the very grounds for their victimization.

Sexuality was perceived as hard to organize and contain, and therefore dangerous, because as a fluid form of desire, it compromised this monolithic sense of self. Theweleit goes so far as to postulate that instances of fascist violence are identity-maintenance processes which 'subsume sexual drives under drives for self-maintenance'.[22] Homosexuality was all the more dangerous as it involved a pleasurable embracing of sameness which compromised distinction and difference, threatening to open the borders of the self:

> Homsexuality is a danger to the *Ganzheitsleib* as it is seen as dismantling boundaries in two possible ways: a return to the original 'unformulated return of the libido' and the foregrounding of anality in a society which seeks to ensure that 'the anus, the ultimate sluice, remains persistently hidden'. . . . Anal penetration comes to represent the opening of social prisons, admission into a hidden dungeon that guards the keys to the recuperation of the revolutionary dimension of desire – 'revolutionary' in that it is a 'desire to desire'.[23]

But while 'it was imperative for "real" homosexuality – the potential for actual *homosexual* pleasure – to remain under lock and key',[24] Theweleit argues that the Nazi regime practised homosexual anal intercourse, paradoxically, to disempower this revolutionary potential of homosexuality as a 'desire to desire'. As a compulsive pleasure, homosexuality undid norms, but as an activity of power, anal intercourse could be used to reinforce the difference between self and other in what Theweleit refers to as an act of 'territorialization'. The strict limits within which it was allowed within the Nazi hierarchy preserved it as an exploitable tool in the maintenance of power within and between ranks: 'since "homosexuality" was never publicly sanctioned, it remained shrouded in obscurity; and it was this that allowed it to play a privileged role in the Right's internal power struggles'.[25] If Theweleit's complex thesis is correct, then it may explain why homosexual activity within organizations such as the British Movement may not be paradoxical to the participants, and for them it does not necessarily negate the organization's homophobia.

Misrecognition

Nearly every skinhead I spoke to in the course of researching this book was committed to left-wing political parties, so their sense of betrayal at the emphasis given by the makers of *Skin Complex* to fascist gay skinheads is more than understandable. As one said, 'I didn't like it because it was far too political – the usual thing, all skinheads are Nazis. I don't like that. Programmes about skinheads should be about skinheads and not Nazis.' As angry letters in the gay press in the weeks that followed attested, many felt that the object of the programme was to portray all skinheads of whatever sexual orientation as fascist or supportive of right-wing politics. To be fair, the programme never pretended to be putting the case for gay skinheads. The programme makers seemed to assume a consensus in favour of gay skins, a consensus founded on the avoidance of certain questions which it was the programme's job to articulate. But gay skinheads are rarely discussed beyond the context of fascism: even accounts of the subculture in the scene-friendly gay weekly *Boyz* address this thorny political question.

But given the strength of the skinhead-fascist association, this is only to be expected. Gay skinheads today have to face up to being mistaken for fascists, particularly those in places and times where far-right politics has some support. Michael Dover now lives in the East End with his skinhead boyfriend Steve:

In the past couple of years, we've had a few occasions when it's been misinterpreted. Someone came rushing up to Steve one night and asked him if he was a fascist. And he said, 'Actually no, I'm not at all.' They said, 'But you've got short hair.' He said, 'The hair doesn't make me a fascist.'

In the aftermath of a BNP victory in a local election in 1993,

quite often in the Bethnal Green area we'd have young schoolboy skinheads coming up to us and saying 'All right mate?' 'cause they actually assumed that if you have short hair you're a BNP supporter. Which is why I wear my pink triangle and rainbow flag.

At the same time, as public knowledge of gay skinheads slowly grows, they have started to become identifiable as gay men: 'We've had cars drive by with people shouting "Faggots!" at us.' Jamie Crofts tells of similar experiences.

I know if I walk along the street, people make assumptions about me. The way things are at the moment (it didn't used to be like this twenty-odd years ago, I suppose) people think you're a fascist, which doesn't bother me, but you have to face up to that. If people confront you, as they do, you can put them right. Having to face that actually makes me think about the issue of racism a lot more than I would have done otherwise, I think.

The existence of gay skinheads in a distinct area of gay subculture does however allow space for far-right activists to move on to the scene. Venues which have come to cater for a clone clientele tend to enforce militaristic dress codes and men-only door policies; as such they have always been open to accusations of covert fascism, particularly from radical activist groups. These venues have found in recent years that a growing number of their customers are skinheads; no doubt, they cater for fashion and fetish skins, but who can be sure that fascists are not present as well – who can tell the difference?

Several straight skinheads I spoke to claimed that, among skinheads, gay and Nazis skins are deemed to look more like each other than the other factions within the subculture; both tend to prefer completely shaved heads (fascist skinheads are commonly derided as 'boneheads'), tight T-shirts and jeans rolled up to reveal knee-high Doc Marten boots. Both these permutations emerged in the early 1980s, from a skin scene that had initially been fairly diverse. One gay skin remembers the differing skinhead tribes at the time:

> Hardcore skinheads – they were just racist, and that was their identity, a lot of hatred and stuff; and genuine skinheads, who weren't particularly racist, – more like the original skinheads, because the ska revival was happening as well at the time, two-tone, a suedehead thing. The identity was different according to details. There were 8-, 14-, 24-hole Doctor Martens, and then you had people who just wore DM shoes; trousers could be cut off high jeans, bleached, or Sta Press, bomber jackets or Crombies and it all said something about the type of skinhead you were . . . 24-hole DMs, tattoos on your face and HATE and LOVE on your knuckles meant you were a hard-core skin. Quite a few of the gay guys had their faces done – rent boys went for that. It was protection; tattoos made you dead hard. If there was some twat trying to have a go, he'd think twice.

While neo-Nazi skins had a political reason to look as threatening as possible, gay men had an erotic interest in the hardest possible image too: both groups seemed to agree on what that was, resulting in an intensification of the masculinity signalled by the previous incarnation of the skinhead. According to one gay skin member of Blood and Honour, erotic interest extended to the 'straight' hard-core skins. 'Yeah, they're straight, but sexuality isn't that cut and dried. Because that particular skinhead image is an exaggeration of masculinity, anyone who adopts it . . . well, there's got to be some interest there.' At the start of the skin revival,

> if you saw a skin, he'd have a grade 4 crop and ordinary boots, that was okay then. But as it went on, the more extreme it had to be: head

completely shaved, 20-hole Ranger boots – it's got to be the hardest image possible. The tattoos on the face are really a straight skinhead phenomenon. As the cult was getting more exaggerated, everyone was trying to be that much harder than the next skin. You never saw that many tattoos in the early days, unless they were roses or Mum and Dad. But then it was HATE and LOVE on the hand, bluebirds, CUT HERE round the neck, it got more and more. Earrings, too: you might have started off with one, but then it had to be more, more extreme. Rings through the nipples: I remember seeing skinheads with nipple rings long before it became popular on the gay scene.

A number of gay skins in the mid-1980s sported tattoos on their faces to distance themselves from fashion skins, who could shed their clothes at the end of the day. It was a measure of their commitment to skinheadism to have their identity literally written on the body.

Steve lives in London. He is deeply suspicious of 'poseur' skins and three years ago . . . he had a tattoo on his neck which included the Union Jack and the words London/Skins later modified to London/England. It is seen by many as a provocation . . . it has led to Steve being banned from some gay pubs and often gives him hassle.[26]

That exclusion only serves to attest to his authentic skin-as-outsider status. He said, 'I'm glad I had it done . . . If anyone wants to have a go at me, I'll give 'em a fight.' Hardness signalled working-class status and authenticity; the hard-core skins and gay skins both historically had an equal investment in looking as hard as possible.

I asked Daffyd Jenkins, the Manager of the south London uniform club the Anvil, whether he thought there was any danger that people might misrecognize a fascist skinhead as a gay skinhead. His answer was unequivocally, 'No':

The difference is pronounced – apart from a very small percentage. You can recognize a straight skinhead with your eyes closed and your back turned. With a lot of skins, you can walk into any bar and see some sights and think, God, that's a nasty piece of work. There are a few real hard-core skinheads who are not allowed on the scene; any Nazi regalia is automatically banned by any respectable bar, we just will not allow it.

In July 1993, however, a black man was attacked by three white skinheads at another venue favoured by gay skins, the London Apprentice, which only added to the controversy over allegations that customers had been seen wearing swastikas and other fascist regalia.[27] This led to the Lesbian and Gay Campaign Against Racism and Fascism picketing the pub, calling for its barring of women to be lifted and a strict door policy to keep fascists out. Drag star Lily Savage openly leant his support to the picket.[28] *OutRage!* had campaigned over similar issues the previous year, before a meeting at which Peter Tatchell, representing the gay activist group, Vicky Pengilley, the venue's director, and the LA's customers were satisfied that allegations of racism were totally groundless.

Referring to the sighting of fascist regalia on the premises, Jenkins firmly believes that

> the incident at the LA was a one-off. No matter what checks you put on the door, people still get in. They only have to stuff a couple of arm bands in their pockets and put them on at a later time, and the venue gets accused of all sorts of things. There was an incident in the early days at my club; two guys turned up in leather coats, and when they took them off, they had SS officers' uniforms on. And the annoying thing was, these guys weren't on the scene at all, they'd just worn it as a joke. It caused no end of upset – letters to the press saying Daffyd Jenkins was a nasty Nazi bastard for allowing this, and all the rest of it.

Liberté, égalité, homosexualité?

A skinhead does not signify fascism as unequivocally as the swastika: not all skinheads are Nazis. However, the distinctions between various skinhead categories are not always clear to the reader (and indeed the wearer too, sometimes). In 1981 an article on Jewish skinheads in *The Times* concluded that 'the picture is complicated: there are black skins, and there are non-violent skins'. But 'the lone Asian walking in an unfrequented street anywhere east of St Paul's cannot tell the inner quality of the skinhead individual or pack advancing toward him. All are equally fearsome.'[29]

Within a scene where all *appear* to be equal, a homosexual context where class differences are elided by a uniform dress code, indulging in power games may seem to be a fairly unproblematic activity. But although the gay scene is supposed to provide space for oppressed identities, within this space some are more oppressed than others. In this homo context, race still acts as a marker of difference which signifies the real experience of social hierarchies in an oppressive and racist society. Issues of racial difference and economic reality question who can afford the luxury of playing with power. So when faced with a skinhead, some decoders cannot afford the luxuries of objective idealism and intellectualizing about various reader-positions. As with the swastika, survival may require recourse to a more fundamental approach to semiotic decoding.

It was this question – who can afford to read a skinhead wrongly? – which informed the approach of *Skin Complex*. The most memorable sequence of the programme was an Asian man in a subway, having to walk through a crowd of skinheads approaching from an opposite entrance. Given the traditional skinhead targets, the lone figure was intimidated as both a gay and an Asian man; he was doubly oppressed. This was articulated on the programme by Shaky Shargill, who said he felt 'intimidated by skinheads both as an Asian and a gay man' because 'you can't separate dress from politics: people will see a skinhead, not a gay man or a liberal man dressed as one'. Echoing the radical-political argument of Lesbians Against Sadomasochism and the GLF, he feels that the use of any power role-play cannot be condoned until the material conditions which create those roles are changed: 'Until racism is ended, the scene can't assimilate the skinhead image.'

The programme illustrated the ethnicity of dominant gay masculine modes, placing the skinhead in the historic context of the macho scene, where each iconic permutation (leather queen, clone, cowboy, etc.) was represented by a white man. Just as the skinhead's association with queer-bashing was used to prove the homophobic nature of masculinity in operation on the macho scene, so the skin's association with racism was used to show how the gay scene has been created by and for the needs of white men. Bruce from Shegun (the Black Lesbian and Gay Caucus) identified this tradition as being 'out of touch with our interests and our needs'. He spoke with a collective voice, accompanied by two other black gay men: for him and those he represented, the skinhead in particular was an unequivocally fascist symbol and, as such, directly threatening and oppressive to many people 'on *sight*'.

In 1986, Isaac Julien and Kobena Mercer argued that the rising visibility of skinheads on the white-dominated gay scene was proof of that scene's racism. 'While some feminists have begun to take on issues of race and racism in the women's movement, white gay men retain a deafening silence on race. Maybe this is not surprising, given the relative apathy and depoliticised culture of the mainstream gay "scene".'[30] The absence of any dialogue on attitudes to race was bitterly ironic given 'recent innovations in subcultural style'. In keeping with the tradition of the radical-left's call to read social symbols in terms of how they are actually understood rather than how they might potentially be read, those styles are decoded within the same discursive terms:

> After the clone look in which gay men adopted very 'straight' signifiers of masculinity . . . there developed a stylistic flirtation with S&M imagery, leather-gear, quasi-military uniforms and skinhead styles. Politically, these elements project highly ambivalent meanings and messages but it seemed that the racist and fascist connotations of these new 'macho' styles escaped gay consciousness as those who embraced the 'threatening' symbolism of the tough-guy look were really only interested in the

eroticisation of masculinity.

Julien and Mercer underlined machismo's continuity with fascism through the racism of that machismo: 'If the frisson of eroticism conveyed by these styles depends on their connotations of masculine power then this concerns the kind of power traditionally associated with *white* masculinity.'

Radical feminist considerations of sadomasochism had similarly concluded that it entailed a respect not just for masculine but for white superiority. Any play with fetishes of dominance and power must accept the prevailing social conditions that signify those fetishes, and is therefore against the needs of anyone who is homosexual, female and/or black. In a chapter of *Against SM* devoted to race, Karen Sims states that playing with identities is a 'white women's issue . . . It comes out of a luxury I don't have'[31] and that the SM movement is 'totally against what I see the direction of Black people having to be in this country and it would totally alienate Black people, it would totally alienate other cultures'.[32]

Nevertheless, 'black' is no more a homogeneous group than 'gay' or 'skinhead'. Skinhead identity obviously holds some appeal for those black men present in gay (and indeed straight) skinhead subcultures. Given that consent is manufactured, however, their involvement is hardly proof of the non-racist nature of those environments – certainly not as far as those who object are concerned. However, the totalizing nature of accusations of false consciousness doesn't leave much space for counter-argument. The political trend in the wake of Queer has been to suggest that the eroticism of a politically problematic practice demands overt interrogation, not condemnation: 'You can't police desire' has become the all-too automatic response to the prohibition of sexual activities.

Arguing against claims that black gay men should avoid skinhead identity becomes all the more difficult when one considers the prominence of SM in gay skinhead sex. Racial difference threatens to reimpose social oppression within same-sex SM scenarios when black people participate as submissive partners. On *Skin Complex*, Bruce voiced particular concern at the signification of racial difference on the SM scene, warning that black men must never take the role of slave. The danger is that subcultural appropriation may redeploy dominant ideology and be read by the wider culture as supporting the naturalized status of that existing oppressive structure. Darlene Pagano cites an example of this from a chat show on San Francisco TV devoted to lesbian SM which featured a white and black couple. 'The Black woman said, "But I like to be her slave" . . . I thought it was very racist of KQED to zero in on that and say, "Look, it's okay; everybody's into it."'[33]

Given the problematic nature of the skinhead, wouldn't it just be easier for gay subculture to reject the look outright?

Get 'em off?

The emergence of scene-based masculine gay identities gave rise to a subculture characterized by sadomasochistic practices and the use of symbols which, at some level, derive their significance of power from a male context. In some cases, those symbols can be fascistic. This may be seen to validate the speculative fears of gay liberationists that masculine codes, even when recontextualized, cannot but redeploy violent patriarchal oppression. The gay skinhead identity is a locus of convergence for all three controversial aspects of the macho model's appropriation of dominant 'rough' masculinity: his role as a fetish and an accumulation of fetishes, his association with queerbashing (hence SM), and his (distantly symbolic, if not actual) association with fascism.

One answer might be for all non- or anti-Nazis, gay and straight, to abandon the skinhead look to neo-Nazi movements: after all, as one writer commenting on complaints from skinheads about prejudice against them, 'Perhaps we should say that kids should not dress in a cliche style if they do not want to be treated as the worst of their kind.'[34] If we refuse to read skinheads as anything other than fascists, those who are not may eventually cease using the code, and at least then we would really know who our enemies were on sight.

But the semiotic fundamentalism of skinhead = fascist only serves to reinforce the far right's project of social homogenization and the fixing of identity boundaries. Malcolm Quinn's analysis of the swastika shows how tautologous signification serves a fascistic purpose and warns that the continued power of the closure of its signification bears witness to the success of the German nationalist project, which constructed symbols – and races – as arrested and static, just as it fixed the characteristics it attributed to other races, whose differences this process naturalized. 'The danger of our current situation is that individual memories of Nazi terror will fade, but that the swastika will continue to be used as a racist symbol uniting far-right groups across Europe.'[35]

The photographer and writer David Bailey presented a more ambivalent opinion than the other black gay men interviewed on *Skin Complex*, where he described queers dressing like skins as 'not fighting skinheads but stripping them visually and culturally of their identity'. Whereas confrontation consolidates differences and delineates identities, capitulating to far-right ideology, this tactic subverts those constructs. Fascist ideology is contested by open signifiers and fluid sexualities. Homosexual identity was feared in Nazi Germany precisely because its apparent ideological inability to be contained meant that it could not find space in, and therefore threatened to deconstruct, the strict gender system which relied upon heterosexuality to naturalize the distribution of labour and social hierarchy.

The tactic of appropriation is problematic, as it may provide space for those who in fact do subscribe to the dominant order. But resisting the closure of an image or identity to a single 'natural' meaning introduces a multiplicity which undoes the phallic power of closure inherent in ideologies of the natural. Skinhead images, and the related SM and macho scenes, are insulting to many people and the culture which endows such images with their oppressive significance should of course be changed. But queer appropriation, in attempting to contest their oppressive significance, may bring about such material changes.

Notes

1. Geoff Pearson, '"Paki-Bashing" in a North East Lancashire Cotton Town: A Case Study and its History', in Geoff Mungham and Geoff Pearson (eds), *Working Class Youth Culture* (London: Routledge and Kegan Paul, 1976), p. 52.
2. George Marshall, *Spirit of '69: A Skinhead Bible* (Dunoon, Scotland: Skinhead Times Publishing, 1991), p. 36.
3. Susie Daniel and Peter McGuire, *The Painthouse: Words from an East End Street Gang* (Harmondsworth: Penguin, 1972), p. 81.
4. Marshall, *Spirit of '69*, p. 7.
5. Peter Evans, 'When Being a Skinhead Becomes Part of Life', *The Times*, 16 February 1981.
6. Marshall, *Spirit of '69*, p. 64.
7. Ian Walker, 'Skinheads: the Cult of Trouble', *New Society*, 26 June 1980, p. 347.
8. Marshall, *Spirit of '69*, p. 9.
9. *Ibid.*, p. 33.
10. Nick Knight, *Skinhead* (London: Omnibus Press, 1982), p. 24.
11. Amanda Mickison, 'Little Skins Talking Tall', *New Society*, 5 February 1988, p. 13.
12. Tom Hibbert, 'Who the hell does Garry Bushell think he is?', *Q*, September 1992, p. 6.
13. Marshall, *Spirit of '69*, pp. 105–8.
14. *Ibid.*, p. 138.
15. *Ibid.*, p. 89.
16. *Ibid.*, p. 141.
17. 'Skins:2', *Out*, (April 1985), p. 20.
18. 'Boot Boyz', *Boyz*, 17 July 1993, pp. 13–14.
19. Mickison, 'Little Skins Walking Tall', p. 13.
20. Hibbert, 'Who the hell does Garry Bushell think he is?', p. 6.
21. Klaus Theweleit, *Male Fantasies, vol. 2* (originally published as *Mannerphantasien* (verlag Roter Stern, 1978)) translated by Chris Turner and Erica Carter (Cambridge: Polity Press, 1989), pp. 274–342.
22. *Ibid.*, p. 278.
23. *Ibid.*, pp. 312–13.
24. *Ibid.*, p. 325.
25. *Ibid.*, p. 337.
26. *Out*, March 1985, p. 20.
27. Reported in the *Pink Paper* and *Capital Gay*, 2 July 1993.
28. *Capital Gay*, 2 July 1993.
29. Richard North, 'The Brain Beneath the Bristle', *The Times*, 22 July 1981.
30. Isaac Julien and Kobena Mercer, 'True Confessions', in Rowena Chapman and Jonathan Rutherford (eds), *Male Order: Unwrapping Masculinity* (London: Lawrence and Wishart, 1987), p. 132. (Originally published in *Ten* 8, Summer 1986.)
31. *Against Sadomasochism: A Radical Feminist Analysis* (San Francisco: Frog in the Well, 1982), p. 99.

32. *Ibid.*, p. 103.
33. *Ibid.*, p. 103.
34. North, 'The Brain Beneath the Bristle'.

35. Malcolm Quinn, *The Swastika: Constructing the Symbol* (London: Routledge, 1994), p. 138.

8

'The hardest possible image'

The previously sublimated queerness of working-class youth culture was aggressively foregrounded in punk. Punk harnessed the energies of an underclass dissatisfied with a sanitized consumer youth culture, and it was from the realm of dangerous sexualities that it appropriated its shocking signifiers: British punk congregated around Vivienne Westwood and Malcolm McLaren's shop Sex in the Kings Road in the mid-1970s, which sold sexual fetish gear as fashion; and the styling of the Sex Pistols was informed by the image of the dangerous rough rent boy. Punk showed that dangerous, threatening, aggressive masculinity was not necessarily heterosexual. Extreme narcissism, the invitation to scorn, became a measure of one's hardness.

It was this valorization of outrageousness which provided a welcome space for gay teenagers to stumble towards articulating a sense of sexual identity. And it was the desire to shock that saw the skinhead emerge, harder than ever.

'Oh my God, the skinheads are back'

'I'd been so introverted', remembers Tony:

> When I got to sixteen I thought, I've got to have a girlfriend; if I get a girlfriend, maybe I won't feel this way. I kept hoping it was just a phase; I really felt like the odd one out, like there was something different about me. So about at about nineteen, twenty, I was going to discos, they were the in thing, but I'd just stand there. My friends would be dancing, and I'd think, what am I doing here? I was really introverted. I wouldn't dance to fast records – maybe just have a smoochie at the end.
>
> So when the Sex Pistols came along I just felt, that's really me. I really identified with it. I needed something to concentrate on where I wouldn't have to think so much about the way I was feeling. The first time I saw punks was actually in 1975. Unless you were part of that crowd, you wouldn't know, it was a very underground scene. I remember being at this very posh disco in Maidenhead on the river. It was quite an in place – people would come from London. I remember standing in there and these four punk girls (although I didn't know they were punks) walked in. I thought, My God, they look brilliant. People were completely shocked.

One had green hair, mad make-up, no bra, green pierced nipples, a see-through pink plastic mac, knickers, fishnet tights and Wellington boots. You wouldn't laugh – you'd think, she looks brilliant, but shocking. When I saw the Sex Pistols, I thought back to those girls and I thought, yeah, that's for me. It brought me out of myself – although not totally, 'cause I still had that sort of dark secret. I changed overnight. One minute I had long, 'haven't-had-my-hair-cut-for-a-year' sorta hairstyle; the next I had bleached, cropped hair. And I went out; the first time, I went to a punk club on my own. I was one of the first punks in Slough, so I went to this punk club in Reading, I went down and I didn't know anybody and within half an hour I knew loads of people. The more I went, the more people I knew. It was so different from discos – nobody talked to you in discos. In time, I got more adventurous and my appearance got more elaborate.

Effeminacy could signal aggressiveness; hard masculinity was not necessarily confined to heterosexuality. So, by the early 1980s, the cultural shift in attitudes to homosexuality and masculinity was pronounced enough for *some* kids growing up gay to start thinking and acting beyond the constraints of the preceding generation. Growing up in Surrey in the 1960s, Daffyd Jenkins had believed that, 'if you weren't a screaming Mary, you weren't a proper queen. The few that were around that were not overtly faggot were oddities in a way' – hence his surprise when a gang of gay skinheads first walked into the Union Tavern in 1969. Fifteen years later, Richard, who now runs the gay skin venue Silks, found skinheads gay-looking even before he came out, so his discovery of gay skins on the scene came as no surprise. 'I think [the skinhead] has always looked gay . . . I've always taken the view for years that by and large the skinhead culture, people who want to look like that, are mostly gay or tend to lead that way.' So the existence of extremely masculine gay men went from being inconceivable to being the expectation – at least to the perception of would-be homosexuals. Yet public knowledge of skinheads had changed little in this time; it was the understanding and expectations of men who identified as gay which had started to alter in the intervening period.

Tony saw a new generation of skinheads emerge from the punk scene. He could remember their predecessors from 1969, when he was thirteen and living in a small town in Oxfordshire:

I can remember people a bit older, fourteen, in Crombies and things like that, hair not skinhead but very short style. My sister was a skinhead too at the time, Crombie, Sta-press, loafers. But she went to the youth club, it was a small town, there wasn't anything like a skinhead scene there. When I was younger I was in awe of her, she was like a Tomboy anyway, with a skinheady haircut, Ben Sherman, braces. I remember going to a village hall disco and there were skinheads there all at one end. Obviously it was a different scene if you lived in London.

I can remember two guys in my class who were skinheads, they were aggressive. There was them and there was the older gang, but if you dressed that way they all stuck together. The only skinheads I mixed with were the ones in my form. I wouldn't hang out with them, they always got into trouble. One of them got his eye shot out with an air-gun pellet once, I remember. I only saw them in gangs at discos, at the youth club.

Skinheads came back in '79, '80. The first time I remember seeing a huge crowd of skins was one day I was in the Kings Road in a pub. The whole place was punk and there were two bars and a big plate glass window. We were just sitting there and the next minute the whole of this huge window came in, it completely shattered, almost like it was in slow motion, there was glass everywhere. Everyone ran out of the pub and the whole pub was surrounded by skinheads. You couldn't get out of the pub. Girls were screaming. It was so dramatic – one minute literally there were just no skinheads at all around, the next there's a big gang of them, about seventy. The police came eventually and I walked past this off licence with this girl I was seeing at the time and I remember this woman pulling down the shutters saying, 'Oh my God, the skinheads are back', like they'd had a ten-year break and they'd suddenly returned. She was petrified.

Suddenly it was punks versus skins. It seemed to me that skinheads were always looking for fights. I was attacked by two skinheads. They approached me – I as going to a punk club in Reading, there was a big gang of us walking down the road but I was straggling behind, and I just turned round and there were these two huge skinheads. One said, 'Give us some money.' I didn't have a chance to say anything, he just head-butted me in the face. I've still got the scar – I needed four stitches in my face. They were just looking for trouble.

When I was living in Slough, there were skinheads who mingled with punks, there were skinhead gangs but also ones who liked going to punk groups would mix with us. There was a phase when skinheads were very anti-punk and then they went through a stage where we all went to the same clubs. There was a pub in Islington, the Blue Boy, where the Angel tube development is now, called Skunks – skins and punks – which tried to mix the two, but it always seemed there was a bit of an atmosphere, and there were always odd stragglers who would try and cause trouble. I went to the Moonlight Club in West Hampstead once, and I was with a group of about fifteen, and this punk lad who I used to hang round with, I used to really fancy him but I wouldn't say anything, he was a boxer. We were waiting to get a train back to Hayes when these two really really big huge skinheads came up to him and started abusing him, saying look at your hair and so on. They were really big guys – I was shitting myself thinking I know what's going to happen. He didn't even say anything, he just knocked them both out. He just punched twice and knocked both out. When we got the tube they were still lying on the platform. And the thing is this guy was really quiet, you wouldn't think . . . but he was a boxer, so he knew what the was doing.

In all seven years I was a punk there were very few punks I fancied. I always, always fancied skinheads. My fantasy was skinheads. Skinheads thought they were harder than punks 'cause punks wore make-up and things, although obviously there were hard-looking punks. I'd go to punk gigs and you'd get skinheads there, they were the ones who always took their shirts off. Some punks would take their shirts off, but skinheads always had really horny bodies, and they'd always all dance together, they'd start wrestling.

But for Tony, there was still some distance between identification and desire. Although at one point he was moving towards skinhead, he never fully adopted the image because of its fascist association, and being a punk brought him enough suspicion as it was. Skinheads were also unequivocally straight for him anyway.

I went around with straight skinheads for so long, so when I see skinheads now in a gay club, it seems odd. For me, when I found out there were gay skinheads, I couldn't connect the two. I thought, they're complete opposites. You look at them and think, yeah they've got a good image, but it's like saying you want to get off with a straight person. I suppose a lot of gay people do, but then, if you get off with a straight person, they're not straight.

For him, skinheads are definitely a straight thing: 'I used to find the scenario very gay anyway – all over each other, arms round each other, shirts off – it's weird.'

'With other gay skins, the sex was very masculine'

Even though the skinhead had (secretly) become institutionalized as a gay type, awareness of this barely extended beyond the knowledge of the participants. For most gay men in the early 1980s, skinhead still meant straight and violent, but the subculture nevertheless provided some answers to working-class youths who felt as alienated from gay subculture as from the rest of society.

Nick grew up at the tail-end of the first emergence of the skinheads, as number four crops were growing into the longer styles of the smooths.

Early on in 1972, '73, the fashion was a throw-off from the sixties' skinhead. I was at school then. I wasn't a skinhead; I had hair, but I wore the clothes. It was sort of mixed; feather cuts, that was a continuation of the skinhead. Sometimes you'd wear Sta Press with boots or loafers, but always a Ben Sherman. It was Crombies then, no bomber jackets; that came in much later. You'd have a handkerchief with a stud through it in your Crombie and your sharpened comb and Durex – 'cause I was going with girls then. Everyone had a metal comb, and you'd sharpen the end of it into a point. And I can remember going to football matches with my mates in Coventry, we'd go to see Wolves, Coventry City, with razor blades in our Doc Martens.

An unhappy childhood and a growing awareness of his sexuality led him to become a skinhead in the late 1970s.

Where I came from, a council estate in Coventry, you weren't gay. Nobody was gay. It didn't matter if you felt gay, you just *weren't*. I went to a normal school and I was an outcast really. I stopped school when I was fourteen, fifteen, because I was too frightened to go; instead, I used to do things like paper rounds. My mates were all drop-outs as well, so they all used to go down the arcades, all on the pin-ball machines, taking trips to the arcades in Leicester Square; that was where everybody used to go, because there wasn't anything else really.

I felt oppressed by everything: by working-class straight guys – if I went to a pub, if I got on a bus late at night, if I went to school, wherever I went I got beaten up or attacked or verbally, in every way. My parents didn't want to know me; I left home when I was sixteen, I left school a week later. I didn't really have any sort of education.

I was quite angry and oppressed in the background I was coming from, and I think that oppression took the form of anger. And the most angry, most aggressive, most violent image I could think of was the skinhead. And also at that particular time, I found skinheads very masculine and I was attracted to masculinity. So basically I took on their identity, if you like. It gave me an identity which I was seeking, and I couldn't really have at that time . . . Being a skinhead gave me an identity, values, self-worth, all the things I was lacking in myself. It was all about finding out who I was, and at that time I was that person, I was an angry young man, and there were a lot of very angry young men.

I think it was a protective identity because it frightened a lot of people and kept them at bay. They were much less likely to come at you if you took on a harder identity. But having said that, you're walking round as a skinhead and other straight skinheads would find out you were gay because – well, people just find out, and that's when the problems arise, they see you on the street and you'd get it from them. You wouldn't get it from the general public . . . Yes, I think it was more a protective thing than anything else, because if you frighten people, they keep their distance.

The effeminate model was losing its stronghold on the scene but macho gay identities had still to firmly establish themselves, particularly in the provinces.

Where I came from in the Midlands, there were a few gay skinheads in Birmingham, and a couple in Coventry, but there wasn't really a very big gay scene. The London scene was very different then; there weren't a lot of masculine gay men around, there was no gym culture at that time, whereas now there is, with men expressing their masculinity through muscles. Back then, that was more in America, you didn't really get a lot of that here, so people were looking for other ways to express that. And I think guys who felt like that expressed it in that way. I was very aggressive, towards gay men as well. You know, tripping up queens, intimidating them, that sort of thing, especially the really camp ones. The skinhead image was rebellious, and one of the things we were rebelling against was 'gay'. We grew up with Larry Grayson and John Inman and we thought, we're not like that.

And then I started coming up to London. I was eighteen, and Subway was going on then, and the Meat Rack; it was a really interesting time. Everybody was the same; Boy George was in a squat, Judy Blame was doing jewellery, everybody integrated and knew each other. And then you went on the gay scene, you met other gay skinheads and you all stuck together, and everybody knew everybody and you wouldn't go with anybody else. All the gay skinheads knew each other and they stuck together. There were a couple of gay skinhead friends from those days in Nick Knight's *Skinhead* book, although they were meant to be straight; a couple of them I used to go out with. All my boyfriends were skinheads. My first boyfriend was a photographer with long hair; he was supposed to be straight, although I knew he dabbled, and I got him drunk, determined to seduce him. I said to him, if we get together, I've got to shave your hair off, you've got to be a skinhead. And I can remember, the first time we ever slept together, I did that. I gave him a number one – no, not even number one, I shaved his head. And then we slept with each other. And we went out with each other for three years.

Nick found that most of the other gay skins he met had also fled homophobic home environments, arriving in London with nowhere to live.

It was definitely a class thing, we were working-class guys. At that particular time I didn't meet any middle-class skinheads. They didn't exist, because middle-class skinheads couldn't have coped with the street, which is basically what skinhead is all about. It's a street culture, it wasn't a fashion thing, 'cause you'd get your head kicked in. I remember getting off the tube at Leicester Square and getting stopped by straight skinheads;

'You're a fucking queer', that sort of stuff. There was a lot of hassle from straight skinheads to gay skinheads. And then there were the others that were more tolerant, really.

People were frightened of skinheads then; frightened, but attracted. For some people that fear was combined with sexuality. At that time there weren't a lot of gay skinheads, so you were part of an élite set. You were more sought after in one way, and in another way more rejected, 'cause so many middle-class queens wouldn't have anything to do with you. But the gay skinheads themselves were the most élitist, they were real snobs. It was like, you know, you couldn't go with that one because he was bald – that's why he was a skinhead; he's not a real skinhead.

Being a 'real skin' compounded the issues of class and sexuality:

It's a big thing for skinheads because they want to believe in themselves. The harder they were, the more they identified with what they believed the image stood for. It's all that thing about being the Real McCoy and street credibility – that's very important, more for skinheads than any other group, 'cause skinhead is a working-class identity, and street credibility is a working-class thing. It's the coolness, knowing where you're coming from, knowing the score, being astute at a street level – I can't explain, it's really difficult . . . something, an essence of working-classness. There's as much snobbery in the working classes as there is in any other class – that's where it comes from, I'm the real thing, 'I come from this' and 'I am this.'

Hardness was proof of one's authenticity, and at this time homosexuality and masculinity were deemed to be incompatible even by gay skins themselves.

The gay men always used to say they were straight, 'cause it meant you were real. I used to do it myself. You had to look hard. That's manifested in whatever . . . more tattoos, for example. At one time, if you didn't have your face tattooed, you weren't the real thing. Tattoos were another sign of how hard you were. You'd have beauty spots on your face, and especially things on the neck – I remember 'CUT HERE', really naff things. It's a working-class thing, spots on your knuckles, really rough DIY jobs in Indian ink. Quite a few of the guys had their faces done – rent boys went for that. It was protection; tattoos made you dead hard. If there was some twat trying to have a go, he'd think twice. I was going to have my head tattooed at one stage, but luckily I went for my arm instead.

According to Nick, although it was yet to be accepted on the scene, skinhead identity operated as an access point for lower-class men alienated by the existing scene identities. 'It meant us working-class kids could spot each other immediately. There was a loyalty there: we were a subculture within a subculture.' The direct signalling of working-class identity still embodied in the gay skinhead leant itself to an older model of working-class involvement in the middle-class homosexual subculture of the early twentieth century.

When I came to London, the look was associated with rent boys and that sort of thing. I think a lot of working-class lads, eighteen, nineteen years old, they were involved because they had no money . . . I think it was a matter of poverty for a lot of people. And you could go to a gay club and immediately, without doing anything, people would know in an indirect way.

To be quite honest, I think a lot of those guys were on the game, working-class guys who had run away and come to London. A lot of them used to go to the Golden Lion pub; at that time, that's what you did. There were a lot of skins there. There were also a lot of strange guys – quite a lot who were drug-fucked. You had to be very careful; they were insane. You'd pick up phone numbers and you'd go and see these guys later. I used to know one guy, he used to have five of us round his house. He was an older guy, about forty-five, trying to be nineteen. He was like Daddy really, we used to hang around him and he used to look after us. There was never anything sexual – he just liked to have us around, watch us.

I used to come up here and everybody used to like the look of me, so I got to go to all the clubs. I used to go out with a very beautiful guy called Joe; he was a skinhead who used to dance at Heaven. He was really beautiful. He used to model in *Zipper* and all those magazines. I didn't do that, but that's how they sort of got on. He'd have older guys looking after him, and I'd have older guys looking after me, and we were going out with each other. But I was good-looking and you survive, don't you? I suppose I traded in on that. I used to get older men who liked me and looked after me rather than a lot of guys who'd go out and do whatever . . . But you are still young and you are still vulnerable.

We either went with each other or other men for money. With other gay skins, the sex was very masculine: wrestling, rough, not much kissing, often none. You'd have a different type of sex with a gang member. They'd only sleep with middle-class men for money. They hated the middle classes because they were oppressed; it was their way of being rebellious.

Middle-class punters expected skinheads to be heterosexual:

I used to pretend I was straight, because that was their fantasy. These men expected us to be hard. The middle classes associated skinheads with being rough and therefore they could have rough sex which they craved but which they wouldn't allow themselves to express. The middle classes were more educated, which repressed some things. And you got a lot of these men who wanted to be dominated, or whatever. A lot of them just wanted me to kick the shit out of them, call them queer bastards, that sort of thing. I think back now . . . how could I have done that? But in those days, I needed the money, so I didn't think about it, I just did it.

The continuity of his role with the established tradition of rough trade was fairly evident to Nick.

The image of working-class masculinity . . . I think it's quite an old-fashioned thing now, but I should imagine, years ago, middle-class men would have a bit of rough on the side; manual workers, soldiers, obviously masculine. I think that's more what it was about, fantasies about rough, working-class masculinity; domineering.

It's quite sad, really, when you look at it, but at the time it wasn't, 'cause you're young and naïve and you don't realize you are being exploited. But maybe you can ask the question, who's exploiting who? We were oppressed in [terms of] money and status and they were repressed sexually, and somewhere along the line we fulfilled each other's needs. But I think it *was* exploitation for a lot of people, 'cause you didn't have any choice really, it was that or starve. A lot of them didn't have anywhere to live; it was the working classes, people who came from broken homes, didn't have anywhere to go, were on drugs, were alkies; from that point of view, they were exploited. Definitely. We made the most of a bad situation, really. You had to survive. I mean, I had some really good, good times, really fabulous.

It was, however, the cross-class liaisons made possible by the rent scene that gave Nick his chance to escape.

I stopped being skinhead when I went away with someone very rich; he educated me and took me to Europe. I suppose I became more sophisticated, and in the society I mixed in then, being a skinhead just wasn't appropriate. In Europe, it was more associated with fascism, and it was embarrassing. I didn't have to protect myself 'cause I wasn't on the street anymore. And I became more educated, discovered literature, met people who could speak five languages . . . I was very lucky. And as I got older, I came to terms more with my sexuality, so I didn't feel the need to be so masculine all the time.

The interaction of London's skin and rent scene was acknowledged by the broader culture. An article called 'The Doc Marten Angels' by Martyn Harris in *New Society* followed the movements of poppers-sniffing skinheads Muttley and Zeb, 'both', says Muttley cheerfully, "right fascists"', who, much to the journalist's amazement, would look after young male Piccadilly prostitutes – for a price:

> The skins also tap the rent boys at the Dilly as part of an informal protection racket. Then if a friendly rent boy has trouble with a customer, Mutt or one of his friends will do him over. In Brewer Street, a rent boy comes up to Mutt and hands him a couple of Benson and Hedges, so it's true. It really is.[1]

Contesting the belief of sociologists that the working-class homeless rent scene was a solution to problems of economics, not sexuality, Nick was adamant that the rent skins he knew were all definitely gay. 'A lot of those straight skins, and even the closeted gay ones, wouldn't have gone near that, they were too frightened. They might have picked someone up, beaten the shit out of them and got the money off them, but that's all.'

Nick would go to Heaven, the Coleherne and the Bell. For the most part, straight skins 'who were NF and violent' and gay skins stuck to separate territories. But there was a crossover section who 'pretended they were straight'. 'The straight ones that were in the closet all used to go to the Last Resort.' This shop on Goulston Street, near Petticoat Lane market in London's East End, was famous at the time for selling authentic skinhead gear; it was also notorious for conscripting skinheads into far-right politics. Ian Stuart of the Oi! band Skrewdriver and a leading figure in Blood and Honour was a regular face there, distributing neo-Nazi propaganda to the customers. Nick went there himself, with the skinhead performer Mick Furbank, whose act, Crucified Skin, romanticized the skinhead as a persecuted outsider through a mythology that drew on Buddhist monks and warrior legends. He was also responsible for some of the most popular T-shirt designs to be sold at the Last Resort. Mick Furbank later came out as bisexual in an *NME* article and made it into *Gay Times*; 'he became an icon for us gay skinheads, because he was really hard, really scary, and he admitted to going with blokes. It made a big difference.'

> It was very intimidating at the Last Resort, there were loads of fascist skins, and they hated gay skinheads. These closets would have a scene with you, but it was all very quiet, nobody knew and you weren't going to tell anybody 'cause you'd get your head kicked in. Some of them were out on the gay scene but in the closet on the straight scene. And the straight guys didn't know, 'cause they didn't go to gay clubs.

The gay skinhead identity provided an (albeit problematic) access point to gay identity for working-class gay men intimidated by the association of 'gay' with the effeminate model.

I had a few mates who'd go to straight clubs but not to gay clubs; but later they'd go, but only with people like me. We were acceptable to them 'cause we were gay skinheads, we weren't like the other faggots. They hated other gay men, or rather resented them. They didn't think they were real men. They'd take the piss out of them, 'cause they [the gay men] were . . . straight, as in not streetwise. 'Fucking wankers', they'd go, 'they don't know what the score is, they haven't been there . . .'

Whereas gay skinheads had adopted the skinhead identity because it refuted dominant expectations, rendered them highly desirable on a gay scene which valorized 'real' masculinity, and provided protection on the straight street, these 'closet skins' adopted the image as a disavowal of their homosexuality.

Being gay challenged your masculinity. So what they'd do is take on a really masculine image and go, 'I'm not gay, I'm not gay', and go queerbashing, 'cause they were fighting themselves, some of them. Some of the worst hardcore skinheads were gay, 'cause that was their fear, looking at what they were, so beating them up was a way of dealing with it. And when they were older, I suppose they faced up to it.

The similarity of the self-presentational strategies of gay and neo-Nazi skins can be explained by their shared investment in looking as terrifyingly hypermasculine as possible; the motivation of those who stood somewhere between the two groups shows that it was not for dissimilar reasons. Nick usually spoke of gay and Nazi skins as unproblematically distinct groupings, often defining them against each other:

Gay skinheads weren't racist. They knew about being a minority. I had an Asian skinhead boyfriend at that time; he never had any trouble. But there was a lot of racism among straight skinheads. It was like, 'He's all right 'cause he's one of us', about looking for acceptance. Not all skinheads were BM members, but among the straights, I'd say 60 per cent were, and the other 40 per cent were more like ska skinheads, like rude boys, more into reggae beat and that stuff.

But the confused territory between the groups, populated by 'closet skins', troubles this simplistic homogeneity: 'Some of the really big fascist skinheads later came out.'

Although Nick's original incentive in adopting the skinhead identity was to contest dominant expectations about his sexuality, it contributed to the establishment of an identifiable gay type for those who would come out later. His perception of the way his gay skinhead gang operated underlines the homosocial structure of skinhead identity and its troubling concordance with heterosexual patriarchal expectation:

It was a very a masculine thing. Men were men. And it was quite tribal, an expression of masculinity, much like athletes in Ancient Greece, it's an expression of the same sort of feeling where masculine men are attracted to masculine men. And the skinhead was the most masculine image at that time.

Kim was one of the hard-core British Nationalist skins who crossed the clearly marked boundaries of hard-core and gay skin scenes that Nick identified.

I became a skinhead in '82. I was only nine or ten when the original skinheads were around, but I could remember them. Nowadays with youth cults, anything goes, nobody's surprised at anything anymore. There isn't even a main cult. But in those days there was lots of coverage. There was something about them even then that I found attractive: I didn't know what it was. I was probably more aware of liking them than I was of being gay then. That was about 1969. Then it all died.

I left school in 1977, punk had only just started, and everybody was walking around in flares and wide ties. Once the punk thing had peaked and it went into Oi!, skins were back, and I'd always wanted to be one. It was even better than the first time in a way, 'cause everything was more exaggerated: the hair was shorter, the boots were bigger, the jeans were shorter. It as a caricature of the first time around, but it seemed much better. When the skins came back at first, they started off with a number four crop, and then they began cutting it shorter as the look became more and more exaggerated. I remember starting work in '78 as a railman at Whitechapel Station – there was a Milwall *v.* West Ham match. The Oi! thing had come along, there were loads of skins wall to wall, but there were hardly any boneheads. Most had number three crops growing out. But the next stage was for people to have Union Jacks dyed, and then shaved, into the crop, and then it was bald heads.

I can remember the first time I went to the Last Resort shop. It was winter at the time, there was snow on the ground; I walked past a couple of times to pluck up enough courage to go in. They sold all the gear; you paid through the nose for it, but it was worth it sometimes. For example, in the early eighties, you couldn't get button-fly red tag Levis *anywhere*. Sometimes, when they ran out of jeans and people still wanted them, they'd ask you to wait while they 'checked the warehouse'. What they did in fact was buy a pair round the corner and sell them on to you with a fat mark-up. I used to get my T-shirts at the Last Resort on a Sunday. It used to shut about two o'clock, when the market shut.

He too found the Last Resort troublingly straight:

You'd just stand there, and then what could you do? And frankly, with the gay side as well, you never wanted to get too involved, you didn't want to say too much. None of the pubs round there would serve skinheads, 'cause they'd lose all their custom. All except the Station Bar – it was run by British Rail, they'd serve anybody. I remember going in there before I became a skin. It was absolutely packed, and it wasn't a Bank Holiday Monday or anything, and it was like a dream come true, my eyes were popping out.

I used to read about the Oi! nights at the 100 Club and at Skunks in *Sounds*, and I'd always wanted to go, but none of my friends were skinheads, and at that time I was twenty-one – most people would say, 'You're bloody well too old for that!' But it was something I'd never fulfilled. The first time I went to the 100 Club, I went without a crop. And I thought I had to get it done after that.

They used to sell these Last Resort calendars, and although I was more interested in the skinhead side than the gay side, it seemed incredible that there were all these topless blokes in it. One of the main photographers responsible for those calendars was gay. But the idea that the skinhead scene would be all about lads taking their shirts off and dancing together, that was incredible, I didn't believe that would happen. But of course it did. I used to go to gigs at the 100 Club and they were really horny. I wasn't there as a gay man having a fantasy about what was around me, like some paedophile walking down the beach looking at kids in swimming costumes; I was there as a skinhead. But there was more than one emotion being released at the same time. When I was standing there 'Sieg Heil'-ing, that was releasing an emotion within me. It wasn't put on like a costume to go there, that was in me. And there was the other side of it as well. The two together in parallel. Fortunately the two didn't mix.

Interestingly Kim talks of the sexual and political attractions of the gatherings as being so separate as to be almost directly conflicting. And sometimes they did conflict: 'The night of the Bermondsey by-election I was at a Skrewdriver gig at the 100 Club, and Ian Stuart got up and slagged off Peter Tatchell, called him that queer foreigner, and everyone cheered, and I did too.'

There was no doubt in Kim's mind that he was gay.

I started going to gay places around the same time as when I became a skinhead. There were clones around in those days, but they tended to be quite old and were always a complete turn-off for me. There were gay skins, I soon found out, that used to go to places like the Black Cap, but they were skinheads first. There were gay mods in there, gay soul boys in there – they just happened to be gay, but the cult came first. Now it's the other way around, in most cases.

My first regular, of all places, was the Laurel Tree in Camden Town. Now it's a happening rock place thanks to the Britpop scene, which is incredible, all these groups have played upstairs and everything, because back then it was one of the worst, most run-down pubs on the gay scene. We only went there 'cause you could get a seat and it was quiet enough to have a conversation. Then we used to go to the Black Cap and the London Apprentice – there were quite a lot of skinheads there, a lot just dressed up – but I think most are like that. That was about '84, '85. Apparently the Asylum at Heaven on Thursday had loads of gay skinheads. Normally because of work I couldn't go, but when I went there was fuck all there. It was a real disappointment.

I knew some gay skins to talk to at the Black Cap and at Bolt's club in North London where they used to have a gay skin night. I thought they were like me – right-wing skinheads that happened to be gay – but I used to feed things into the conversation step by step and check out their reaction, and they weren't, they were just students who had put on the gear for an evening to live out their fantasies, and then go home and get changed and go back to art school the next day.

I used to see Nicky Crane at the Bell. Loads of gay skins used to go there. He got barred: there was someone in a wheelchair and he made the comment 'they should all have been in the camps'. There was a big fuss about it in *Capital Gay*. The scene can be very sensitive about that sort of thing. I've got two bomber jackets, one with No Remorse and Skrewdriver patches, and one that's plain. It depends where you're going, because some venues won't let you in. Some places don't worry. But the LA, they won't let you in there with those badges on. I've had abuse from gays. I was out once wearing No Remorse patches and someone came up to me who was pretty much the worse for wear and said, 'Oh, so you're into that shit then are you?' I told him to piss off. I know skins who'd've decked him.

Nick's observation that the straight and gay skin scenes were very much separate is born out by Kim who, although he saw no contradiction in being gay and being a nationalist, lead a double life.

On one occasion I'd been out to the Black Cap, and I was travelling on the Northern Line from Camden Town, and Ian Stuart was sitting opposite, on his way back to King's Cross. And although he didn't know my name, he recognized me from The Last Resort. He was like, 'Hello mate, how are you, where've you been?' and I said I'd been out drinking. 'What pub?' I had to think quickly, carefully make one up, because he'd probably been in most of them and got barred from most of them. And with everything I said, I was just digging myself deeper and deeper. But luckily nothing came of it. There was another time when a skinhead asked me where I'd been, and I can remember struggling for an answer, 'cause you never knew how much they knew. They'd probably have been really surprised if they'd known the truth. These days, right-wing skins know about the gay adoption of skinhead clothes because there've been things in *Blood and Honour* about it. But in the mid-eighties, it was unheard of.

This growing awareness has made them nervous. 'Yeah, 'cause you're under attack from all sides. A lot of skinheads are paranoid, especially ones who've had a lot of tattoos and can never escape from the image at all.' The growing perimeter of this knowledge has stopped the skin image from allowing him to pass. 'I never felt that people thought I was gay when I walked the street. But now I know they do.'

In the early 1980s, Nicky Crane was the only face from the gay scene that he ever saw at straight venues:

I knew he was gay and he knew I was. He'd never acknowledge me at the gigs, he'd look right through me. And yet, when I saw him at a gay venue, he'd nod. But he had to separate that side of himself. I always got the impression I wasn't the only gay person there: I couldn't have pointed people out, I didn't actually know any other gay men there. But for me it was always just below the surface.

There used to be this Dutch guy who'd film the gigs. It was really obvious he was gay to me: I talked to him and he tumbled straight away, so we'd chat. On one occasion, when Skrewdriver was playing West Kent, he needed someone to hold the light. He couldn't really trust the other pissed up glue-sniffer boneheads, so I did it. My claim to fame is that I was on stage with Skrewdriver helping to film them. He knew I was gay and I knew he was gay. But to me, the whole scene, it was all so obvious that it was all there just beneath the surface, it didn't need to be stated.

Kim has always fancied only skinheads. 'If he wasn't a skinhead I wasn't interested.' He has only ever met sexual partners on the gay scene.

You never knew what you were dealing with in a straight venue. No matter how pissed you'd get, to me there was always that . . . after all, you were dancing with people stripped to the waist, arms round each other anyway. So you could do all that without anyone ever tumbling what was going on. But who knows? Perhaps the guy next to me was doing the same thing. It wouldn't surprise me. There's always an element of self-preservation in people that stops them going too far. Even when I went for a piss, you'd look dead ahead, not dare to look to either side. But the fear was exciting. Even though I was a part of it, I knew I wasn't quite – there was 10 per cent that wasn't. There was an element of excitement, 'cause it felt like you'd infiltrated. They weren't all muscly, and some were really ugly, but you remember the muscular ones, the sensible tattoos.

In common with most others, Kim uses the priority of the skinhead component of a gay skin's identity over his sexuality to decide whether or not someone is authentic. Referring to some National Front skinhead rent boys he knows, he says, 'Even though they're gay, to me they're still skinheads first – they didn't dress like that to pull more punters. They probably got punters in the first place *because* they're skinheads; and because they're skinheads, they're unemployable.'

Evidence of far-right loyalties are also high on his list of criteria for determining authenticity.

When I'm out, I grade people. If someone's got nationalist badges or Union Jacks, that's something. Fashion skins wouldn't wear anything like that. White laces – I know on one level it's superficial, it's all image, but trendy skins, fashion skins go near that, they wouldn't 'stoop that low' as they'd say. So if I see patches, Skrewdriver, Nationalist badges on T-shirts, 20-hole rangers, white laces, there's a pretty good chance they're real, 'cause they're showing a bit more commitment.

He believes an association with the right is what makes skinheads sexy to all those who admire them, even if it's disavowed.

There's a lot of people I've met, who love that image, and they'd love to be like that, but they won't step over the line. Probably 'cause they're too politically correct – that's what it comes down to. I know a lot of gay people who think I'm beyond the pale because of the right-wing thing, they can't accept that. But I also know they fucking wet themselves. Although they're not skinheads themselves, they love it all, but they can't actually accept it, because it's just not on. I think, more fool them.

Kim's last straight skin night out was at Skrewdriver's final gig in September 1992. 'Thanks to *Time Out* – if they hadn't publicized the Anti-Nazi League demo, I'd never have found the venue.' The gig was held at a pub in Eltham, and the conflict of nationalist with anti-fascist demonstrators resulted in violence and the police being issued with riot gear.[6] Nicky Crane wasn't there, because it was soon after they'd broadcast *Skin Complex* on Channel 4, where he'd come out. That was the main talking point: everyone was laughing about it, 'Did you see it?' they were going. It's interesting that they made a point of having watched it.

When I went to the toilets, which were covered in nationalist stickers from all round the country, I was more aware of the sexual side of it than I had been in the past, because I hadn't been to an event like that for so long. By the end of the evening with all the songs and the 'Sieg Heil'-ing, the nationalist side of things, which I'd forgotten about, took over, and I wasn't even conscious of the other [sexual] bit.

I've been a member of the Gay Skinhead Group for two years. I feel duty-bound, but to be honest. But I realize that – and it comes back to the Rainbow Alliance thing again – the gay scene is very suspicious of anything like that. So to get publicity, they got to be seen to be ultra-politically correct. The good old GSG have to dilute everything for acceptance, and I'm not interested in that bollocks. What I'd like is the gay boneheads club (which you could never do, because you could never get it publicized) which would not be about going on about the original skins being into ska, the Trojan record label and sideburns – fuck that! We want fucking boneheads, with jeans rolled up to the knees, 20-hole boots, CUT HERE round the neck. That's what 90 per cent of the gay skins are into, even if they don't adopt that themselves; that's what it's all about.

The macho scene

Neither Nick nor Tony happened across the gay skinhead scene which had quietly continued, tucked away in a corner of the developing macho venues, since the end of the skins' first era. As Michael Dover said, 'in the early seventies, there was a great time when virtually all the skinheads you used to see were gay; you didn't see that many straight skinheads for a long, long time in the early seventies'. The post-punk revival saw a new wave of recruits to this scene, where the ages of the original skins technically disqualified them from being part of a 'youth' subculture. 'At that time I noticed contemporaries still clutching on', Mike Dow recalls, 'and many are still dressing that way, but I saw the emergence of young guys who had never known the first wave of skinheads were now dressing in that way.'

This British macho scene had become a confused fusion of skin, biker and leather queens, with other masculine signifiers (biker gear, military styles such as camouflage gear, combat trousers and flying jackets) corrupting the skinhead image. The wholesale importing of the clone from the United States later in the decade consolidated this subcultural practice. It was no longer a matter of aping heterosexual masculinity: butch was definitely a *gay* thing. The diversity of clone types was demonstrated by the macho drag of the most mainstream proponents of this subcultural development, the American pop group the Village People: biker, cop, cowboy, construction site worker, native American and army officer. The scene had become a Village, and the macho queens the ruling set. But they also demonstrated how closed the open secret of gay machismo was when their appearance on a chat show failed to signify anything queer to a fellow guest, the right-wing political campaigner and arch-homophobe Anita Bryant. The most popular skin venue at the time shows how important the American influence was on establishing the importance of the macho scene in British gay subculture. 'The London Apprentice would have been the most popular venue for gay skinheads then', says Mike Dow. 'Michael Glover, who started the LA, had seen leather bars and cruise bars in the States and it was his intention to bring that style of bar to London.'

The fact that popular opinion in the early 1980s saw skinheads as fascists did not deter potential recruits from this scene.

By and large most gay men who adopted that look fought very hard to keep the image. Queens are very strange things in a way, if they like something and find it sexy then nothing's going to stop them. They're not terribly politically correct and I don't think it bothered too many of them. They knew that they weren't fascists anyway. One or two of them were, but only one or two. Most of them just thought it was sexy and weren't gonna give it up.

But this gay skin, close cousin to the clone, was something quite separate from the straight skinheads of the time. 'I don't think there was any crossover. Straight skins were dancing to Oi! and gay skins to early Hi-NRG.'

At this time gay skinheads started to organize themselves as a subculture within a subculture. In 1985 Mike Dow, the publisher of the national gay newspaper, *Out!*, used his title to run a two-part feature on gay skins with an ad for the newly established Gay Skinhead Movement.

The GSM is a new national movement whose aims are to encourage skinheads to come out and meet others. It is a social group strictly for skinheads only and hopes to put skins from all over the country in touch with each other and will attempt the difficult task of breaking down the barriers between gay and straight skins to generate an atmosphere of tolerance and understanding.

The newsletters included listings, personal ads, and information on shops, tattooists and bands. 'I used the newspaper to get the ball rolling', says Mike. 'Initially it was a contact service for guys who were interested in skinheads – they could just write in and then newsletters would be drawn up and sent out. But I soon passed it on because I didn't have the time.'

The GSM folded in 1988. 'But there was still a need to try and continue something like it', says Chris Clive.

So Mick Shaw started the Gay Skinhead Group up in Derby. He was a real skinhead, into all the music and all the things like that. In 1991 he wanted out of it because he was emigrating to Holland. So he advertised in the magazine, 'Anybody want to sort of help me out?', so I said 'Yes.' 'Great!' he said, and I landed up with the whole lot on my plate. I've been doing it continuously now on my own for about four years.

The GSG provided a role similar to the defunct GSM. 'It's a social group. I try and get people into contact with each other. If I travel up to Manchester I can ring a couple of the members up and say, can you put me up for the night? That sort of thing. Obviously there are other motives as well, which are fine.' Chris edited a quarterly fanzine, *Skinhead Nation*, a ten-page A5 'zine. 'I wish I got more contributors; 90 per cent of it's written by me. I do get stories in; some of the longer stories. People pay £10 for a year's subscription. It only just covers the cost of photocopying and postage. It doesn't make a profit.' This would be mailed to members with a supplementary list of personal ads. 'The contact list isn't like all these other ads, it just has the name and the area they're in, and a couple of code letters to say what they're into, basically. Nothing explicit.'

We have members in America, Canada, Singapore, Brazil, quite a lot in Germany and Sweden . . . when I took it over it wasn't international at all, but I've had interviews in various international magazines, Czech, Holland, Belgium, Germany and the States. These magazines get around . . . people just keep joining, so if I go abroad I can ring people up and find a place to stay.

When Chris took over the GSM in 1992, there were forty members; by the time of his death in May 1995, membership had grown to over the two hundred mark.

Skinhead Nation became part of the extensive international network of skinhead fanzines, and drew inspiration from the 'official' British skinzine, *Skinhead Times*. The back cover of the Winter 1994 edition of *Nation* was devoted to lamenting its demise and praising the paper's mastermind, George Marshall. 'He wouldn't let us advertise in his paper at all', claimed Chris. 'He wasn't anti at all, not at all, he just didn't have that sort of coverage, it's all full of music stuff, loads of record ads.' However, with queerness rendered invisible by the uniformity of the skinhead, some gay ads would slip in.

I did notice that, in the columns, a couple of our members were advertising, usually to sell something, or for penfriends – and we all know what that means. There used to be this ad in there for the guy who runs Rangerskins, who are an outward-bound group, going abroad in tents, that kind of thing. Now he managed to advertise in there because obviously George didn't know that it was a gay outfit.

Objections

The increased visibility and organization of gay skinheads in the mid-1980s saw a corresponding rise in the vociferousness of political objections to their presence on the scene. The formation of the GSM heralded the first regular gay skinhead night since the demise of the Union Tavern's Tuesday nighters. The first of the GSM's Moonstomp discos was held in 1985 at the London Lesbian and Gay Centre Gay in Farringdon Road. It marked an occasion for sexual dissidents with a commitment to radical politics to voice their discontent with the mode of masculinity represented by gay skinheads. John Byrne recalls,

> We all went there on the first night, but we had trouble, 'cause there were a lot of lesbians there and they objected to us and called us Nazis and that; they were quite upset. So it moved to another bar in King's Cross, and they had a lot of meetings there. That only finished when more and more non-skinhead people came, until skinheads were in the minority. I don't think they had a strict enough door policy.
>
> There was also a club called the Craven, near Heaven in Craven Street. It was a gay club and pub, upstairs with a camera entry system; the skinheads moved in there in the mid-eighties. About 98 per cent were skinheads or skinhead admirers. There were a lot of closet skinheads, especially in a place like the Craven, you used to get a lot of 'straight' ones as well as gay ones, but nobody cared. It only closed when they redeveloped Charing Cross station in the late eighties.

By the mid-1980s, the numbers of post-punk skin were dwindling. But the skin look was still popular with young gay men coming out on the scene because, as a stark contradiction, it was fashionable among the alternative-trendy end of the gay scene. Figures like Michael Clark who, at this time, moved between hard punk and skinhead-inspired street clothes with a slightly camp twist (a knicker-flashing kilt, cropped jeans slightly flared) were transferring the energies of the gay/fashion scene, focused around legendary clubs like Taboo and the early days of the Pyramid, to a broader audience via the alternative tastes of the arts editors of the style press, the newspapers and Channel 4. Young fashion skins congregated at the Bell in King's Cross. According to Mike:

> That was where the skinhead look crossed over with the fashion look. Guys who were wearing short hair and DM boots and jeans – is that a skinhead? Well no, it's a look that's close to it and derived from it, but it isn't really a true skinhead because there were a few more refinements that set them apart.

To non-skins, however, they looked too close for comfort: 'The reaction is usually curious and cautious. At the Bell in King's Cross, reaction ranges from pure lust to political disgust.' So said one gay skin in a feature on the increasingly popular macho type which appeared in the innovative gay lefty arts magazine *Square Peg*. It devoted a three-page spread to gay skins in the summer of 1986 in direct response to the 'concern raised by lesbians and gay men over the skinhead image and its connections with racism and violence, which was catalysed by media reports and the Moonstomp discos organised by the Gay Skinhead Movement'.

In an effort to undermine the simplistic assumption that skinheadism is intrinsically fascistic, the piece underlined the role of black culture in skinhead history, stressing that they borrowed 'the trilby, the crombie and ska music from young London Blacks. It was common to see skins and rude boys dancing together in SE London halls and pubs, to the likes of Prince Buster, Desmond Dekker, the Maytals and the Upsetters.' The image's adoption by neo-Nazi movements was then identified as a recent historical development.

At this time, there still seemed to be no doubt that gay skins epitomized the opposite of what the straight mainstream expected of gay men. This was implicit in the interviewer's question, 'Is the public ready for gay skins?' and in one respondent's assertion that 'By being a skinhead, I can't be called "not a man".' Gay skins have yet to impact on public consciousness: the interviewees are read unambiguously as fascists, by both straight and gay people. All voice their opposition to racism and fascism and dispute that that's what the skinhead represents, while admitting that their appearance does lead them to be treated as such. They distance themselves from straight skinhead culture with phrases like 'I'm not a usual skin', 'they're wallies' and 'they can't understand gay skinheads', and the argument of the piece is that gay skinheadism as a completely separate phenomenon from broader skinhead subculture and its associations. By 1986 gay skinhead subculture is well enough established for the respondents to be able to move exclusively within the gay scene; the territories are more consolidated than Nick's experience of the early 1980s, with almost all the interviewees claiming to know few or no straight skinheads.

The conclusion to the piece – 'it's a shame that those who make a blanket criticism of all skinheads can't see gay skinheads for what they are: gay men who have *adopted the fashion as a sexual image*' – considers it a sexual appropriation operating merely at the level of style, with a reassuringly obvious, apolitical motivation: 'Sex and sexual fantasy seem to be the main reason for adopting the boot and braces style.'

Significantly, authenticity does not seem to be a concern among these skins. Although the working-class origin of skinheads is acknowledged several times, individual respondents identify themselves as middle class and this seems to involve no sense of contradiction. This way, perhaps, the fascist connotations of the skinhead image can be left with the real thing; this is different, a gay thing, an unproblematic reappropriation with all the difficult political overtones left behind with the original owner. Other gay men and lesbians still saw it as a straight thing, however. 'Their presence in gay pubs and places is looked upon in much the same way as if they were straight', says the writer. One talks of 'gay people's hostile reaction'; another claims 'Lesbians have come up to me and asked if I'm gay.'

The skinheads themselves voiced differing perceptions of the expectations of the gay scene. One saw his identity as an individualist rebellion against existing models of gay identity: 'I don't like the trendy fashion of the gay scene and skins can't be made respectable', while another saw it as a viable model of gay identity: 'I see it as a fashion style for the gay scene.' While for some their skinhead identity pre-dated their coming out by several years, presumably facilitating their emergence on to the gay scene, others adopted the skinhead image *after* being on the scene as a favourable alternative to other more well-established macho identities in the clone tradition. 'I find it sexually attractive as I like the masculine look and don't like facial hair', says one; 'gay skins are associated with rough sex and I am interested in power games', says another. 'I don't like leather culture and the seemingly conservative and middle-classness of SM bars.'

Slippery skins

Accompanying the interviews in *Square Peg* was a piece called 'Why I'm a Skin, by the Brother'. A personal, almost poetic meditation of a gay skinhead's sense of his own identity, it forms part of a collective gay subcultural exercise to rewrite skinhead mythology in a way that renders it accessible to gay men. Those authenticating aspects of the skinhead which would have precluded its circulation within and throughout gay subculture – the requirement that participants be working class and straight – are erased, and the skinhead is instead cleverly authenticated by siting its origin in the pre-social realm of the 'natural' world.

The piece presented a highly romanticized view of the skinhead as an outcast, 'silent, menacing, utterly alien'. 'If he is clever he is the eternal outsider, using his image to constantly vary and contradict himself, able to walk anywhere, his passport the astonishment of the sharp mind in the brainless stereotype . . . He is an anarchist not because he rejects rules but because they cannot be applied to him. They slip off.' He comes to symbolize the alienation, isolation and heightened sense of individualism experienced by many gay men growing up in a heterosexist society. The popularity of the romanticization of the skin extended beyond the confines of gay mythology, however; Mick Furbank's semi-mystical vision of the Crucified Skin, as sales of his T-shirt attested, was very popular with straight skins.

Abstracting the skinhead from the historical conditions which shaped 'his' emergence, 'he' no longer signifies a collective class identity but an individual beyond all social categories. There may of course be a personal motivation here: 'the Brother' was not in fact born in an urban working-class environment but 'remotest and desolate suburbia'. A similar redemption of the mythology is at work in Mike Dow's chronicle of gay skinhead subculture which had appeared the previous year in the free paper *Out!* Here, the non-class-specific nature of gay skin subculture, which should threaten to de-authenticate it, renders it *more* real:

> Generally speaking, gay skins come from a far broader background than straight skins. Many are found in highly respectable and skilled jobs . . . It could be said that the gay skin is the true skin, because he cuts across education, employment and environmental barriers.
>
> He has usually decided to become a skinhead after consideration and preparation for some sacrifice, not simply because he comes from a tower block in Canning Town and his mates are doing it.[2]

This piece is fairly exceptional as a pro-skin piece which does not shy away from addressing the complex questions raised when an image which has come to represent fascism is adopted. The writer believes that the skinheads' desire to find a position outside society from which to articulate an anarchist politics explains 'why they became fascist, because there was no other political base uncolonised by the teachers, social workers, police'. And violence to immigrant communities is apparently due to the fact that 'they are more alien to suburban England than skins can ever hope to be'.

These two moves – individualizing skinheads and rendering them class-free – have significant implications on the discourse of authenticity, which is still an important factor in the identity of 'the Brother'. Dislodged from the context of working-class culture, this skinhead authenticates his masculinity through recourse to nature in bestial metaphor. The text refers to skinheads as 'big mad animal boys' and the uniform becomes 'a hide . . . reduced to the function of an animal's coat; his boots are his hooves . . . He is pure sex because no intellectual drives can be read into him.' Indeed, one remnant of the class legacy remains in the stance he takes against bourgeois intellectualism; he sites himself in opposition to 'all the art students and *i-D* wallies, all the *Square Peg* readers'.

This bestialization of the skinhead uniform renders it natural, pre-social, so the Brother can then remove the antisocial skinhead from the exchange of signs. Unlike all other self-presentational strategies, which are subject to the transient significance of ever-changing fashion, the skinhead look is now (and retrospectively) safely secured, essentially fixed in what it means. 'The skinhead is beyond fashion and cannot be assimilated', his clothes are 'anti-clothes'. This was a common belief: Mitch, a skinhead from Newcastle, claims in *Out* that his skinhead identity is beyond style: 'It's my way of life. Teddy boys and mods have come and gone but they all still look as though they're wearing a fashion. Being a real skinhead has nothing to do with a fashion. It's shouting, "I'm a skinhead."' The signifier is closed to representing nothing but itself.

This has interesting implications on the skinhead's mobility. Once, the skinhead sought to secure and police boundaries. Now, 'a clever gay skinhead can cross every boundary going'. He can even walk among those he hates 'and yet feel utterly at home in their world'. The skinhead is able to function in any context but not become implicated in or transformed by them. The literal antisocial status means he is a stable site which renders him able to float freely through society. To use Theweleit's analysis, he can now move with all the dangerous fluidity of homosexual desire without compromising the phallic totality of his self.

With the authenticating origin of the mobilized skinhead sited beyond the social, it can now be relocated from heterosexuality to homosexuality: the writer confesses, 'I was dead scared until I found their sexuality was usually like mine.' By the late 1980s, then, masculinity and the myth of the skinhead had been shaken up enough for the skinhead's whole-hearted adoption as a gay type.

Notes

1. Martyn Harris, 'The Doc Marten Angels', *New Society*, 24 May 1984, pp. 307–9.

2. Mike Dow, 'Skins: 2', *Out*, April 1985, p. 20.

9

The Queer Appropriators:
Simulated Skin Sex

If the gay skin was the bogeyman of radical gay politics of the 1980s, then the 1990s saw him championed precisely because of the politically incorrect nature of the desire he embodied. This was thanks to the wide-scale interrogation of the lesbian and gay political agenda which had dominated since the early Liberationist days: Queer. The Q-word itself was the very 'bad', oppressive term that Liberationism had sought to quash with the assertion of 'gay'. For their issue devoted to 'The Politics of Queer' in May 1992, *Gay Times* chose to represent the public face of Queer with a topless skinhead behind bars, recognizable as Michael Flaherty of the London queer SM club Sadie Maisie. Across the Atlantic, Queer film-maker Bruce la Bruce's 1991 film *No Skin Off My Ass* had celebrated the skinhead as the romantic outsider, an erotic focus beyond the confines of the recognizable closet of gay identity.

'"Queercore", née homocore, the cut-rate, cut-throat, cutting edge of the homosexual underworld', was an American fanzine scene born out of 'a desperate need to create an alternative to the extant gay community'.[1] Bruce la Bruce, growing up in early 1980s Toronto and alienated from the 'gay community', found that punk made more sense of his sexual dissidence. Whereas 'the gay underworld used to be a refuge for misfits . . . now punk had become the repository of lost souls'. But he discovered the punk scene could be fearful of sexual dissidence: 'I even fell in love with a skinhead who hated fags, and, during our tempestuous relationship, got the shit beaten out of me on more than one occasion.' If gay skins were a manifestation of self-oppression for gay radicals, this relationship marked la Bruce out as one fucked-up queer. But then, as he is proud to admit, 'I am not now nor have I ever been a likely candidate for the position of GLAAD poster child.' (The Gay and Lesbian Alliance Against Defamation campaign for positive lesbian and gay role models and the banning of negative ones in the American media.) Homocore, 'the bastard child of two, once exciting, volatile underground movements, gay and punk' was born when he set up the fanzine *JDs* (standing for juvenile delinquents, underlining the way queer identity and youth subcultures derive from the same energies of dissatisfaction). The 'zine reappropriated glossy gay images with punk attitude: cut, paste and photocopy. His self-oppressive relationship with a skinhead made it to celluloid with *No Skin Off My Ass*, which he refers to as his 'first porno' and sees as a logical progression from *JDs*.

The film opens with a camp hairdresser (la Bruce himself), very much in the Wildean tradition of the aesthete (bad thing number one: an oppressive stereotype), discovering a skinhead on a park bench (bad thing number two: a self-oppressive sexual object). He takes the skinhead home, where they play out various quasi-sadomasochistic games (bad thing number three), the fascist undertones of such play made manifest in a dream sequence which sees them saluting in a quasi-Nazi scenario (bad thing number four). Working-classness now has no function other than to eroticize the difference between the skinhead and the queen who discovers him; in fact, we later learn that the skinhead is middle class. The skinhead gives little away; although he eventually has sex with the hairdresser, he never identifies as gay (bad thing number five . . .).

The film eroticizes the ritual of head-shaving (which humorously allows the roles of the protagonists to dovetail neatly: after all, what else would a hairdresser and a skinhead get up to?), which confirms the skinhead's alien-ness in his uneasy relation to all possible social positionings: head-shaving becomes a stripping away of social signs which fix the wearer's identity. His appearance signifies 'skinhead', but what does that mean? Not working class, not heterosexual, not queerbasher. 'Skinhead' has become blank; it refuses to situate itself with any clarity within the social. In his reticent manner, he refuses to explain himself, refuses to be read in a way that makes complete sense.

This film articulates the romance of the skinhead as one who exists beyond the intelligible organization of the social; in Britain, meditations by British gay skins on skinheads had similarly mythologized the figure in the previous decade (Mike Dow's *Skins* and *Square Peg*'s 'Why I'm a Skin, by the Brother'). And this mobility extended beyond fantasy: the popularity of this underground film with gay American middle-class audiences attested to the extent to which the skinhead has become decontextualized enough from its straight British working-class context to allow it to be intelligible to them. The skinhead had become a Queer hero precisely because he was excluded from liberated 'gay'-ness both as a sexual object and a viable gay identity. He was a misfit, and it was that very outsider-ness to the world which 'gay' had become that Queer championed.

While Queer embraced politically problematic and unsound pleasures and motifs as a 'challenge against the 1980s gay gentrification of sexual identity',[2] others seized this as an opportunity to generate previously silenced or disavowed debates: Queer questioned the radical-left dogma of democratized sameness demanded by liberated homosexuality. If power difference as the erotic drive of sadomasochism was ideologically dangerous and therefore 'against the interests of lesbians and gay men', then queers wanted to know why it was so sexually attractive. Dismissing it as politically unsound simply swept the matter under the carpet. It still went on; people were just ashamed to talk about it. Queer allowed once politically problematic questions of 'dangerous' desire to be articulated rather than disavowed. In fact, some modes of Queer derived directly from those lesbians who, in the 1980s, had argued for SM in the face of its disavowal by radical feminism.

The consequences of Queer are stark. It seems difficult to imagine a piece such as 'When Difference Is (More Than) Skin Deep', which was published in a collection called *Queer Looks* in 1993, appearing in a lesbian and gay publication in the 1980s without much controversy. In this, the democratic sameness of partnerships required by radical lesbian politics with its (gender-, race-, class-)separatist tendencies is questioned by queer cultural critic B. Ruby Rich. She refers to this as 'lesbian bed death' caused by 'overmerging, by the dissolving of self into (too like) other', and says the debates around SM in the 1980s 'were clearly attempts to introduce "difference" into same-sex couplings as a strategy for maintaining eros. As such, the roles made perfect sense at the level of strategy despite the arguments made at the level of ideology.'[3] She proposes not only that social difference is required by lesbian relationships as an erotic dynamic, but that this difference is best articulated in the field of race, arguing that 'queers have the potential for a different relationship to race, and to racism, because of the very nature of same-sex desires and sexual practices'. The extent to which problematic questions of the erotics of racial difference had previously been disavowed is illustrated with the example of Marlon Riggs' landmark film, *Tongues Untied*. Ostensibly autobiographical in structure, the film ended with the sentiment 'Black men loving black men is the revolutionary act.' It was 'a repudiation of cross-race bonding', despite the fact that Riggs' own lover was white.

The consequence of Queer could be seen in *Skin Complex*, where a black gay skinhead said that he was attracted to the image precisely *because* of its transgressive potential. He was not supposed to look at skinheads because they were supposed to be homophobic and racist. Here, difference is dangerous and, for this person at least, all the more erotic for it.

Queer

It is difficult to talk of Queer because the label was applied to and claimed by so many voices of protest at the mythic 'gay community' on both sides of the Atlantic that by the time it had made a sizeable impact on the politics of 'lesbian and gay' it had become almost meaningless. I was asked to attend a conference in 1994 called the Queer Atlantic where British and American writers were invited to discuss the different deployment of queer in our respective countries. What emerged however was that this binarism of British/American modes, signalled by the Atlantic, had already been successfully exploded, not by a unity, but by a multiplicity. There were at least as many notions of queer floating free in the discussion as there were speakers.

This was partly due to the fact that most of us had happened across Queer in various ways, as lesbian activists, AIDS activists, film-makers, artists, poets, academics and club victims. Queer, although motivated by similar dissatisfactions in many sites, was always diverse. There was, of course, the Queercore, punk-inspired bunch of misfit fags. One strand was informed by AIDS activists, who, pissed off with watching their friends and lovers die while nothing was being done, felt the issue was too urgent for polite campaigning. Another was motivated by the fact that middle-class white gay men continued to hog the 'lesbian and gay' agenda, with the requirements of women and people of colour rarely addressed. An academic strain saw that the categories 'lesbian' and 'gay' were too historically, geographically and ethnically specific to be useful in understanding certain modes of sexual dissidence. Another branch was in the visual arts, with queer film-makers feeling limited by the subcultural requirement to use only sanitized positive role-models, preventing them from asking difficult, important questions about sexuality and (more importantly) making good films.

All together, Queer voiced dissatisfaction with and a distance from the narrow definition of 'lesbian and gay', characterized by a stroppy attitude. A 'Queer Power Now' leaflet distributed in London in 1991 declared, 'FUCK THE LESBIAN AND GAY COMMUNITY'.[4]

If postmodernism was straights catching up with camp, as Andy Medhurst has famously remarked, then Queer was lesbian and gay politics catching up with postmodernism. The claim that Queer activism put the camp back into campaigning brings this process full circle. A brief consideration of theories of the postmodern is necessary to understand how and why Queer came to transform identity politics. These theories also account for the simultaneous emergence of the skinhead and Gay Lib.

'The 1960s represented the end of the long reign of the modern, liberal consensus'[5] and this was manifest in the liberationist activism of various disenfranchised groups contesting the white, straight, male, middle-class ideology that passed itself off as consensus. This was the Death of Man, the collapse of the modernist concept of centred objectivity. But this mistrust of coherent ideology paradoxically threw the alternatives, through which this mistrust was politically articulated, into doubt also. Thus Lyotard says that 'one of the outcomes of 1968' was 'a perception of the failure of . . . revolution':[6] a loss of faith in coherent ideologies (of Marxism, of Liberationism). Modern(ist) science is the ultimate normalizing authority, the discourse of objective universal truth, and 'Marx and Engels, like their rivals, subscribed to the "modernist" dogma of scientism'. Marxist-derived liberation or revolutionary politics were therefore equally as suspect as dominant liberalism.[7]

The very concept of history was also debunked with the cynical realization that it is not a teleology of progress towards 'a universal emancipation'. Lyotard saw this cynicism motivating 'reactive or reactionary attitudes or utopias'.[8] The skinhead can thus be identified as an intensified conservative recourse to pre-existent identity models in the face of cultural change: 'When the real is no longer what it used to be, nostalgia assumes its full meaning.'[9] Skinheads looked idealistically to a mythical past, while the other reaction, the utopian, looked forward to a mythical future: the late 1960s' counter-cultural critiques from those marginalized by normalizing universal perspective in the form of radical identity politics – the GLF, for example.

Both strategies, although mutually opposed, acknowledged the fragmentation of society and exhibited a modernist desire to reconstruct some form of social homogeneity or a coherent subject, be it an 'authentic working class' or 'gay male' identity. Liberation appealed to essentialist definitions of homosexuality and consequently relied on the notion of a homogeneous 'gay community' wherein all were united by the commonality of homophobic oppression. However, such a centred, universal cultural model elides differences within the 'community', falling foul of the same modernist notion of consensus that it aims to oppose. In asserting and presenting themselves as monolithic, liberation groups were reproducing (albeit minoritized) consensus ideology. In an effort of disavowal, they intensified the stress on the 'realness' of their constituencies. This is the paradox of counter-hegemonic action: the social mobilization and empowerment of oppressed groups through identity politics in a time when coherent identity, as an oppressive concept, was itself in question.

The impossibility of 'communities of oppression' was realized as the fractured identities reproduced themselves as factions within gay and other marginalized political groups in the 1970s and 1980s. But this made the formation of community all the more urgent, as resistance has to be articulated around some sort of commonality. Lyotard has written of the impossibility of radical political formations where oppression 'demands, and in a sense promises, community. But this community is yet to be. It is not yet realized. For the first time, maybe, communities begin to conceive themselves in terms of promise, in terms of obligation, and in so doing they are conscious of not being real.'[10] The formation of radical communities involves an investment of faith in a *future* promise of community as something yet to be realized. Drawing on the writings of Derrida, Laclau and Mouffe, Queer theorist Judith Butler uses the phrase 'incalculable futurity' when referring to the paradox that renders the materialization of radical politics impossible. Political formations are haunted by 'what Mouffe refers to as part of the not-yet-assimilable *horizon* of community'.[11] The ideal of a radical inclusivity is impossible, but this very impossibility nevertheless governs the political field as an idealization of the future that motivates the expansion, linking and perpetual production of political subject-positions and signifiers.'[12]

The difficulties – indeed, perhaps the impossibility – of delineating a political community and negotiating differences within it, only serve to emphasize the need for the community's existence. While years of Liberation politics may have led many to question the reality of the 'lesbian and gay community', the need for an anti-homophobic project by people who could agree on some common response to homophobia was still as urgent as ever. Queer marked a point in the early 1990s when some of those committed to anti-homophobic political projects started to question the use of terms such as 'lesbian' and 'gay' by exposing, exploring and expanding upon the differences within the homogenizing label of 'homosexual'. The implications are still being felt and there is still much work to be done: Butler writes in 1994, 'the thought of sexual difference within homosexuality has yet to be theorised in its complexity.'[13]

The radical diversity of Queer

Queer, drawing on the academic developments, contested the essentialist discourse which characterized liberationist notions of lesbian and gay selves. This was manifest in the centrality of the calls to 'come out' played in their tactics: the sexual self was the 'real' self, deep down inside, masked by the surface of the social self. The idea was that, the more people there were 'out', the closer we would get to 'Liberation'.

Postmodernism not only refuted that essentialism, it also interrogated the notion of progress, of teleology, of history advancing towards a better future. Queer politics saw this in its recognition of the impossibility of homogeneity: sexuality is seen to be socially constructed and the gathering under the banner of 'Queer' is strategic and provisional, not essential. The very name of an early Queer activist group, Queer Nation, ironically acknowledges the impossibility of a gay community while recognizing the strategic importance of assembling one.

Queer acknowledged that coherent – and therefore confined – sexual identities are oppressive. As all identities are prescribed by an oppressive social order, to conform to any, even a marginalized or outlawed one, is to capitulate. An 'acceptable', albeit abject and distanced, territory has been created for homosexual identity: the ghetto of 'gay'. Brian Rafferty wrote in *New York Queer*, 'Gay identity is an unspoken conspiracy between gays and straights. Each authenticates the other . . . whenever you hear someone talk about gay culture, think about how important it is for straights that there be such a thing.'[14] Eve Kosofsky Segdwick has called this approach a 'minoritizing' model of homosexuality: 'that there is a distinct population of persons who "really are" gay' and that such a category exists 'because of its indispensableness to those who define themselves against it'.[15]

Therefore the very concept of sexual identity, that sexual activity renders you classifiable as a certain type, is a cultural con. Radical Queerness seeks to dispense with it altogether: Mancunian Queer group Homocult, who share with Homocore an aesthetic (of cut, paste and photocopy) as well as an ideology, refuse to see sexuality as grounds for identity politics. Such a strategy exploits the universalizing model of (homo)sexuality: 'that sexual desire is an unpredictably powerful solvent of stable identities'.[16] For Homocult, social class is the only true organizing principal.

Destabilizing identities – or rather, to expose identity as inauthentic – may be the ultimate goal, but material conditions simply do not allow the refusal of identity. The difficulty is that the dominant dictates the terms: attempting to destroy identity by existing beyond it (a literally utopian project) will not prevent its reimposition. The dilemma is encapsulated in the 'Queer Power Now' leaflet: 'FUCK BOUNDARIES. FUCK GENDER. FUCK LABELS.' Queer power is itself dependent on the label 'Queer' (hence the inconsistency and indeed impossibility of Queer as a label). If Queer destabilizes the site safely delineated by 'homosexual', from what stable site does queer politics articulate itself? Is the critique of identity a feasible site for a new identity politics? You're on shaky ground. Some may be queer, or postmodern, or camp enough to understand the constructedness of identity and the provisionality of territorial boundaries, but the dominant main-stream for the most part is not aware of this. Theory may prove that identity is illusory, but a refusal to label oneself will not stop the dominant from categorizing and oppressing on those grounds. As long as people (who live in a practical, material world) are marginalized, identity is not defunct.

Eve Sedgwick, while acknowledging the usefulness of the homosexual category to homophobes, attributes the failure to dismantle the homo/hetero binarism in part to 'its meaningfulness to those whom it defines'.[17] The age may be post-modern and post-consensus, but it is not post-homophobic. Behaviour will always lead to identification by others; a group's non-conformity will simply result in a coherent queer identification and exile to the ghetto of identity, otherwise its members will be assumed to be straight. Either is a fairly unproblematic categorization. As Judith Butler has stated, 'it remains politically necessary to lay claim to "female", "queer", "gay" and "lesbian" precisely because of the way these terms, as it were, lay their claim on us prior to our knowing'.

Hence the explosive diversity of Queer politics. Some queer groups sought to destroy the very category of sexual identity; some deconstructed and tactically reconstructed terms such as 'lesbian' and 'gay' to create a site from which to articulate anti-homophobic projects; others simply re-embraced the liberationist agenda, but with a stroppier attitude. This was illustrated in various 'Queer' reactions to the film *Basic Instinct*, which starred Sharon Stone as a seductive, murderous bisexual. Queer activist groups in New York picketed the première and early screenings in 1992 because Stone's character was a 'negative representation' of lesbianism. (They put the 'camp' back into campaigning by giving away the plot.) At the same time, Queer academics and critics applauded the character's power, sexiness, autonomy and refusal to conform to society's standards.

If the goal is to expose the inauthenticity of identity, surely it is better to use identity tactically rather than to dispense with it altogether. One tactic is to work from the base of existing models of sexual identity but refuse to be confined within them, fluidly undermining them by spilling out into straight territory from the ghetto; for example, Queer Nation's 'Nights Out' (visibly occupying straight clubs) and *OutRage!'s* kiss-ins in 'public' (straight-dominated) spaces. The unapologetic transgression of boundaries was queer: but didn't the unproblematic realness of those lesbians and gay men taking part simply reinforce those boundaries?

Word made Flesh

This problem with boundaries, delimiting the Queer constituency, was played out on the door of the club scene. Queer was a manifestation of a cynical attitude towards organized politics (another symptom of a postmodern loss of faith in truth, history and teleology) which had resulted in a wave of apathy hitting even the most politicized sites, such as student union lesbian and gay societies. Queer drew its inspiration from radical pleasure, not radical politics: the club scene. In 1992 Paul Burston wrote of the way in which Queer played on the increasing interest in genderfuck and cross-dressing to 'align its message with the energies of the club scene rather than conventional gay politics'.[18] The open nature of the gay club and bar scene which developed around Old Compton Street in London's Soho in the early 1990s has been taken as evidence of growing Queer confidence:

A number of commentators have stressed the design of the new bars themselves, which are light, open spaces with huge plate-glass windows . . . This is contrasted with gay venues in the past, where the distinction between interior and the street was clearer . . . In these new venues, gay men are not hidden behind closed doors. Straight passers-by can look in and observe . . . We are highly visible.[19]

But Jon Binnie acknowledges the way in which this assertiveness can lead to exclusionary practices which only reaffirm homo/heterosexual difference.

He quotes from *Boyz*, 'But there are still one or two straight people in the street, which annoys Stuart from Brixton. "They should block off each end and set up gay checkpoints."' Binnie comments, 'Statements like these (even if ironic) are ridiculous given the proliferation of diverse sexual dissident identities. How could it be done? It's hard to tell what straights look like any more.'[20] For now the market, which had previously been restricted to the (putatively lucrative) pink pound, was potentially extended to anyone with enough money and little enough homophobia to calmly accept the discovery that the bar they were sitting in was in fact gay.

It is on the door to queer clubs that these questions of how to distinguish and whether to exclude straights have been played out. I was involved in the setting up of a Queer night, Flesh, in Manchester's Haçienda in October 1991. We declared it a 'serious pleasure for dykes and queers', much to the disgust of most gay men over the age of thirty: the angry calls I had to take from the managers of well-established 'gay' venues in the north-west surprised me. What had interested me more in that slogan was the fact that we had to gender-differentiate, because Queer had already become male-dominated. It was important to appeal to dykes because Manchester's scene had a notorious history of gender-division. The prospect of men sharing space with a high proportion of very visible women offended some gay men too, used to men-only and male-dominated spaces. There were also objections from the established scene at our use of straight staff.

So, before we had even opened, Flesh's opposition to the norms of homosexuality was already evident. It also asserted itself in opposition to the norms of heterosexuality. In those early days of Flesh, the door policy was predicated very much on a separatist agenda. This was partly because we had to compensate for the club's reputation for being very hard and very straight; there had been a notorious amount of gangster activity associated with the club. Drag queens and self-made freaks, hand-picked for their ability to scare straights, were employed to cruise the queue, challenging people on their sexual identities.

But, of course, such an exercise was ridiculous: any straight who looked glamorous, or odd, or gorgeous, or freaky, or who was prepared to snog someone of the same sex, could get in. No doubt some straight-looking lesbians and gay men were excluded. In trying to enforce the categories of gay and straight, the labels came to seem increasingly meaningless. When the takings dropped in 1993, this separatist, minoritizing definition of queer started to look both economically as well as ideologically unsound. For various reasons, then, Flesh's constituency was potentially limitless. When the club was featured on Channel 4's youth show *The Word*, one of the organizers said, 'Flesh is for everyone, it's about doing your own thing.'

Queer, in a very real sense, had dissolved boundaries to the extent that 'lesbian', 'gay' then 'straight' and finally 'queer' began to lose their meanings.

How do these spaces remain sexed as queer if anyone can gain access? It had profound personal implications: one of the organizers of Flesh, as well as many of the regulars, discovered that sexuality was indeed fluid enough to spill over from homosexuality into heterosexuality in such a way as to problematize both terms. I know many confirmed-straight male clubbers who, having managed to sneak in, found their way to homosexual identity via sex with the club's dazzlingly seductive drag queens. The accusations that had been levelled at us in the early days by many spurned heterosexuals, that our door policy stank of Queer fascism, started to ring true.

Eve Sedgwick shifted the debate from essentialist/constructivist to minoritizing/universalizing models. Her view of queer would seem to belong to the latter strategy – that potentially *anyone* could be queer. Indeed, at 'The Queer Atlantic' conference when it became clear that we were each working according to a different definition of Queer, she stated that, for her, Queer was anything which assisted an anti-homophobic project.

This was a major criticism of Queer – its inconsistency: 'One minute you can be straight and still be Queer', noted Paul Burston, 'the next we're talking genetic separatism – all straights are bigots and we're caught up in The Straight War Against Queer Love'.[21] There are two points to be made here: first, to argue for such a consistency is to fail to acknowledge that oppression does not operate in any singular or coherent way. The tactical diversity (or, less euphemistically, factionalism) of Queer did reflect this, and as such its 'failure' to achieve a coherent manifesto or strategy should have been recognized as an achievement. Secondly, stroppy attitude characterized all modes of Queer, and this was manifest in such inconsistency. Inconsistency prevents radical moves from being incorporated for the purposes of the very ideology they oppose.

Judith Butler, aware of its socially provisional status, wrote of the inadequacy of 'lesbian' as a description of her subject position. However, one word, some form of identity, is needed: 'There is a political necessity to use some sign now, and we do, but how to use it in such a way that its futural significations are not foreclosed?'[22] Alan Sinfield identified this as the very question Queer tries to answer: 'The task is not to select the one true word that ultimately speaks our essential name, but to keep devising strategies to outmanoeuvre hostile appropriations: to keep moving.'[23] In other words, inconsistency, far from being a fault, is a useful tactic: To erect identity boundaries and then move them, always shifting goalposts to avoid own goals, to confuse the dominant's pigeonholing and to expose the provisional constructedness (as opposed to permanent naturalness) of social categories. Speed is important, as the lack of the marginal's economic and cultural power in face of the dominant's dictation and (re)definition of the terms available means that these movements can be quickly recognized, recategorized and defused by the dominant. Rapid and incongruous recombination of those terms may break their 'natural(ized)ness'.

But can we ever move fast enough? The problems on the door at Flesh demanded a definition of a Queer club, and, therefore, of Queer itself. If it means being different from the norm, *how* different from *whose* norm do you have to be to get in? Various strains of Queer set up their own criteria. Queer lost its appeal for me when someone claimed (with no noticeable trace of irony) they were *queerer* than anyone else because they liked getting fucked with an iron bar – and they didn't care about the gender of the person holding it.

The very fact that the club scene has incorporated Queer back into itself is read by some as a neutralizing move in the name of capitalism. Assimilation is inevitable for all projects of semiotic subversion. 'Any active dissent can be commodified, turned into a product useful for the maintenance of capitalism', writes Sadie Plant. 'Dadaists, surrealists and situationists all realised that anything they produced could be integrated into the structures they opposed.'[24] She writes this in response to Stewart Home's call for a three-year art strike in order to frustrate the dominant's ability to assimilate subversive culture. Her own solution is for artistic subversives to recognize, side-step and expose dominant recuperation of their efforts: like Alan Sinfield's exhortation for Queer to keep moving.

Both the Queer appropriation and the punk revival of the skinhead can trace their tactical lineage back to Situationism. It is in the anarchist skin novels of Stewart Home, themselves a queer appropriation of Richard Allen's work, that these histories converge. Home has been putting Situationist theory – what he has called 'Positive Plagiarism' – into practice since he formed the punk band White Colours in 1982; in 1994 he edited the first critical anthology of essays about the Situationist International. What began as a gathering of semiotically subversive intellectuals in the late 1950s, the Situationist International inspired the aesthetics and anarchist politics of the near-revolution in Paris of May 1968, which heralded the arrival of 'Liberation'. It is also considered by many to be the beginning of subcultural analysis and directly inspired Malcolm McLaren's considerable involvement in the birth of punk.

But it seems one can never move fast enough. Assimilation is inevitable, and assimilation is death. 'I hate the word "queer"', wrote Bruce la Bruce in 1995. '"Queercore" is dead.' Watching *Who's Afraid of Virginia Woolf* had reminded him

> how you can create something out of a desperate need, and make it so convincing that not only you but others around you start believing it too. But, well, when it becomes an international phenomenon or something, and people start referring to your imaginary creation as 'legendary' and 'important', it's time to deliver the telegram proclaiming that your blonde-eyed, blue-haired son is dead. It's time to move on to the next game.[25]

The death of Queer

The presence of a Queer identity is impossible. As a a tactic of 'FUCK BOUNDARIES . . . FUCK LABELS', to say 'I'm Queer' is to categorize oneself in a way Queer disavows. As soon as it is recognizable, Queer's radical potential is extinguished. As soon as Queer was explained, as soon as the word entered popular currency, it evaporated. The Q-word was already being spoken of as 'last year's thing' by the time *Gay Times* came to devote the bulk of its contents to the discussion of Queer in May 1992. Indeed, Richard Smith's piece in that issue announced that it was already over: 'times move on and if you don't move with them and cling to the wreckage of past victories and former glories still wearing your star jumpers and flares. . . you only make yourself a laughing stock. . . perhaps it's time to start looking post-queer'.[26] Three months later the magazine ran a feature by Paul Burston called 'The Death of Queer Politics', which stated that the movement's demise was not so much 'the end of Queer Politics as an acknowledgement of the fact that Queer Politics never really existed.'[27]

To some extent this has to be true. Queer as a radical political movement was predicated on 'incalculable futurity', just as much as the Liberation politics that preceded it. And if all radical groups have to negotiate the unrealness of the terms of their constitution, then how much harder for a project such as Queer, concerned with the interrogation of the very notion of identity. I've already shown some of the problems faced in sorting out who was to be included in the Queer nation, and a further difficulty, often cited as the cause of Queer's demise, also concerned the terms of its constituency: this celebration of diversity was always allegedly dominated by white middle-class men.

In terms of Butler's incalculable futurity, Queer was an impatient temporal leap towards the promise of a political solution, and this was manifest in the very word itself, stolen from dominant discourse where it served an oppressive function. As such those who took the word chose to ignore the opinion that the dominant group dictates the terms as they operate *in the present*, and took an imaginative leap into a future when those supposedly dominated might dictate the terms. And in so doing, they *were* dictating the terms: 'Queer' lost its derogatory status. . . for some. (The popularity of the Q-word in the early 1990s tended to conform to generational groups, and most of the British gay press was in the hands of gay men over thirty. The company responsible for Britain's most widely-read lesbian and gay title forbade mention of Queer on the grounds that the term might offend some readers.)

But the fulfilment of a political promise premised on the yet-to-be-realized was, and could only ever have been, forever deferred. Queer was always doomed to be what Charlotte Raven has called 'a spectre of its own imminence'. Once its impossibility is acknowledged and it is consigned to the past, when could it ever have really been present? How could Queer ever have existed in the here and now? One moment it is yet to be, the next it's last year's thing.

Richard Smith's fashion metaphor is highly appropriate: Queer was a fashion(able) attitude. Indeed, Queer's death was attributed to its proponents' classification 'as style rebels without a cause, complete with a wardrobe full of radical-chic t-shirts'.[28] Perhaps the most visible success of Queer was in fact the popularity of 'Queer as Fuck' T-shirts (a variation of the Inspiral Carpets' 1989 'Cool as Fuck' T-shirts) which dated in even less time than they took to lose their shape. From those in the industry who have to know about it, to those who consider it a frivolous irrelevant capitalist luxurious wasteful extravagance, to those who just feel left behind by it, many people are wary of fashion. There is a mistrust of style and artifice in the face of the real, along with fears of exclusion, élitism, distraction, of time moving too quickly and of being left behind. The trouble is that fashion always exists in hindsight because as soon as something is announced as being fashionable, it's over.

Fashionability then becomes a struggle to remain beyond the confinement of scrutiny and the ethnology of the fashion press. Queer was about moving fast to evade sexual categorization. Both require an almost instinctive, seemingly unintellectualizable *attitude*.

If Queer evaporated in its explication, its energies derived from its refusal to explain, to account for itself. A common reason given by many gay skins for dressing the way they do is 'it's just a sexy look'. This has often been criticized as inadequate, as a refusal to interrogate; it is a Queer tactic. The realm of fashion and style is a highly appropriate, maybe even the only, site for successfully disrupting identities in a postmodern society. Back in the early 1980s, Klenk and Chesebro speculated (correctly) that style might be the arena for such new modes of activism: 'Whereas the political challenges of the sixties were discursive and products of the mass demonstration, in the 1980s rhetorics of confrontation may be decidedly non-verbal and interpersonal in nature.'[29]

Skin deep

The emergence of the gay skinhead may well have been initially motivated by a reactionary concern with dominant, straight masculinity. But the effect is more radical. To return to my identification of skinheadism as a reaction to the recognition of postmodernism: skinheads emerged as an anti-style, articulating a fixed authenticity in reaction to the social mobility of mod fashions. Queer skinheads expose skinhead 'realness' as just another style in a fluid fashion system, and the authentic masculinity of the skinhead as a simulation.

The image of the gay skinhead, as a postmodern appropriation and operation on the level of style, may be read as a Queer tactic. Semiotic fundamentalism, with its essentialist tendencies, empowers the very system which delineates and distances its categorizations by accepting such identity distinctions, nailing the lid on the gay ghetto and closing decodings to the algebra of skinhead = fascist. Queer, in refusing semiotic fundamentalism, opens this ultimate signifier of masculinity as a site of contestation of the meaning of man, 'avowing the sign's strategic provisionality (rather than its strategic essentialism) . . . preserving the signifier as a site of re-articulation'.[30]

Queer appropriation in the arena of identity – the assumption of the identities from which gay men are supposed to be excluded – serves to undermine identity in the destabilizing of borders and exclusions: difference, the function of the oblique in binarism, gives way to sameness, and in so doing undermines the authority of same/different. In *Gender Trouble* Judith Butler championed the presence of straight 'norms' in lesbian and gay subcultures: she saw their new context problematizing those norms. This argument was articulated in the face of a decade of radical-feminism's utopian project to build a lesbian identity outside the organization of the social, beyond phallic law.

The more insidious and effective strategy it seems is a thoroughgoing appropriation and redeployment of the categories of identity themselves, not merely to contest 'sex' but to articulate the convergence of multiple discourses at the site of 'identity' in order to render that category, in whatever form, permanently problematic.[31]

Historically, this came at a time when sadomasochism and the associated lesbian 'stereotypes' of butch and femme were still bad things that had to be eradicated. Butler's answer is not to dispense with these identities but to intensively redeploy them. This would result in a multiplicity of identities which might undermine not only the dominant notion of a coherent homosexual, and heterosexual, type, but identity itself. 'Straight' modes of behaviour circulating within gay subculture 'can and do become the site of parodic contest and display that robs compulsory heterosexuality of its claim to naturalness and originality.'[32] 'If subversion is possible, it will be a subversion from within the terms of the law, through the possibilities that emerge when the law turns against itself and spawns unexpected permutations of itself.'[33] Opponents of such appropriation dismiss the Foucaultian notion that sexuality is placed within and dictated by the matrices of power, and that there is no prediscursive libidinal expression or potential, as an acceptance of oppression. But acceptance does not preclude change: hyperacceleration of the circulation of these oppressive terms available may serve to undo them.

This undoing of gender has become known as performativity: the theory that the *signs* of identity (and gender, for studies of subjectivity show the two to be mutually constructive) are in fact primary to the mythology of gender identity, 'in the sense that the essence or identity that they otherwise purport to express are fabrications manufactured and sustained through corporeal and other discursive means'. This leads to the conclusion that 'genders can be neither true nor false, but are only produced as the true effects of a discourse of primary and stable identity'.[34] Drag serves to expose this as it 'fully subverts the distinction between inner and outer psychic space and effectively mocks both the expression model of gender and the notion of a true gender identity'.[35]

Macho drag

Most gay skinheads probably do not operate as part of a conscious tactic but as just another scene-based identity. But as an appropriation – the taking of what is not proper, entering where one does not belong – of dominant *masculinity*, structurally the skinhead is not so far removed from the scene's appropriation of femininity: the drag queen. Both may be read as examples of genderfuck. The performative nature of the gay skinhead denaturalizes the categories involved: homosexual/heterosexual, effeminate/masculine.

While the emergence of masculine dress codes on the gay scene was a reclamation of natural masculinity (and all its associated patriarchal privilege) for some, other observers saw the subversive potential of the new look as a form of macho drag which signalled its distance from heterosexuality through exaggeration. Chesebro and Klenk's scene survey uncovers a bartender who 'recognises that these styles are in fact costumes and a product of external manipulations'.[36] Several other sociologists similarly trace the clone look as a *conscious appropriation* rather than uninterrogated redeployment of heterosexual masculinity, remarking on a transformation in the cultural crossover: 'the clothes are worn differently . . . from the way they are worn by "real men". They are much tighter-fitting, especially tailored to be erotic and sensual as possible . . . These subtle changes and transformations of objects infuse the style with a new meaning of eroticism and overt sexuality – that is, they are used explicitly to make one appear sexy and attractive to other men.'[37]

> Gay men all over town (and around the country) trimmed, shaped and refitted the shaggy casualness that was the real essence of the original straight image . . . What emerged was a deliberate new style which does not say, 'I am a straight construction worker' but rather 'I am a post-liberation gay man!'[38]

It is the awareness of the drag effect among those sporting macho styles that leads Jamie Gough to reject this as 'an attempt by gay men to make themselves more respectable. Empirically this is dubious in that the styles adopted do not actually look "normal": even a clone outfit does not look "normal" and, far from being a disguise, advertises you as gay.'[39] 'To be sure, gay masculinity is not in any simple way "real" masculinity . . . it is more self-conscious than the real thing, more theatrical, and often ironic.'[40]

This drag-consciousness is evident to many gay skins today. One proudly told me of his retort to activists campaigning outside a men-only venue about the covert fascism of gender-exclusive door policies. 'Leave it out', he said. 'Can't you see it's all just drag?' Another, who has worked in the management of men-only venues for over a decade, told me that he had always believed his identity, and the macho scene in general, was about gay men showing how real they could be. 'But I can't believe that any more', he now says. 'You see all these men making such an effort with their outfits, fussing over the details . . . I have to admit that these days I see it all as so much drag.' It is no coincidence that several of London's most popular drag performers can be seen out on their nights off as skinheads in men-only venues: female impersonators make great male impersonators too.

The fact is, however, that in addition to these macho drag queens there are gay skinheads who sincerely believe in their right to claim a 'genuine' skinhead identity. But these skinheads who successfully 'pass' do not necessarily work against the boundary-dissolution effect of drag or performativity: passing the boundary patrol is the first step to infiltrating the enemy camp. This would surely subvert and insidiously undermine the dominant notion of '(assumedly straight) skinhead', which, research suggests, is even more troubling for the dominant:

> gay masculinity conveys a message to others, particularly heterosexual males. The gay male who is known as both gay and masculine challenges the sensibilities of heterosexual males far more than the effeminate gay male. Under experimental conditions researchers have consistently reported that effeminate gay males are more tolerated and less aggressed against than more masculine gay males.[41]

(This needs some qualification: studies have also found straight men to be more accepting of straight-acting gay men and more hostile to effeminate men. This is the double bind of a heterosexist social organization. Gay men are required to be simultaneously invisible *and* conspicuous so that they can be marginalized.)

Emphatic reimposition of dominant notions of gender by queer skins who only look queer in fleeting glimpses may undo those notions more effectively. Gay men who sincerely claim an authentic skinhead identity prevent the phenomena from being written off as just dressing up, and this infects the *whole* system – all skinheads – with a hyperreal drag effect. Seeming to be a 'good copy' ('real' skinhead) rather than a 'bad copy' (drag skin) may conceal the homosexual identity of the wearer under the assumed straightness of skinhead; but should that homosexuality be suddenly revealed, the good copy is exposed as a bad copy, exposing all other skinheads as copies and throwing their status into doubt: 'good/bad' becomes extremely problematic. Thus once the queerness of a 'genuine' skinhead is exposed, *all* skinheads become drag queens as all look the same. 'Parody makes obedience and transgression equivalent, and that is the most serious crime, since it cancels out the difference upon which the law is based',[42] writes Baudrillard. Parody exposes the real as a simulation, so the drag effect of gay skins has implications for straight skins too.

Even while heterosexualizing the origin of the skinhead, Chris Clive acknowledged its inauthentic status: 'A lot of the skinheads do it because they're trying to put on an image of what they're probably not. They're trying to look macho and butch when deep inside they're probably not. Which makes them get away with it, of course.' So it's not so much a matter of gay men trying to be real men, as all men trying to pass as real men while trying to disavow that effort and deception. In the case of the skinhead, that often manifests itself through emphatic recourse to authenticity. In the present age of simulation, Baudrillard sees this intensified recourse to notions of the 'real' as cultural disavowal of the death of reality that simulation exposes.

Simulated skins

Performativity exposes gender as a simulation: 'Gender is a kind of imitation for which there is no original.'[43] The relation of gay skin to 'real' skin is exposed as being of one of copy to copy rather than imitation to original. In the age of simulation, signs no longer refer to any reality, the mutually sustaining difference of real/representation, only to each other and a system of exchangeable equivalences. 'Simulation is no longer that of territory, a referential being or a substance. It is the generation by models of a real without origin or reality: a hyperreal.'[44]

Queer appropriation of skinhead imagery exposes the bouncers of identity, the border guards of territory, as simulations, and opens the sites of 'origin' they guard. Now anyone who looks like a skinhead is in fact a real skinhead – when creating a simulation, 'you will find yourself unwittingly in the real, one of whose functions is precisely to devour every attempt at simulation, to reduce everything to some reality'.[45] The 'function of the real' can be seen imposing itself in the intensified recourse to the myths of 'reality' ('I *am* a real skin, because . . .') motivated by 'real' skins' proximity to and awareness of fakes. Eventually, you have to give up. Even George Marshall, custodian of the essence of (straight) skinheadism, acknowledges the outcome: 'Anyone can claim to be a skinhead and as long as he looks the part, who's to say he's not?'[46] Similarly, Richard, who runs London's sole skin-only club, says, 'Genuine skins *are* fashion skins – there's no difference. What is being a skinhead? I don't know what it is. It's not a matter of role-play. I don't see how I play any part. I am me, and it's just how I want to dress.'

The parody of gay skin drag has become the blank parody of postmodern pastiche, and this is a recent historical move. When discussing his first sighting of gay skinheads in the Union Tavern, Daffyd Jenkins says, 'These were skinheads – they weren't macho Marys, but they were gay.' In 1969 he could distinguish 'real' from 'drag'. But this distinction cannot be made in 1995. 'What's the difference between real gay skins and macho Marys? It's very difficult to tell. It's like, what's camp? Everybody recognizes camp, but nobody can describe it to you.' The exaggerated masculinity of skinheads has a drag effect on all skinheads.

Skinheads were always already simulations. The 'original' skin was supposed to be a reassertion of a working-class identity at the level of style. In fact, it was an exercise in nostalgia creation: the look did not refer to an origin in a previous class model but a contemporary bourgeois stereotype. 'The accent, like the clothing, is constructed from the cartoon worker, the navvie. Skinhead style takes the bourgeois caricature of its own class (dumb and violent) and makes it yet more extreme.'[17] This look was then authenticated by positing itself in an anteriority articulated through nostalgia: a myth of origin, a second-hand authenticity, obscuring the fact that it was a bourgeois image of the male worker adopted by working-class boys in the *absence* of a working-class identity. The nostalgic myth of a homogeneous working-class community was created performatively and operated not in relation to reality, but in relation to other like images: skinheads dressed to look like each other.

As a result of its punk *revival*, this simulation of white working-class hardness was further exaggerated. The skinhead, as the identity of fixed authenticity, is challenged both by its own status as a reappropriation and the subculture's post-punk diversity. 'When the real is no longer what it used to be, nostalgia assumes its full meaning. There is a proliferation of myths of origin and signs of reality; of second-hand truth, objectivity and authenticity.'[48] Hence the panicked claims to the genuine status of 'real skinhead' by various factions, each with its own version of the subculture's origin and true meaning.

The historic involvement further queers the straightness of this lost origin anyway. John G. Byrne is by no means the only gay skin photographer whose pictures have acted as access points to skinhead subculture for straight lads. John's pictures have been popular with skinheads around the world since he started taking them in 1980; indeed, it was one of his pictures that was selected to grace the cover of the first volume of *The Collected Richard Allen*. His choice of models is motivated to some degree by his sexual interest: 'I like to take pictures of skinheads that I particularly like myself, personally. I know most of them anyway. Some are gay, some aren't – or they're bisexual. They're all very masculine types.' The documentary, 'natural' feel of his pictures is a conscious reaction to the over-styled nature of most gay photography, but that 'natural'-ness is problematized by the *conscious* avoidance of heavy-handed styling: naturalness is just another style.

> I don't like arty-farty pictures that you usually see in gay magazines. I'm not against them being taken, but they're just so usual, they're far too artificial. I like to take pictures that look like people you'd see in the street that you'd particularly like. I don't like posing them too much – it's unavoidable sometimes, but I try to do pictures that are not too posed.

The skinhead is reproduced in the dominant culture, for consumption by heterosexuals, within a homoerotic frame: John's pictures sell as well in gay sex shops as in skin venues. Those straight lads who take John's pictures as a basis for their own hard, straight image are using a (homo)sexualized image of a skin, who may well himself have been gay, as a reference point. Who's copying who here? Who owns the copyright? Were skinheads ever the property of heterosexuality? This is further complicated by the fact that homosexuality has authorized the skinhead. When the Victoria and Albert Museum ran an authoritative exhibition on youth cultures, *Streetstyle*, in 1994, the skinhead dummies were clothed in items from John Byrne's wardrobe. John called the V & A after reading about the museum's request for authentic skin items in *Skinhead Times*.

> The funny thing was, they had the skinhead stand with my clothes on one side and they had the gay section on the other side. The gay section had a lot of very effeminate clothes on it. I'm sure a lot of people have got different views about fashions, but I thought it was strange they didn't have some more butch clothes on the gay stand.

With the straight origin queered, and therefore lost, in this way, 'Queer appropriation' is a contradiction in terms: Queer, as ever, erases itself. The assumption inherent in this phrase is that gay men appropriated the prepackaged product of natural masculinity embodied in the skinhead at some point in the mid-1980s. This is still commonly believed to be the case, even among many gay skins. But Queer would seek to destabilize those very sites of 'gay' and 'straight' by exposing the illusory nature of their stability. An appropriation is predicated on the notion of rights of ownership – that certain qualities are inherent to certain social types. Queer tells us that all property is theft.

Gay skins have been involved from the start both as subjects and as agents of the dissemination of the skinhead image; the official pictorial history of 'straight' skinheadism is gay. The gay skin is not an example of Queer appropriation because skinheads were *never* completely straight. At times they've been gay: but they've always been queer.

Drag exposes heterosexualizing norms as a dynamic of intensified reproduction and disavowal. 'The parodic or imitative effect of gay identities works neither to copy nor emulate heterosexuality', writes Butler, 'but rather, to expose heterosexuality as an incessant and panicked imitation of its own naturalised idealization.'[49] This is symptomatic of culture in the age of simulation: the hyperaccelerated way in which modern technologies reproduce the 'real' through their simulation only serves to undo that reality.

It was not only on the gay scene that the image of the skinhead was being endlessly repeated. The skinhead may have been too threatening, or seemingly anti-style, to undergo assimilation into the mainstream in the preceding years, but the post-punk image existed in a decade when the hyperacceleration of images was far more intense. This manifested itself in the interdependent sites of advertising, fashion and pop, where the skin look was cut up, the label lost and the origin forgotten.

Model skins

Although the media coverage of the post-punk skinhead in the early 1980s bound him to the notions of mindless violence even more successfully than his 1960s predecessor, the emergence of skinhead simulations in the signifying industry of advertising later in the decade saw its undoing. In 1986, Stephen Wells in the NME could write of the skinhead's partial assimilation into the mainstream. With advertising agencies deciding that hippies, rockers and punks were 'aged and faded, the skinhead is being rehabilitated as the only widely recognisable youth stereotype left . . . a naughty but nice Care Bear cuddly. So meet the mediaSkin — saving people from falling buildings, behaving on tube trains, joining YTS schemes, drinking pop . . .'[50]

This assimilation was only partial, though. The exchange-value of the *word* 'skinhead' with the notions of mindless male aggression was still in operation: the advertising agencies using skin imagery tellingly felt the need to deny that shaven-headed boys in boots and braces were actually skinheads. Allen, Brady and Marsh were responsible for a series of animated Weetabix ads where five biscuits were anthropomorphized into four DM-booted bald lads and a pig-tailed girl. The lads threateningly advised youngsters to eat the cereal: ' . . . if you know what's good for you,

you do. We're the Weetabix, OK?' In their styles and mildly aggressive behaviour, they gesture towards 'skinhead'. But Peter Rayworth of the ad agency said, 'We never call them skinheads . . . Skinheads have all sorts of unpleasant connotations . . . They're aggressive, they're sordid, they sniff glue and they mug old ladies.' Billboard and magazine ads for the Youth Training Scheme featured a portrait of a scary-looking skin, as did TV ads for the soft drink Tizer. And Persil washing powder was advertised in a thirty-second commercial showing a topless young skinhead having a bit of bovver with a washing machine. The agencies responsible for these adverts all claimed that 'their boy is . . . just an average youth who happens to look like a skinhead'. Only those responsible for the *Guardian* ad, which used 'a nasty looking bastard . . . more your sordid, glue-sniffing old lady mugger, all flailing limbs, plastic bomber jacket and bleached jeans', admitted that they were depicting a skinhead; and this was deliberately to undermine expectations of skinhead behaviour.

The convincing and well-researched deployment of actors in these adverts further served to undermine the notion of a genuine skinhead. Do real skinheads who become actors remain real skinheads when they play skinheads, or are they just acting? Gay skin Wolf embodied this paradox as a model with the Ugly agency in the late 1960s: his qualification for this job was his identity as a *real* skinhead. Profiled in a 1971 *Daily Mirror* feature on skins, which significantly hailed him as 'the model skinhead', he sited himself at the origin of the movement:

> I've always been a skinhead. I was a skinhead even before the word was invented. When I was twelve or thirteen I decided I didn't want to be a hairy and had my hair cropped. The boots and the braces and the Crombie have always been around in my life.[51]

This would have made him a skinhead in 1961. He went on to say that skinhead life is 'booze and birds, in that order. Birds are all right in bed, but out of bed, no dice. Women don't fool me in the least. They're very selfish. They're born to exploit men. But they'll not exploit me.' Presumably this misogynistic contempt is supposed to underline his heterosexuality/ authenticity for *Mirror* readers – the significantly gendered term, 'male model' carries certain overtones.

The Bovver Boots model agency ('East End kids, Equity punks, Skin 'Eds a speciality') was set up in the mid-1980s to cater for a shortage in convincing youth subculture members available to advertising agencies. Questions of authenticity are no longer relevant: Ben Brooks, who played a skinhead in an advert for Tizer, joined the agency as 'a stout, long-haired drama school drop-out'. He is certainly not the real thing, then, but he is *convincing*. Promotional culture exposes the skinhead as a simulation, a challenge of performance; it is simply a matter of looking the part.

So, by 1986, although the label 'skinhead' was still beyond approval, the *visual image* was circulating fairly unproblematically within the dominant culture as a signifier of '(roguish) youth' rather than '(violent) thug'. The label had come off, and the layers of association were slowly starting to peel away. As a copy among so many other copies, the skinhead *look* becomes detached from the significance of 'skinhead', which, from the statements given by the very people using the imagery, still carried connotations of violence and fascism. The Manager of Bovver Boots significantly felt the need to stress, 'I would never knowingly employ a National Fronter . . . I wouldn't use anyone who runs down gays.' Thus the style is subject to what John Clarke defines as 'defusion': where 'a particular style is dislocated from the context and group which generated it, and taken up with a stress on those elements which make it "a commercial proposition", especially their novelty'.[52]

Fashion

Elements of the skinhead look had also been circulating, earlier in the 1980s, at an unconscious level. The same myths of authenticity which had originally inspired the skinhead wardrobe informed the 'Hard Times' look which emerged around 1981. A reaction against the artificial, effete excesses of New Romanticism, this was a manifestation of the gloomy zeitgeist of Thatcher's early years, articulating an earnest acknowledgement of the realities of economic depression and high unemployment. It was back to style basics: distressed denim and leather, no frills and rough machismo.

'Hard Times' informed the political dress of members of radical-left groups throughout the 1980s. Eschewing the capitalist conspiracy of fashion, which encouraged you to buy clothes you did not need, their self-presentational strategies drew from supposedly fashion-resistant sites: shaved heads, rolled jeans, Doc Marten boots and workwear that justified itself through its practicality and formed a reaction to fashion. This was not an attempt to emulate skins, but was motivated by similar ideological concerns to posit the wearer in a utopian authenticity outside or beyond fashion.

In 1986, the very year that 'The Brother' was reiterating the 'real' skins' belief that 'the skinhead is beyond fashion', the skin look was becoming fashionable among gay men, while fashion was cutting up the skinhead and sticking him back together.

To assert his fixedness, the skinhead has to stand outside the fashion system. As Baudrillard has written, 'There is no such thing as fashion in a society of caste and rank, since one is assigned a place irrevocably, and so class mobility is non-existent';[53] the skinhead asserted a nostalgic yearning for a familiar, fixed society in reaction against the class mobility of the mods. Therefore, in a society where fashion exists as a sign of social fluidity, he must withstand the tides. And the fashion system needs him to be kept outside: it needs seemingly constant, seemingly exterior standards against which to define its fluidity.

Ever-changing fashion, which characterizes the ever-changing yet ever-present 'now', is the discourse of social change at the level of appearance. It is the indeterminacy of fashion as a fluid system that makes people nervous: the late capitalist hyperacceleration and circulation of images, their subsequent identification and immediate redundancy, threaten to leave you behind. This leads to renewed efforts to establish '(good) taste', which can be seen as the reappearance of the real in this discourse of simulation. 'Taste' passes itself off as absolute, asserting itself in terms such as 'timeless' and 'classic', disavowing the fact that it changes each time it is used to authorize developments in fashion. Taste denies that there is no consensus, for with the loss of consensus, 'there is no criterion for the role of taste'.[54] It is this dynamic which drives postmodern cultural overproduction, and which was all too apparent in the fashion press of the 1980s, which sought to chart changing trends according in terms of (absolute) taste. If taste *were* monolithic, we wouldn't need a fashion press to chart its changes.

The speed with which the press assimilated new developments in fashion at this time simply hyperaccelerated the speed of change. The way hyperaccelerated culture exposed reality as simulation was evident in the rapid succession and then overlapping of revivals and revivals of revivals: a consequence of punk, by the end of the decade the very notion of 'revival' became meaningless as the present simultaneously consumed and was submerged by various pasts. This only served to validate the subsequent proliferation of titles: there was *more* need for *more* press so that one could keep abreast of these numerous rapid changes. Fashion mags became 'style bibles', and two very different approaches to the nature of style were evident in two influential youth-targeted monthly titles. Glossy, real-bound and consistent in its design evolution, *The Face* pursued an agenda of (modernist) cool with a distant, ironic attitude and defined 1980s taste. Marking itself in opposition to the more established title was *i-D*. For much of the decade printed on rough paper and stapled for effect rather than need, with graphics comprised of distressed photocopies and sticky labels, it championed kitsch and a postmodern trash aesthetic.

i-D's punk DIY attitude was summed up in a 1987 spread titled 'The Appropriators': 'When garments like denim and MA–1 flying jackets become too popular, an artistic burst of customizing soon turns then from a uniform back into a unique outfit . . . THE FAMILIAR IS BEING APPROPRIATED AND DEFILED BY THE IMAGINATIVE.'[55] Acknowledging that all social signs are by definition cliches, the DIY aesthetic reasserted individuality (doing-it-yourself redefines the 'self') with incongruous accumulations, trying to prevent closure through an overabundance of signifiers – loads of logos crammed on to lapels or safety-pinned on to backs; 'buckles on hats' and bottle-tops on Docs. The body became the site of the hyperacceleration of signifiers. The write-up was accompanied by Polaroids taken by Wigan of clubbers in London's Delirium in tailored jackets and flying jackets customized with badges, carefully placed rips, safety pins, suedeheady bowler hats. The effect was a solution to the uniform effect that the clothing industry could produce in bulk. It also had political appeal in its use of second-hand clothes: recycling was in, and the trash aesthetic was cheap.

This was the deconstruction of fashion, literally ripping clothes apart and stitching them back together. The look, along with the D-word, found its way to the catwalk five years later as fashion caught up with theory. But the consequences were more immediate: clothing ensembles were being exploded. Bits of uniforms could be picked off and reconfigured into new outfits. This in fact had been happening throughout the decade. The very definition of Levis and bomber jacket as anonymous wardrobe basics in 'The Appropriators' spread showed how these elements of the skinhead ensemble, once so rare, had become so popular that they had found their way into every high street in Britain. As these individual satellites shot out of the orbit of 'skinhead', they carried with them a tacit memory of skinhead.

With this explosion of the skinhead came the enforced myth of its origin as beyond fashion. *The i-D Bible* of 1987 included a feature on 'Classic Looks', a crash-course in (predominantly working-class) youth cultures which, since the post-punk era had chased revival-mania, had all come to have contemporary significance. Skinheads form the first entry. Significantly, under 'Crossovers' appeared 'Gay skinheads: DM boots, bleached jeans, bald heads and personal stereos.'

Pop

No one ever accused Bros, the outrageously successful chart band of the late 1980s, of being skinheads, although they were often justly accused by gay men of looking like queens. But their early styling (cropped hair, tight white T-shirt, Levis jackets and rolled jeans, MA–1 flying jackets, DMs) derived from the skinhead via the gay scene. The decontextualizing, designifying techniques of the 'Appropriators' philosophy was evident in the presence of Grolsch bottle tops on their Doc Martens and in the absence of any skinhead signification.

Individual elements of the skinhead uniform had always served a metonymic function to some degree. A 'skin-head' is a shaved head: with no clothes, it is only the shaved head of the cover star of the Queer *Gay Times* that communicates a sense of 'skinhead-ness'. DMs, in being dubbed 'bovver boots' signified similarly: the meaning of the Docs on the cover of *The Young Londoners* was clear. But with the uniform broken up, individual elements floated free in fashion. They could then be reassembled in similar configurations without explicitly invoking the associations skinheads had once carried. Loosened from the associations of fascist, queerbasher, racist, straight and working class, they could move in contexts which were non-fascist, middle class and queer. With the skin look cut up, the label lost and the origin forgotten, elements of the skinhead look found their way into radical gay groups via the Hard Times-derived activist uniform. But, even though he had been semiotically blanked, those connotations continue to haunt the skinhead as obsessive memories, sexualizing him in the threat he once may have represented.

Within a few years, skinhead styles were being worn without any longer signifying 'skinhead'. Alongside the recognizably skinhead ensemble being worn elsewhere in gay subculture, a fragmented, defused version of the look, losing coherence as an articulation of 'skinhead', became part of a distinctive urban homo style: Doc Martens, Levi 501s, denim jacket, cropped hair, bomber jacket. Its recirculations, reproductions and repetitions had seen it mutate into something other than skinhead. These elements had been circulating beyond the confines of skinhead in earlier decades on the macho scene. But by 1988, these elements broadly said 'gay man/homosexual/queer' rather than specifically a 'macho queen'.

This look was consolidated by the proliferation of images of out-gay pop stars such as Jimmy Somerville and Marc Almond. The media interest afforded to these stars only served to popularize and spread still further this new skinheadish gay uniform. Nick attributes not only the popularity of the gay skin look, but also its ability to be taken up on such a wide-scale and the loss of its inherent 'working-classness', to the diffusive context of pop in the mid-1980s.

> There wasn't any middle-class skinheads in the early eighties, no way! Well, I never met any. Earlier in the eighties, it was more about revolution, a working-class identity. Middle-class men couldn't have coped with it. They just weren't streetwise. That was later, when it became . . . softer. People had slightly longer hair, it was around the time of 'Small Town Boy', Jimmy Somerville, that time, when it became trendy, I suppose. I think Jimmy Somerville had a very big influence. He had a type of look that wasn't exactly skinhead, but a move on from that. He had short hair, bomber jacket, he was a working-class boy, lots of people related to him; I think he had a big influence on the gay scene, definitely, I think he really did, a huge impact for working-class gay men.

The ubiquitous image of the pop star – significantly presented as a *gay* pop star – had three important implications. It consolidated a new (hard, masculine, skinheadish) gay image for straight people; the skinheadishness of the image opened gay identity to working-class men; and, in turning this permutation of the skinhead look into a (mere) style, equivalent to and exchangeable with other fashion choices, it became accessible to middle-class queens. 'He presented a working-class image for working-class men to latch on to. And then other people started to adopt that image, the middle classes started to ape it. Suddenly it was a fashion thing rather than a class thing; it moved on.'

Gay skin Nick remembers the way pop had defused the suedehead in the early 1970s through the styling of one of the most popular and innocuous bands of the decade. 'The Bay City Rollers picked up on the suedehead with their feathercuts and boots.' In fact, the person responsible for the band's famous outfits (parallel three-quarter-length tartan trimmed trousers, tight shirts, braces and boots) was the designer of the suedehead-like costumes for *A Clockwork Orange*.

If dressing like/being a skinhead was no longer problematic for gay men, neither was it problematic for a feminist pop star. An early interview with Sinead O'Connor in *i-D* in 1987 serves to illustrate the way a skinhead appearance no longer signified 'skinhead'. Pictured in rolled Levis, DM boots, braces, white T-shirt (with shoulder pads) and bowler hat on her shaved head, 'she's got skinhead haircut but doesn't like skinheads'.[56] The title 'An Irish skinhead folk-singing fashion victim?' acknowledges the cultural unintelligibility of the contradictory accumulation of cultural signifiers.

In conclusion

The adoption of skinhead imagery by gay men can be read as a Queer tactic for two reasons: it is the unapologetic embracing of a bad object choice, and it serves to assert that which should not be included within the realm of the 'homosexual': real masculinity. Being a real skinhead is shown to be simply a matter of looking the part because those whom the category should exclude do it so well. Consequently, the real masculinity that the skinhead was supposed to embody is shown to be a simulation: gender, identity and reality are exposed as hyperreal simulations with no origin. The mythic stable site to which the skinhead is supposed to refer – straight masculinity – is destabilized by a history of homosexual involvement. And fashion's deconstruction of the skinhead allowed a skinhead-derived look to become the dominant urban gay uniform even among those who ideologically opposed skinhead styles on the scene. With gay men unwittingly looking like skinheads, dressing up as skinheads and being real skinheads, the skinhead as a symbol of straight, white, working-class masculinity is queered: potentially *anyone* can be a skinhead – even if they hate skinheads.

Notes

1. Bruce la Bruce, 'The Wild, Wild World of Fanzines', in Paul Burston (ed.), *A Queer Romance: Lesbians, gay men and popular culture*, p. 186.

2. Matias Viegener, 'The Only Haircut That Makes Sense Anymore: Queer Subculture and Gay Resistance' in M Gever, J Greyson and P Parmar (eds), *Queer Looks* (London: Routledge, 1993), p. 128.

3. B Ruby Rich, 'When Difference Is (More Than) Skin Deep'. *Queer Looks*, p. 318.

4. Keith Alcorn, 'Queer and Now', in *Gay Times*, May 1992, p. 24.

5. Charles Lemert, 'General Social Theory, Irony, Postmodernism', in Steven Seidman and David Wagner (eds), *Postmodernism and Social Theory: The Debate over General Theory* (Oxford: Blackwell, 1992), p. 42.

6. Quoted in Michael Newman, 'Revising Modernism, Representing Postmodernism: Critical Discourses of the Visual Arts' in Lisa Appignanesi (ed.), *ICA Documents 4: Postmodernism* (London: Free Association Books, 1989), p. 134.

7. Steve Seidman, 'Postmodern Social Theory as Narrative with a Moral Intent', in *Postmodernism and Social Theory*, p. 59.

8. Jean-Francis Lyotard, 'Complexity and the Sublime', in *ICA Documents 4: Postmodernism*, p. 23.

9. Jean Baudrillard, *Simulacra and Simulations* (New York: Sémiotext(e), 1983), p. 12.

10. Lyotard, 'Complexity and the Sublime', p. 23.

11. Chantal Mouffe, 'Feminism, Citizenship and the Radical Democratic Politics', in Judith Butler and Joan Scott (eds), *Feminists Theorise the Political* (New York: Routledge, 1992), pp. 369–84.

12. Judith Butler, *Bodies That Matter* (London: Routledge, 1993), p. 193.

13. Butler, *Bodies That Matter*, p. 240.

14. Brian Rafferty in *New York Queer*, quoted in Keith Alcorn, 'Queer and Now', *Gay Times*, May 1992.

15. Eve Kosofsky Sedgwick, *Epistemology of the Closet* (London: Harvester Wheatsheaf, 1991), pp. 83–5.

16. *Ibid.*, p. 85.

17. *Ibid.*, p. 83.

18. Paul Burston, 'The Death of Queer Politics', *Gay Times*, August 1992, p. 24.

19. 'Trading Places: Consumption, Sexuality and the Creation of Queer Space', in David Bell and Gill Valentine (eds), *Mapping Desire: Geographies of Sexualities* (London: Routledge, 1994), p. 194.

20. *Ibid.*, p. 197.

21. Paul Burston, 'The Death of Queer Politics', p. 23.

22. Judith Butler, 'Imitation and Gender Insubordination', in Diana Fuss (ed.), *Inside/Out: Lesbian Theories, Gay Theories* (London: Routledge, 1991), p. 19.

23. Alan Sinfield, 'What's in a Name?', *Gay Times*, May 1992, p. 25.

24. Sadie Plant, 'When Blowing the Strike is Striking the Blow', in Stewart Home (ed.), *Neoist Manifestos/Art Strike Papers* (London: AK Press, 1993), p. 37.

25. Bruce la Bruce, 'The Wild, Wild World of Fanzines', p. 186.

26. Richard Smith, 'Papering over the Cracks', *Gay Times*, May 1992, p. 29.

27. Burston, 'The Death of Queer Politics', p. 23.

28. *Ibid.*, p. 24.

29. James Chesebro and Kenneth Klenk, 'Gay Masculinity in the Gay Disco', in James Chesebro (ed.), *Gayspeak: Gay Male and Lesbian*

Communication (New York: Pilgrim Press, 1981), p. 92.

30. Butler, 'Imitation and Gender Insubordination', p. 19.

31. Judith Butler, *Gender Trouble: Feminism and the Subversion of Identity* (London: Routledge, 1990), p. 128.

32. *Ibid.*, p. 92.

33. *Ibid.*, p. 93.

34. *Ibid.*, p. 136.

35. *Ibid.*, p. 137.

36. Chesebro and Klenk, 'Gay Masculinity in the Gay Disco', pp. 95–6.

37. Gregg Blachford, 'Male Dominance and the Gay World', in Kenneth Plummer (ed.), *The Making of the Modern Homosexual* (New Jersey: Barnes and Noble, 1981), p. 200.

38. Andrew Kopkind, 'Dressing Up', *Village Voice*, 30 April 1979, p. 34.

39. Jamie Gough, 'Theories of Sexual Identity and the Maculinisation of the Gay Man', in Simon Shepherd and Mick Wallis (eds), *Coming On Strong: Gay Politics and Culture* (London: Unwin Hyman, 1989), p. 131.

40. *Ibid.*, p. 121.

41. Chesebro and Klenk, 'Gay Masculinity in the Gay Disco', p. 101.

42. Baudrillard, *Simulations*, p. 40.

43. Butler, 'Imitation and Gender Insubordination', p. 21.

44. Baudrillard, *Simulations*, p. 2.

45. *Ibid.*, p. 39.

46. George Marshall, *Spirit of '69: A Skinhead Bible* (Dunoon, Scotland: Skinhead Times Publishing, 1991), p. 104.

47. Ian Walker, 'Skinheads: the Cult of Trouble', *New Society*, 26 June 1980, p. 346.

48. Baudrillard, *Simulations*, p. 12.

49. Butler, 'Imitation and Gender Insubordination', p. 23.

50. Steven Wells, 'Diamond Geezers', *New Musical Express*, 20 September 1986. Quotations in the following paragraph are taken from this article.

51. *Daily Mirror*, 8 March 1971.

52. John Clarke, 'Style', in Stuart Hall and Tony Jefferson (eds), *Resistance Through Ritual* (London: Hutchinson, 1976), p. 188.

53. Baudrillard, *Simulations*, p. 84.

54. Lyotard, 'Complexity and the Sublime', p. 22.

55. *i-D*, June 1987, pp. 53–7.

56. *i-D*, May 1987, p. 5.

10

What Does It All Mean?

To end with a conclusion would be highly ironic. Any such ending would be at odds with my argument that the queered skin's value is that he opens the closed signifier of masculine authority. It would in any case be impossible to come to a single conclusion about a category as diverse as 'gay skins': the phrase refers to so many gay men, queers and other non-heterosexuals that have lived as skinheads for so many different reasons over so many years. As the phrase 'gay skinhead' dissolves each of its constitutive terms by erasing the difference in their mutual opposition, the phrase itself starts to become meaningless. Literally: as attested by the refusal of all those gay men who dress like skinheads but claim no relation to the word. Gay skins aren't even 'gay skins'. They're just gay men.

Is this a good thing or a bad thing? On a grand scale, in the greater field of normalizing heterosexual masculine structures, it's a good thing – possibly – that the discourse of masculinity can no longer unproblematically predicate itsef on the alignment of heterosexual/homosexual with hard/soft and authentic/artificial. But first, the down side. If you find the appearance of skinhead offensive it's an extremely bad thing. Certainly on a local scale, at a subcultural level, some of the consequences are troubling.

The gay skinhead is both a cause and a consequence of the masculinization of gay male subculture. The gay mainstream now expects and requires machismo as the dominant behavioural mode of gay men. Go to almost any gay club in any large British city and you'll see sweaty, topless, muscly, shaven-headed punters. Not so long ago they were the exceptional go-go dancers, held aloft on podiums as ideals for others to admire and emulate; as desire has collapsed into identification, these days the dancefloor is awash with them. And therein lies the paradox: we can talk of a 'gay mainstream' because gay subculture in the 1990s is so diverse; and yet this mainstream would seek to homogenize its diverse constituency through macho codes.

'Butch' is a gay thing: I've never heard a straight man use the term, except when mimicking queens. Even if hard masculinity is not attainable by all gay men, it is expected that all gay men will desire it. Such is the strength of this ideal that any gay man who professes otherwise is treated with suspicion. In 1994, while working on the editorial team of *Boyz*, the scene-based gay weekly for men under twenty-five, I wrote an article celebrating girly boyishness and lamenting the fact that only straights did it these days. This evinced a very angry fax from a reader (and *Boyz* articles rarely stir up readers' emotions enough to inspire such reactions). It was addressed to Ms Angel (Murray Angel was my *nom de plume*): 'Who does she think she is? . . . I'm gay because I'm a man and I fancy men . . . Just because I'm gay, it doesn't mean I can't be a real man.'

In 1995, while the *Boyz* pin-ups were as hard and beefy as ever, style mags from *L'Uomo Vogue* to *Interview* to *The Face* were celebrating the sexiness of skinny, girly male models. Not because they were challenging or weird, but simply because they were beautiful. 'Saying it loud, fey and proud', wrote Nick Compton in *The Face*.[1] 'Look in '95 at who is peddling the extreme gender stereotypes . . . the stalwarts of proud-to-be-gay Old Compton Street crew struggling with the bar-bell of manliness.' Perhaps these days hetero/homosexual aligns with hetero/homogeneity.

Cultural change is never even, and the effects of the late-1960s' masculinization or 'butch-shift' are still being felt. Some of the older gay skins I interviewed still believed that the skinhead was an intrinsically straight phenomenon, that 'straight masculinity' was something beyond the territory of homosexuality. The extent to which a mode of masculinity can claim to be gay when heterosexuality is its (however distanced, however 'lost') referent is questioned by David Forrest, who writes of the young man coming on to the urban gay scene in the 1990s:

> he appears to have moved away from seeing himself and being seen by others, as a 'gender invert', a 'feminine' soul in a 'male' body, and towards seeing himself as being seen as a complete (that is, 'real') man.[2]

But then Forrest questions this change with the observation that 'personal ads in the gay press appeal for "similar straight-acting partners"' and that drag is still a popular scene phenomenon. Have gay men arrived at authentic masculinity? Or is gay masculinity an emphatic disavowal of feminization? Is it still the effeminate model that drives gay modes of identification?

This takes us back to the Freudian definition of the double nature of the fetish as a disavowal and acknowledgement of castration. If femininity is the state of having been castrated, and masculinity the state of almost always about to be castrated, then straight masculinity is the fear of impending castration, and gay male masculinity is the dynamic between the fear of castration and the possibility that one is already castrated (phallic difference is disempowered in gay sex, and the accusations of effeminacy still haunt the culture). Hence emphatic recourse to macho fetishes, a denial of one's already having been castrated: this is a masquerade of masculinity. But this is the very tactic straight men use to prevent castration, and the double nature of the fetish would suggest that this fear of already having been feminized haunts straight male subjectivity too. What gay masculinity reveals is the masquerade of *all* maleness.

And that has to be a good thing.

All men together

Another problem at a local level but with possibly radical consequences is the status of men-only clubs. Gender separatism is a thorny issue; while radical feminism espouses women-only spaces as sites of resistance to patriarchy, it has informed many of the objections to clubs with exclusively male door policies. It is significant that men who object to women's tents at Pride tend to prefer men-only venues; the enforced phallicism of the macho scene *would* blind them to the nature of patriarchy, runs the rad fem argument.

Historically, gay skins have gravitated towards venues that cater for an exclusively male crowd, and there *are* problems with men-only clubs that have yet to be accounted for. It is not just women but femininity that is excluded: drag queens (with the exception of stage acts) are usually barred from such venues. In 1991, radical Queer group Homocult caused panic on the Manchester club scene when they issued a statement claiming that butch dykes with strap-ons had infiltrated a dimly lit backroom in a men-only bar. The uproar exposed a distinctly gynaphobic tendency on the scene as butch queens worried about whether they'd been penetrated by women.

Queer should (and in this case did) seek to subvert such gender consolidatory contexts. But Queer also argues for radical pleasure – any pleasure derived from a source beyond the discourse of normalizing sexuality. It asserts the right for people to enjoy politically problematic sexuality on the grounds that they are pleasurable without having to justify the ideology of that pleasure (Queer means never having to say sorry . . .). This validates the argument that, as men-only venues tend to be mainly concerned with sex, and as male homosexuality is about men loving men, women *need* to be excluded. But this may be articulated through (and indeed motivated by) misogyny – passing such venues, I've heard too many abusive terms hurled at women by the men on the door.

However, the existence of men-only gay clubs does subvert the binarism of homosocial/homosexual on which patriarchy is predicated. In their marginalization or enforced exclusion of 'the feminine', these venues accord with the demands of dominant masculinity; likewise in the homosocial nature of their constituencies. But they resolutely claim this in the name of 'gay', and the consequence may be paradoxically queer. Not only does homosociality become a requirement of the homosexuality against which it should define itself; homosexuality may be seen as a logical consequence of enforcing homosociality.

So, even while he asserted that skinheads are essentially straight, one gay skin who was present at numerous punk and skinhead gigs in London in the early 1980s remembers:

> It was always my fantasy to go with skinheads, I found the whole image a total turn-on. Skinheads always had really horny bodies, and they'd always all dance together, they'd start wrestling . . . They always had their shirts off, all over each other, arms round each other – I used to find the scenario very gay.

Another gay skin from that era recalls his first visit to an Oi! gig:

> The idea that the skinhead scene would be full of lads taking their shirts off and dancing together, that was incredible, I didn't believe that would happen. I used to go to gigs at the 100 Club and they were really horny. You were dancing with lads stripped to the waist, arms round each other, so you could do all that and get a real kick out of it without anyone ever tumbling what was going on. I was the only gay person who was gay there, as far as I know. But who knows? Perhaps the guy next to me was thinking the same thing. It wouldn't surprise me.

Skin clubs looked gay, and gay clubs look like skin clubs: when a 1994 episode of the Granada TV crime drama series *Cracker* needed to set up a neo-Nazi skin rally, a vast number of local scene queens were recruited – and they looked the part.

Closing the signifier

I've argued that, as a culturally unintelligible body, the gay skin queers the skinhead and all the discourses of natural white working-class masculinity he embodies. In my optimistic Queer reading of the gay skin, I've assumed that the image has been exposed as a mere style and that those previous 'real' meanings only remain as half-forgotten phantoms. Of course, as I stated in my introduction, it is far more complex than that: ideology is never so neat. There are overlapping communities of knowledge, overlapping and contradictory epistemologies within those communities. Which notion of skinhead does the gay skin disrupt, and for whom?

A measure of the extent to which skinheads and association with them, however distant, ironic or even queer, continue to remain politically suspect came in 1992 when the pop star Morrissey played an open air gig in Finsbury Park, North London. The Mancunian singer and prolific lyricist's work with the Smiths, who disbanded in 1987, had shown a Wildean influence, lyrically, aesthetically (flowers) and erotically (early Smiths' lyrics where characterized by a fascination with rough young lads from a distant admirer). These lyrics had been celebrated for their lack of gender specificity, and in interviews he espoused the destruction of normalizing categories of gender and sexuality: in the 1985 *Smash Hits Annual*, he declared, 'I don't recognise such terms as heterosexual, bisexual . . . These words do great damage, they confuse people and they make people unhappy so I want to do away with them.'

However, perhaps Morrissey became aware of the futility of gender-free utopias in gender deconstruction (listeners read whatever gender-grid suited them into his work, and his own identity was subject to the same appropriation, with gay and straight fans arguing that he was 'theirs'), and came to embrace more explicitly conservative modes of gender: his first solo release was called 'Suedehead'. In the years that followed, football hooligans, National Front supporters and racial abuse started to feature in his lyrics, and skinheads appeared in videos and on stage backdrops. In May 1991 he voiced his delight at the rising number of 'skinheads in nail varnish' among his fans. He even visited John Byrne to discuss the use of one of his pictures for the sleeve of his 1994 compilation LP, *World of Morrissey*. Exacerbating the controversial use of British nationalism as a focus of his work were comments mourning the death of Englishness, championing British football hooligans ('I understand the level of patriotism, the level of frustration and the level of jubilance') and accepting racism ('I don't really think, for instance, that black people and white people will ever really get on or like each other.')[3]

But it was his association with skinheads that both acted as confirmation of this and proved to be most controversial in its own right. When Morrissey appeared at a weekend open-air festival in Finsbury Park on 8 August 1992, 'his affection for skinhead and nationalist imagery', commented the *NME*, 'was given its most public display ever'. He walked on wearing a silver lamé shirt and draped in a Union Jack to a stage decorated with a monumental blow-up of two (female) skins. Such imagery was evident elsewhere that day, but in a far less ambiguous context: Madness were headlining the gig, whose unwelcome skinhead/NF following, dating from the band's original emergence from the post-punk Two-tone ska scene, meant that there were fascist skinheads in the audience; and nearby, National Front and British Movement members were being mobilized to attack a Troops Out march in the area. Morrissey abandoned his set half-way through and cancelled his gig on the following day; his press office released a statement saying his removal was due to projectiles and a 50p thrown by a 'National Front skinhead'.

While many skinheads in the crowd interpreted the combination of the skinhead backdrop, the British flag and a lamé shirt as an ambiguous distancing from and ridiculing of British nationalist skins (according to John Byrne, 'the Nazis skinheads thought, "How dare they? It's our flag and no-one else's"'), the rock weekly the *NME* saw it as an unambivalent identification with the imagery. A team of journalists concluded that 'cavorting with the Union Jack, with all its ambiguities, and surrounding yourself with the paraphernalia and imagery of the skinhead cult' moves you away from a celebration of Britishness (itself questionable) into 'entirely different and altogether more dangerous territory'.[4] Whilst conceding that 'the cultural signals of shaving your head and wearing boots have remained confusing', given the spread of skinhead Nazism across Europe, they questioned the suitability of their images for Morrissey to play with, 'however cleverly'.

Trying to render Morrissey's non-heterosexuality intelligible, he was read as homosexual. The unstated belief that was central to their objection was that *homosexuals can't be skinheads*. This is almost made explicit when the report underlines skinheads' reputation for 'violence against blacks. And, for that matter, homosexuals . . . Is Morrissey fascinated by the idea of racism, by the look of violent skinheads, to the extent of being oppressed so much that he falls in love with his oppressors?' they asked, unwittingly echoing the objections that had been levelled at the gay scene's appropriation of skinhead imagery.

In Britain, it could be argued, the signification of the skinhead has been kept open because here the image has some subcultural diversity, having been subjected to revivals and appropriations by various political groups. Internationally it's another story. But British skinheads can at least argue that the image has never been fully closed to signifying 'fascist'.

But there is a geographical qualification on this. Every day, in certain areas, thanks to the efforts of neo-Nazi groups, the skinhead is violently closed to signifying fascism. In the East End of London, the underground neo-Nazi organization Combat 18 employs skinhead imagery to terrorize its targets. But the East End also has a high proportion of visible lesbians and gay men, and is home for a large number of gay skins.

The same alignment of 'skinhead' and 'fascist' is also occurring globally, and far less ambivalently, as far-right groups in Europe, Australia and parts of the United States have imported skinhead imagery as the uniform for its urban terrorists.

Concern at gay skinheads by anti-fascist groups was at its strongest in Britain in the early 1980s, when the image had close public associations with fascist groups; those ideological battles are being played out today in Europe, most notably in Germany where, since the fall of the Berlin wall, local neo-Nazi groups have increased their influence. A study by Eberhard Seidel-Pielen and Klaus Farin published in summer 1993 found that over 40 per cent of the skinheads they interviewed identified themselves as right-wingers; a similar number labelled lesbians and gay men as 'enemies or opposition'. Yet they estimated that 450 of Germany's 8,000 skinheads were gay. The lines are therefore more clear-cut in Germany. The international group for gay immigrants based in Berlin, Schwule Internationale, voiced its opposition to gay skinheads, stating that 'in Germany, the term skinhead is a self-designation, which stands for brutal violence against foreigners, gays and minorities'.

Things came to a head in June 1993 when the German Gay Skinhead Movement, set up in September 1992, announced that it would be attending a lesbian and gay demonstration as a separate group, inviting *all* skinheads along to fight for the right for skinhead imagery to be accepted on the scene. Opponents saw this as an opportunity for Nazi skinheads to attend. The German GSM claims to be closely allied to Skinheads Against Racial Prejudice (although this is disputed by opponents) and a co-founder claims that the group is anti-racist, with neo-Nazis barred and prospective members with a neo-Nazi past having to denounce that past and serve a trial period. A report in the *Guardian* concluded that 'gay people outside the GSM are still asking why the group's members dress in the same style as their ideological enemies, the neo-Nazis . . . For them, the existence of the gay skinhead movement still encapsulates the ultimate contradiction.'[5]

Skinheads unambivalently signify fascism in large areas of Europe. John Byrne says, 'they have to grow their hair in a longer style because there's such a thing about Nazi skinheads in Germany that it's positively dangerous to walk about as a skinhead whether you're a Nazi or not'. When I interviewed Chris Clive, he was entertaining a visitor from Stockholm whom he'd met through the Gay Skinhead Movement: 'He's a proper skinhead and he thinks it's great here, because he can't walk around Switzerland like that but he can in London. In Switzerland he gets attacked by straight non-skinheads, because they'd think he's a fascist and a racist.'

As the skinhead is repeatedly closed to an image of fascistic normalization, perhaps the gay skin is all the more necessary to awaken the wider culture constantly to the fracturedness of this image of white working-class masculinity. For the fascist deployment of skinhead iconography seeks to limit its circulation to fascist contexts. Fascist ideologies seek to violently enforce the phallic authority and legitimizing centrality of Man which dictates the available signs and fixes them within a mythologized discourse of authenticity. This was evident in Goebbels' restriction in the use of the swastika. The contexts in which the symbol appeared had to be strictly controlled, because, as Baudrillard's theory of simulation shows, each repetition of an image seeks to undo the reality to which it refers, and the hyperacceleration of a sacred image reveals it to be kitsch. Kitsch threatened the fascistic semiotic project of closing significance to tautology. Kitsch renders all symbols equally exchangeable, confusing private and public, the trivial and the transcendental.

Those who manufacture kitsch often find themselves in conflict with those organisations which have traditionally mediated between the private and the public realm, such as the church . . . On the one hand these organisations see kitsch as a challenge to their authority; on the other, they realise that their own sacred symbols of communal transcendence stand a hairsbreadth away from vulgarity and profanity.[6]

In 1988, a year after *i-D* celebrated the cutting up and sticking on of multinational corporate logos in 'The Appropriators', cheap, mass-produced religious iconography was enjoying a vogue on the (straight) club scene, manifest in the designs featured on flyers, the sale of tacky plastic icons in trendy clothes shops, and the popularity of a range of T-shirts from a company called Big Jesus Trashcan; emblazoned with Renaissance images of Christ and Mary printed in dayglo colours, they were essential clubwear. The construction of taste – usually self-regulating checks on what should and should not be represented in public – is an important aspect of social control and the delineation of the public realm. Hence Goebbels' need to condemn 'pictures of artistically low value, with self-illuminating swastikas' in drafting the *Laws for the Protection of National Symbols*.

The repeated representation of that awe-inspiring, terrifying mode of (straight white) masculinity in the wrong context renders the skinhead kitsch. By refusing to respect him, to worship at a distance, by claiming and reproducing him, gay men have committed a sacrilegious act.

The skinhead thus kept as an open signifier through the contradictory claims on him, he can never fulfil his ordained function as the phallic naturalization of masculinity and fascistic tautological signification.

Fucked-up skins

Skinhead and gay identities are oppositional sites in the dominant discourse on masculinity: the natural against the unnatural, the authentic versus the inauthentic. If the creation of conspicuously visible homosexual identities merely contains dissident elements and serves to authenticate natural heterosexuality through its otherness, then the appropriation of a skinhead identity maps authentic masculinity on to the feminized body of the gay man and destabilizes both terms. Whatever the intentions of individual actors, gay skinheads shift the emphasis of the second term: from passively being ascribed a fixed identity to actively threatening to consume the primacy of the first term by exposing the interdependence of both sides and dissolving their difference through sameness. The opposition of natural versus the unnatural gives way as the whole system is denaturalized as 'gay' queers 'skinhead'.

That's the theory, and it would seem to work in practice. Consider these complaints against the queer appropriation of the skinhead voiced by a gay member of the neo-Nazi skin organization, Blood and Honour:

Mick [of Skinheads Against Racial Prejudice] claimed on *Skin Complex* that Blood and Honour have really fucked up the skinhead scene. Well, I'd say it was the other way round: the gay skinhead scene has fucked up the straight skinhead scene. When I first became a skinhead and was walking down the street, you might have a bit of hassle from people, you know, 'Nazi bastard', that sort of thing. Nowadays they say, 'Batty man'. It doesn't matter who you are – they've never seen you before, you could be covered in White Power tattoos – that's their first image. You get that reaction from straight blokes. For me, the gays have fucked up the Nazi skinhead image.

Growing awareness of gay skins in broader culture has made straight neo-Nazi skins extremely nervous, to the point where adopting a skinhead identity becomes unattractive.

You're under attack from all sides. A lot of skinheads are paranoid, especially the ones who've had a lot of tattoos and can never escape from the image at all. It must be worse for them. People are pointing the finger. No doubt about it. The gay adoption of the skinhead image has completely fucked up Blood and Honour. It's become the complete opposite of what Blood and Honour is about. In London, if someone sees a skinhead, they don't think, 'Blimey, is he gonna beat me up, is he gonna mug me?' No, they think, 'There's a bloody fairy.'
   All the things I used to fancy skins for, the gays have adopted now. It was the boots, tight jeans, shaved head. Years ago, if you saw a skin with a grade four crop and ordinary boots, that was okay, but the older I get, the more it had to be the hardest image possible: completely shaved head, Ranger boots. Now the gays have got the hardest possible image. I remember seeing skinheads with nipple rings long before it became popular on the gay scene. But now it's all associated with gays, unfortunately.

For those who wish to preserve the skinhead as an image of conservative masculinity, the discovery of people unaware of its queer appropriation comes as a relief: 'The other day, this cab driver . . . He couldn't believe a skinhead could be gay. Which is quite reassuring to hear.' But such innocent individuals, who continue to read the skinhead as exclusively straight, white and working class, are becoming increasingly rare: 'That's why I say gays have *corrupted* it.'

Notes

1. Nick Compton, 'Likely Lads', *The Face*, August 1995, p. 51.
2. David Forrest, 'Gay male identity', in Andrea Cornwall and Nancy Lindisfarent (eds), *Dislocating Masculinity* (London: Routledge, 1993)
3. Adrian Deevoy, 'Ooh I Say!', *Q*, September 1992, p. 63.
4. Danny Kelly, Gavin Martin and Stuart Maconie, 'This Alarming Man', *New Musical Express*, 22 August 1992, p. 16.
5. Jean Jacques Soukup, 'Schism of the Skins', *Guardian*, 6 July 1993.
6. Malcolm Quinn, *The Swastika: Constructing the Symbol* (London: Routledge, 1994), p. 119.

Index